UNHINGED

Unhinged

JOE R MEYER

Contents

Dedicated to those whose voice feels forgotten, lost in the crowd and the art of a blog gives you the freedom to say and be you. This is my voice, my narrative, locked in time for all to see my pinpoint in time.

Foreword

Blogging gives me the ability to truly soul search each day, gives me a chance to express my true self, my emotions, happiness, sadness, depression and slew of emotions. For those who don't blog, have no interest in blogging, writing or even sharing your thoughts with others, I understand it can be difficult to be vulnerable. In the world of blogging, I am really no one, I am no one, but what blogs give me a single point in my life that readers can experience with me.

This second volume tends to go more in depth, and I continue to find my voice and I continue to find my voice as I become more open. In all honestly my wife reads my blogs and is very encouraging but also doesn't always understand why I share such intimate things about myself, and my life and I tell her this is my form of therapy, why spend one hundred dollars an hour with a therapist when I can write for hours freeing myself of afflictions. I know it's not that easy but its pretty free.

The reader of my blogs may not really care about my life, but may some do, I will never know as my blogs which are created on WordPress though my blog Joe R Meyer Creatives. Some of my blogs are very tame such as celebrations and milestones, but some are angry, pain stricken, frustrated as you can see, I am in pain at times and some of my thoughts see me pushed to the edge of suicidal ideation as I discuss the thought of death and self-harm. I am obliviously still here, writing away but ultimately this blog book is a window to my soul, a window meant for my wife and daughter at times, so they have something tangible of who I am, was and how I think and thought if I am no longer here. That is one the reasons I turned these blogs into volumes, not necessarily for the world to read, although I elated you want to share my writing journey with me, but ultimately this is a time capsule for my daughter to know me. Growing up with my mother and father, I truly didn't get to know my parents in the way I wanted to and being that my mother passed in 2015, I will never get that back, pieces of her lost forever. My dad is still alive and well, but mute at times about his life, his feelings, and who he is. I hope that makes sense, often with our parents we grow up with them, they raise us, but do we really know them in the way we should. I get most parents are and can be private about their struggles, but I don't want my daughter Mikaylah and my wife Delia. Although my wife is fully aware of my pain, and it pains her to hear me see me this way, but my daughter doesn't know my pain, as she is on twelve, why would I put that affliction on her at such a young age and carry that burden, no I prefer when she older she read my blogs and will have a better understanding to who her father is and was in the event I am no longer here.

There I go again, talking about my death as if its imminent and deep down I pray I have years and years of time with my family, my writing, my blogs and books to leave her something with my voice, this blog is a part of my voice, I own it.

Part I – Mental Health

Chapter 1

Why is Suicide Stigmatized In Society

January 23, 2023

I often think about death and some of you may read my posts and some may seem kind of dark and I understand that, because I do think dark thoughts at time.

For some reason a thought as been nagging at my mind, which why is it that society finds suicide wrong and in Christian beliefs sinful. I get that when one commits suicide they are taking their lives in their own hands and ending it and from a Christian perspective we are taking our lives which don't belong to us but to GOD. There are many arguments I struggle with because I think about the many that do commit suicide every day, feeling this is their only choice and many times its they last option as they have fought life to be happy, to survive and for so many reasons. Suicide is personal to each person and although for many we do not know why, we tend to think well that person is just not happy with their life, they suffered with depression , maybe they were physically in pain and it was too much.

Why should people have to suffer and Live through it

The question I often want to ask people is why should one suffer in those painful ways and keep pushing forward with life , when at the end of the day, no one truly cares that much and is wiling to help that person feel a sense of relief.

I know myself that I at times feel like a failure in this life, yes I have a family, a wife and daughter whom I love dearly, but at the end of the day I want them to be ok, be safe, have food in the stomachs, shelter and the things they need and even want. When a person feels they can no longer do that for his or her family why should they feel the need to live and suffer and watch their family suffer. I really don't think they should and if that persons make the choice to end their life, they should be able too end it.

Often society will look at suicide with sadness and ask why and even stigmatize the person for ending their life, such as saying well that person is going to hell or that person was weak, they didn't think of those in their life when they did. But I guarantee those are actually they people they are probably thinking of the most when the end their life.

Society is at Fault for today's Suicides

Often times its societies fault that makes those who end their life possible, such as setting the expectation that your life will not have meaning until you have wealth, live in a nice home, this amount money in your bank account and even the type of career you . I often struggle to look even online as celebrities and the media flaunt their wealth and their vacations and money basically telling society that you are nothing unless you have what we have and by the way you will never have what we have. One could say will just ignore those messages, block those people but unfortunately its not easy because everywhere you turn you have society throwing that your life.

Social Media
a 'Silent Killer' of your Mental Health

On the flip side people are saying be happy, love yourself, accept yourself, spend time with your loved ones, life is short as you never know your last day. All true in a way but at the end of the day we are alone although we live on a planet of 8 billion people. 8 billion that are being told each day that are being told well if your NOT a billionaire , then you are nothing, if don't have social status, you are garbage, if you can not influence others and make a living, they your life is worthless.

How can one complete this these messages every day, many can't.

I am certainly not advocating to go and end it as you should at least talk to someone about how your feeling and work to resolves those feelings. But at the end of the day, this is your life and this may be the only way you will feel at peace.

Suicides are devasting but people overcome the loss and move on

Deep down yes there will be people who will be shaken and destroyed emotionally for you ending your life and will ask why, honestly tell those in your life why, give them closure, it's the least one can do. Your family, friends and loved ones will eventually recover, although they may have a permanent scar from the loss and have survivors guilt which is not intended when people leave this world.

LEFT BEHIND

Families and communities deal with life after suicide

By Dwain Hebda

The numbers surrounding suicide are shocking — and the most shocking part may be that no one knows precisely how prevalent the problem is. Last year the Centers for Disease Control and Prevention (CDC) reported that slightly fewer than 43,000 Americans died by their own hand in 2014 — the highest number in 30 years.

As sobering as that is, no one – least of all the CDC itself – believes that number to be anywhere near accurate due to sketchy reporting. In fact, a recent West Virginia University study suggested wide disparities in the number of overdose deaths listed as accidents versus suicides, particularly in the South.

Whatever the number, it pales in comparison to the millions upon millions of family members left behind to cope with a loved one's final act. What follows are stories of three such families and one community coming to terms with who they lost, what they've learned and how they face each new day.

People are suffering each day, people have made great efforts to stop people from suicide, especially in the United States, creating Hotlines open 24 hours a day, which in our call is Dialing 9-8-8 – Basically a suicide hotline. I can only imagine all those individuals who call, text or chat with people on the edge of ending it. Maybe these hotlines stop someone from ending it, maybe it doesn't because at the end of the day that person is truly going to see if what they don't make a difference.

Many years ago I attempted to end my life on February 7, 2007. I was twenty eights years old, suffering with depression, low self-esteem, obesity , alone and without a job. Everything in my life was a mess, when in reality it should have been ok. I was educated with a bachelor's degree, working on my MBA, living at home in a dismal environment , a home full of depression and no hope for the future, so I felt it was time. Speaking with you today, as you see I am still here, but people my sister at the time came home at the exact moment I was attempting to end my life and she saved me, but in reality I believe GOD saved me as he gave her a sickness to come home exactly at that time.

My attempt did affect my family, especially my mother and my sister who has devastated to have witness me jumping off a latter hanging myself. From her account she had super human strength pushing me up and loosening the rope around my neck when I fell to the ground. Moment later ambulance and police arrived to whisk me away to the hospital for a 72 hour hold, where I was then transferred to an outpatient mental facility. I then got out in a few weeks, began seeking therapy and medication eventually getting better, finding work, finding the love of my life, getting married, having our only daughter and here I am today.

I of course still struggle from time to time, as I was diagnosed about 20 years ago as being Bi-Polar with manic depression. I do not currently take meds, but choose to exercise, eat better and work to ease my mind on other things like writing and spending time with my family.

At the end of the day, I would do anything for my family, if it because myself or those I would choose them meaning their lives I would work to preserve instead of mine. I accept that I am going to die one day and accept that my soul will go to Heaven even if I choose to take my life one day as I know Jesus loves me and accepts me. Some of you may feel I would go to Hell but in reality the bible speaks of nothing of suicide as an unforgivable sin, because if you give your heart to Jesus you will be saved. Jesus accepts and knows we are flawed as people and when someone commits suicide and believer they are not themselves, but still gave their heart and life to Jesus. Jesus I believe to be a loving and gracious GOD and although Jesus would want us to live he understands we are flawed and full of sin. Its sinful to take ones life, but GOD is loving and accepting of us.

The reason I say this is because many people one who says they love and accept Jesus end their lives, many who are pastors , pastors who struggle like you and I making the choice to end it, I believe they are in heaven.

PASTOR GREG
LAURIE ON
SUICIDE
In Memoriam
Jarrid Wilson

I know this message may seem strange in the sense of advocating to live life to the fullest, be happy and just accept the difficult times no matter how hard. That your happiness is material to staying alive even though staying alive brings you great hardship and pain. Others will try to say well its tough for lots of people and that's life.

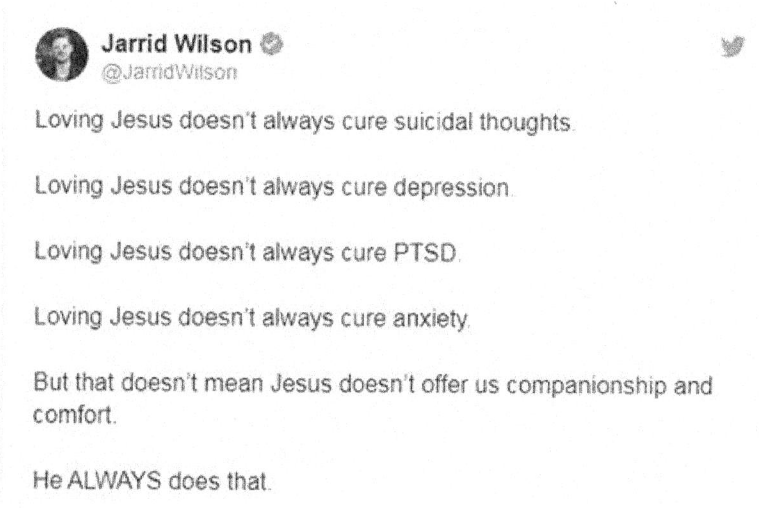

Jarrid Wilson
@JarridWilson

Loving Jesus doesn't always cure suicidal thoughts.

Loving Jesus doesn't always cure depression.

Loving Jesus doesn't always cure PTSD.

Loving Jesus doesn't always cure anxiety.

But that doesn't mean Jesus doesn't offer us companionship and comfort.

He ALWAYS does that.

The Reality is Society could care less if Your commit suicide

The reality is society doesn't care if we die, if people end their lives. People ultimately will only care about their own existence, so again why does society make such great efforts from stopping individuals to end their life. The same argument could be those who are in right to die states as many states feel that is not morally right to ask to end your life by a medical professional even though your in great pain and terminal. One recent case is a women who was arrested for killing her terminally ill husband, a decision they both agreed too,

What's amazing is that in society rules and laws are in place but often times the laws in place meant to protect people do not and even judges overrule decisions allowing murders and killers back on the street, but when we want to choose our own death, people are not allowed to have a say.

I can understand that society should not advocate to end your end and make campaigns to kill yourself, but honestly more needs to be done for those who are vulnerable, society needs to stop half ass attempts. People I believe are hurting for many different reasons, but I believe it all boils down to how you and I treat others. I am someone who believes we should all be informed of those decisions if we decide to end our lives and know yes we are affecting people in our life, they will be hurt, scarred for life, but at the same time I believe people will understand there are whose who struggle each day to hang on to this life and cannot.

NATIONAL
SUICIDE
PREVENTION
LIFELINE™
1-800-273-TALK (8255)
suicidepreventionlifeline.org

If you are experiencing depression and feel that you want to end your life, I encourage you to talk to your loved ones, a therapist and call 9-8-8 and speak with someone. Do everything in your power to make that your last and final solution.

Chapter 2

Is it Ok to Hate yourself?

April 2, 2022

Is it OK to hate yourself? Most would say NO! But I did for most of my adult life. Throughout my childhood and into adulthood I was told by a grandparent I was worthless, a f**k up and never amount to anything and for the most part he was right because I let his words dictate how to live my life.

I was until the last few years I realized I have value. I've been married since 2010 and my wife god bless her has told me I am valuable, when my daughter was born and now that she is 9 she tells how loved and valuable I am and I believe them both.

For many out there who struggle with self worth remember you are worthy , Precious and don't let anyone dictate your value or you'll feel the effects for years and sometimes the rest of your life.

Love your imperfections, weaknesses because you have a lot more strengths then you realize.

We are all in this world together and although I still have trouble valuing myself I tell myself to STOP.

Here is a picture of myself 5 years ago at my worst state. Heavily overweight with a lot of financial stress taking care of my family as the sole provider. Although this caused great stress I put value in my family and stop do, they are my rock and of course my faith in GOD.

Here is before and after and although I can't guarantee I'll stay like in pic 2 I'll work hard to maintain my 60 pound weight loss.

Many of us struggle with our weight, it's been a life long battle but I keep working towards it daily. I love myself more each day but sadly still depend on affirmation from my manager and colleagues to remind me of my value.

I feel I'm better today then I have In years and although #finances never seem to be easy I work at and keep a healthy state of mind as depression and anxiety inflicts at times.

I know I'm valuable and have each day as a re-do if I screw up and do at times.

I look at myself five years and I know I hated myself. I worked full time , part time and even Lyft on the weekends I was tired and burnt out. Let's not get to this point it's not worth it.

We live in a #culture of work hard to the point of exhaustion even death. Spend time with loved ones, friends and put value in what matters yourself, your faith if you have one and remember you are loved.

Have a great weekend and Keep punching!

Chapter 3

How attempting suicide changed my perspective

February 26, 2022

The life changing moment in the making

It was February 7th, 2007, I was 27 years old and depressed, fully of anxiety and ready to throw in the towel. Like so many at that age, it's a tough age. I am educated having been a few years out of university and studying for my graduate degree at that time, but I felt it wasn't enough I wanted more. I grew up in a very dysfunctional home like so many that will say we all did. I grew up with my mother, sister and verbally abusive grandfather, dad was still in the picture as my parents were divorced. Growing up from the age of five years old I was told how worthless I was, made to do hard labor (Not chores) by my grandfather.

My mother between a rock and a hard place did her best to provide but we depended on him who I referred to El Diablo (The devil) because of how he treated myself, sister and mother (his daughter). My mother fought tooth and nail to defend me and my sister from his cruelness, but it was hard because again she depended on him for food and shelter, being a single mom and with low income it was tough, but we never went without the necessities such as food, shelter and clothes.

One would ask why my mother didn't just leave the devil and cut on our own and the answer to that is tough because my mother like so many have to make tough decisions to keep the family intact and at times has to make difficult sacrifices and she did. But the damage he inflicted on me and maybe my sister is felt to this day even though he died in 2016.

I will never understand why my mother went searching for her long-lost father who I feel abandoned her as a child, but even my mother can't answer for that because she died in 2015 at the age of 56 years old.

Many grow up with similar situations or worse like homelessness and physical abuse and turn out ok and some don't. I did not turn out ok, as I grew into adulthood depression started to affect me around 16 years old as I would make visits to the school psychologist but even that didn't help. Graduating high school, I worked to live a normal life going to college and then dropping out for a short time because I was too depressed to focus on what to do with my life.

Life as an Adult and its struggles

Eventually moving out at 19 years old to live with my father and my grandfather who at the time suffered from Alzheimer's helping to take care of him. Living with father was not the healthiest place to be either as it further pushed me into depression and my father was in way supportive of my mental health needs, I was left to myself to figure it out.

Over the years I got worse, still maintaining school and work and tried to live my life rightfully but I struggled with indecision on the direction of my life and career which depressed me even further, I was lost. Part of the problem was I felt so alone, as I had little or no friends to support me and I searched for love getting rejected regularly because of my overweightness. I was always searching for love and relationships even in high school often rejected which painfully hurt me.

In 2006 I was working in financial aid for a college and my aunt suddenly pasted away in her forties, someone who I loved dearly and was always supportive of me which sent me spiraling. I quit my job and spent time at home which was a big mistake being that home was the most depressing place there was.

What I looked like back then in 2006:

Truthfully in those years I should have just tried to make it on my own, but I was to be scarred for the kind of commitment, so I stayed. It took years to recover my career again after my after me quitting I was going deeper into depression. Being depressed I would sit, watch TV and eat, which caused my weight to balloon further pushing me into depression harder. I still worked to get jobs and I did but those were short lived, and I usually quit after a few weeks. I did not drink or do drugs that has never been who I was.

Gone, gone almost gone but not quite

Deeper and deeper I went until one day on February 7th I had another Job interview, expecting when I got there to get the job but was told they had no job offerings even though I was set up for an interview. Therefore, some reason set me off as before going home I got lunch , went home ate my lunch. For some strange reason I decided it was time to end my life as life was not worth living anymore, thinking who would miss me anyways.

I decided to go to the garage and look around, find a old piece of rope and finding a latter outside and a long pole as I swung the rope over the pole ready to complete the deed. At this exact time as I was climbing the latter I looked back and saw my sister come to the backyard, but I still jump nothing was going to stop me from doing this, so I jump as I felt the rope tighten around my neck I quickly blacked out. I suddenly remember screaming from my sister who in a fit of strength pushed my 230-pound body up and bring me down as I looked up at her crying calling for help, I was too lost to know what happened.

When suddenly police and fire came quickly taking me a way to a hospital for a 72-hour observation before I was sent to an outpatient facility for treatment. I was there for two weeks before being allowed to leave, where I quickly saw a psychiatrist and given a healthy dose of meds to stabilize me all while I was still in school. My neck from rope was destroyed suffering from rope burn, but in some way that woke me up to my life.

The return to normal

Slowly things got better, got a stable job, finished my graduate degree and in 2008 found Love with my now wife and then in 2013 having my daughter. One could say the rest is history but truly my wife and daughter were my life savers. My sister of course saved my life from that fateful day which will always be a sad reminder to her as she always remembers and it's hard to discuss because of the trauma she faced too.

Why I am telling you all of this, is because Life is precious and at that point in my life, I didn't see life like that. I saw life as what I can get out of it Money, career and I had none of that. Even today I am a typical Joe, but in a much better place. Does my depression still sneak up, it still does as that will never go away, but I know how to cope better today.

Often times we forget how grateful we need to breathe and live life thinking life is something deposable and it's not. I get we all struggle some more than others, but we must fight on. We unfortunately live in a world where people commit suicide each day and those people and families lose loved ones never to return. Even though you may not see it you are valued, and love and we need to see it for ourselves. It took a long time for me to see this myself but glad I am here to spend my days with my beautiful wife and daughter, sister, father and brother-in-law.

You are valued

Don't ever let anyone family, friend or foe make you feel like you have no value, you must believe you have value, and you do.

Wherever you reside, whatever country you're from, don't let people and society tell you otherwise. I believe for many years I was unvaluable as a worker and a person because I was told so. What I have seen in these last couple years with COVID is that life is precious, and we need to all appreciate and not give up the good fight.

Here I am today:

If you ever feel the need to take the drastic measure to end your life, please talk to someone immediately by calling the suicide hotline at: 1-800-273-8255

Chapter 4

How Society views the Obese today

February 13, 2022

I often think about what I have accomplished in this life of 42 years old. At times yes I am disappointed in my professional place in the world but am working on moving up each day, I just can never give up. One of major goals accomplished in 2021 in my weight loss. Losing more then 55 pounds and being the thinnest I have been ever. Why is this important, because for most of my life I was fat kid. The kid that everyone other then family looked down upon as they measured my self-worth by my pounds and the scale number.

The reality is living in this world we have split seconds to gauge someone's worth by not even speaking with them just visual. Living in the United States we live in

Obese world, but people in my opinion are not completely to blame.

We live in a fast-food nation of getting it quick, its too hard to cook and living on the cheap which is not always the healthiest. I should know because McD's, Burger King and a slew of other fast food where and are my favorites at times. Even in the Fastfood world there are not really any healthy options even if they claim healthily, because of the amount of salt, fat and trans fats, add in the preservatives and in all honestly people wonder why people develop illnesses like cancer it could all be to what we eat.

Growing up Mom did her best, she cooked for me and my sister, home cooked meals, but often times did not have portion control. I was bullied for my heaviness just like your typical movie where the fat kid gets beat up at school, picked on and mocked. In our adult life its no different as society pushes the perfect image of what you should look like today from influencers to celebrities.

Ill admit my family in general have struggled with our weight, it is a battle and part of it could be our genetics, as many people on my mother's side suffer from weight issues. Now that doesnt take away the fact I love my family as is. But growing up, I often searched for someone like a girlfriend to love me back as an equal and often times my weight prevented that.

I know, I know Fat people find love too, but for me it was a different story, no one wanted me until I met my wife Delia which was in 2008 when I was in my late twenties, but until that point, I had no girlfriend, even in high school I was highly rejected which led me to have low self-esteem. My low self-esteem was primarily due to the fact that I grew up in a home with my grandfather who told me each day that I was a piece of shit, I was worthless which I believe late in life.

I will never claim I will never go back to gaining back the weight I fought hard to lose, but it could and if that was to happen, I need to accept myself, but I will sure try to keep it off and lose more if possible. My weight loss is not due to starving myself, but good old-fashioned exercise, eating better and less as we CAN ALL DO IT with a little motivation.

The sad fact is that I have grown to despise Fat people in a way, thinking they could easily work to lose the weight if they wanted to, but don't. I know that sound really harsh and judgmental and its because losing weight has its benefits to more energy, looking and feeling better and people will respect you more and treat you more human.

I know we all have our struggles in life and many of you will say who am I to judge, but really I am because I am the perfect example in a way of what life can be like to live heavy , which sad to say many of those who struggle with obesity can live shorter lives, even some of my favorite actors died so young like John Candy, which he should be alive today, but I believe his weight was a factor.

I look to my daughter to teach her healthy habits so she doesn't struggle like I have as she is only nine years old, at her age I was a porker, and she is fairly thin which is great, but I know my genes will carry over to her if she is not careful. I see so many fat kids today and its really sad parents allow their kids to get like that. Some of you may say well those kids are growing; they need more food.

Often times its what they are eating and no portion control for kids teaching them from a young age of what not to look like and what can happen if they are not careful, which is being despised by society for being fat. The pain of being Fat at a young age is real and hurtful because often times kids learn from a young age to value a person on their size, but really society teaches that too at a young age by what we see in media, movies and magazines that thin will always be in.

The whole love yourself as you are just unrealistic, because we have to depend on others to love us and treat us with respect and often times they will not based on the scale. Some of you may say I am wrong for my opinions, but I can speak only to my own story as if you have struggled with weight maybe you have had the opposite which is great for you.

Look at yourself in the mirror and if you are not happy with what you see, go out and change, eat less, exercise more get tough until you reach that goal of what you feel your ideal self looks like, I know I am now. I wish I had done this in my youth maybe I would be at a different place in my life , more successful because of that simple factor.

John Candy, Comedic Film Star, Is Dead of a Heart Attack at 43

By GLENN COLLINS

John Candy, the outsized comedian who brought a manic bonhomie to his starring roles in some of Hollywood's most successful comedies, including "Splash," "Uncle Buck" and "Cool Runnings," died yesterday in Mexico where he was acting in a movie. He was 43 and lived in Los Angeles.

The cause was a heart attack, said Anna Perez, a spokeswoman for Creative Artists Agency, which represented him.

Stephanie Pond Smith, a spokeswoman for Carolco Pictures in Los Angeles, said that Mr. Candy died in his sleep at his residence near Durango, Mexico, during the filming of "Wagons East," a Western comedy in which he was starring with Richard Lewis. Production was suspended and it was unclear whether the film could be completed.

Worked in Children's Theater

John Franklin Candy was born in Toronto on Oct. 31, 1950. After taking drama courses at Centennial Community College there, he worked at a variety of jobs before landing his first professional acting work as a member of a children's-theater group. Eventually he won roles in television commercials and low-budget Canadian feature films.

In 1972 he was accepted as a member of the Second City comedy troupe, and became a regular performer and writer for "SCTV," the group's television show, in 1977. On "SCTV," he wrote and performed in comic skits, playing opposite the show's other stars, including Harold Ramis, Eugene Levy and Andrea Martin.

He was featured in the show when it moved to network television as "SCTV Network" in 1981. Mr. Candy won Emmys in 1981 and 1982 for his comedy writing on the series.

"My big break came in 1972 when I got involved in the 'Second City' in Toronto," Mr. Candy said in an interview. "Then I was traded to Chicago, and I started my 'Second City' training there."

Played a Polka Musician

Mr. Candy's most memorable character for SCTV was that of Yosh Shmenge, a clarinet player in a polka band, and he kept returning to the role. In 1985, Mr. Candy co-starred in a comic pseudo-documentary for HBO, "The Shmenges: The Last Polka," and in 1990, in the comic blockbuster "Home Alone," Mr. Candy played the leader of a polka band.

His major film breakthrough was in the 1984 hit "Splash," which also made the careers of Tom Hanks, Daryl Hannah and the film's director, Ron Howard. Mr. Candy played the role of the hero's ne'er-do-well brother, Freddie, and Janet Maslin wrote in The New York Times that the film "would not be nearly so successful without the bulldozing presence of John Candy."

"The mere sight of the tubby Mr. Candy is funny enough," Ms. Maslin wrote, "but the spectacle of him playing racquetball really is something to see."

Girth Added to His Appeal

A devoted sports fan, Mr. Candy was a co-owner of the Toronto Argonauts of the Canadian Football League. In addition, with the actors Dan Aykroyd and Jim Belushi, he was part owner of House of Blues, a chain of blues bars and restaurants.

The 6-foot-3-inch Mr. Candy, who weighed more than 275 pounds at times, often complained to interviewers about his seemingly endless struggles with diets. Nevertheless, his girth was a key to his appeal on film.

Mr. Candy was frequently cast as a sympathetic, stumbling, ordinary guy, and often played the slob. Among his other films were "Stripes" (1981), "Summer Rental" (1985), "Little Shop of Horrors" (1986), "Spaceballs" (1987), "Planes, Trains and Automobiles" (1987), "The Great Outdoors" (1988), "Speed Zone" (1989), "Who's Harry Crumb?" (1989), "The Rescuers Down Under" (1990), "Delirious" (1991), "Only the Lonely" (1991), "Career Opportunities" (1991), "Nothing but Trouble" (1991) and "Once Upon a Crime" (1992).

Although many of his films were smash hits at the box office, critics took him to task in recent years for his choice of films, chiding him for some lackluster roles and feeble scripts. Mr. Candy won favorable notices, however, for his performance as the down-at-the-heels coach Irv Blitzer in the 1993 box-office hit "Cool Runnings," about a Jamaican bobsled team. Mr. Candy recently completed the Fox Television movie comedy "Hostage for a Day," his directorial debut.

He is survived by his wife, Rosemary; a daughter, Jennifer, and a son, Christopher, all of Los Angeles.

Universal Pictures

John Candy in his starring role in the 1989 film "Uncle Buck."

This is me! and I will continue to work hard to be a better me in 2022, so what are you waiting for, go and be your best self NOW!

Some of you who read this may feel I am putting down the larger boned people and I am not, I just want us to be better and when I say us I mean weight challenged. I often think of Homer Simpson on the episode when he was fat and how people treated him.

Chapter 5

Accepting Yourself in Today's World

February 19, 2022

Recently I had the pleasure to watch Rocket man the bio pic of Sir Elton John and I must say I quite impressed with his life and the impact he has made with his music and just his humanity throughout the world. Now mind you I am not sure how accurate this story to the real life of Elton John and frankly it shouldn't matter, it was a great film in my opinion. What I loved was the struggles Elton had with his family and how he was able to overcome those incredible difficulties.

Family does truly make a difference in our abilities to sometimes succeed in life and be prepared for a bright future. But many in life don't experience a solid family life such as two parents in the household who are devoted to raising well balance kids. Some of you may be saying well my mom or dad were single parents and they did great and I say I am one of those who was always raised with my single mom who did an incredible feat with raising my sister and I on pennies, but It could have been better.

For those who have read my blogs you will know that I am a difficult relationship with my grandfather in which I lived with along with my mom and sister. My grandfather who I believe never genuinely loved me put me down for most of young life and most of adult life. I was never good enough and he made sure to remind me each day, but in survival my mother made a choice to keep us afloat so I don't fault her for that.

Feeling acceptance is so key to our development in this life, not only be accepted by others but accepting yourself as is. What brings this thought to mind is that recently I had a young co-worker graduating college, starting out her life in the most wonderful way. A young women who I see as intelligent and hardworking and has the world in her hands. There is a hint of jealously in my tone because I look back in my own life and I ask myself what have I truly done in my life to be impressed about.

Yes I am a husband and father but I look back at my life and wish I could be a better provider, but One the reasons I feel I have failed is in my career. Now I am not saying my jobs that I have taken are bad or the companies I have work for are bad, actually they are decent, but it could have been better. Right now students are graduating High school and college starting major chapters in their life.

I think back when I was graduating high school as it was exciting, the future looked bright I was going to college and ready to begin my life. I was ready until early on I started to fail miserably being in college away from home, homesick and not prepared for college, so I made the choice to go back home with no resistance from family.

A choice I regret, but I know back then I was not ready and I didn't have the confidence and the self-acceptance to push myself. This was something that affected my life until today and I don't want anyone's life to be affected in that way. I encourage those who struggle with this to know you are not alone, you are special just the way you are.

One of the struggles so many deal with is comparison as in comparing yourself to others life path as I have done so much in my life. When I look at someone my age, my level of education for example and they go off to be successful while I feel stuck in neutral it hurts me. Many others may feel this way like when will I move into gear and never do at times, it may be because you have never truly accepted yourself.

Being in my forty's now, life has passed me by pretty quickly and it continues to keep going unrelenting and unstopping, so what can one do to overcome this, here are some ways.

1. **Set an Intention**

Set the intention to acknowledge that self-loathing simply doesn't lead to a satisfying life, it actually leads you nowhere. If you intention in life is to have self-acceptance which it should be we will find ways to appreciate who we are and our strengths. It starts with good thoughts and creating a chain reaction to continue those positive thoughts, its that important.

1. **Celebrate your Strengths**

We all have strengths no matter if you can't see them right away, but its important to recognize what those are. Hone in on those strengths and abilities by writing them down helps put those strengths in black and white. If you are having a tough time coming up with your list, name one strength each day. Start with something basic like "I'm a kind person" to start.

1. **Consider the people around you**

What kinds of people do you surround yourself with? Those people in your life make all the difference as mention in my personal example. Those who bring you down are not the people you need in your life even if they are family. Create those boundaries even if it means cutting those out of your life and see you blossom like never before.

1. **Forgive yourself**

We tend to be our worst critics preventing us from self-acceptance. Forgive yourself and move on, it's as simple as that. It's important to learn from mistakes, make efforts to grow and accept you can't change the past.

You make your decision best for you at the time, but I won't lie it would be nice to have a time machine to go back and correct those choices at that time maybe our lives would be different then today.

1. **Shush your inner critic**

The inner critic can be the most powerful voice for good and the bad. We all have that voice but many will push the inner voice aside, some listen constantly like I do. It's important to know that inner critic is not always helpful in your quest for self-acceptance but still valuable being self-aware.

1. **Grieve the loss of unrealized dreams**

Many of problems of self-acceptance come from our inability to reconcile who we are as compared with the idealized dreams of our youth. Maybe you dreamed of becoming a doctor or Lawyer but instead ended up in business and think about it constantly. I do that to this day, I think what if I had stayed in my first college and finished, what if I joined the military, What If, What IF's constantly if my head, but I realize that doing that does more harm then good.

1. **Be kind to yourself**

Many people are hesitant to show even a shred of self-kindness because they se it as selfish or undeserved. By the keys to self-compassion is to understand that weaknesses are part of the human experience. Coming to accept who you are involves loving yourself because of your flaws, not in spite of them.

Chapter 18- My Road to a Better Me Starting with My Weight

April 23, 2022

This year has been unlike any other year with COVID, the pandemic and shutdowns resulting in many of us struggling to be healthy. Now if you have maintained an active lifestyle and were not about to let a pandemic stop you then I applaud you. Prior to March 2020 I was regularly hitting the gym five days a week with a consistent training routine of weights and cardio but not eating as healthy as I knew I should have been.

The gym was always something so important to me I would go rain or shine, morning or night it didn't matter, but then that all changed for many of us. Most gyms naturally closed due to COVID, but some did stay open with an attempt to keep everyone safe. Living in California where there is probably a gym in every city that made a huge impact on those of us who said it was not safe to journey to a daily sweat box and risk exposure to COVID.

So like most gyms my local gym was no different, which pretty much has been closed close to a year now. I often think if I miss the gym and to a certain degree I do but realized that I am able to work around the gym by going to my free resource the local park. When the shutdowns started to happen, I was probably like many shocked that society of hording goods, restaurants, malls and many businesses even churches were forced to close which was pretty depressing to watch. Like many my family and I huddled indoors while I have the opportunity to work from home, my eight-year daughter soon took her elementary school online via zoom but my wife who works in hospitality had to still go to a physical place.

Over the course of weeks turning into mouths many of us adjusted how we ate relying on fast food and ultimately trying to relieve the stress of our new reality for many that lead to food and lack of exercise, hey many of us were just try to deal. I was no different with the gyms closed I took the approach of living in fear for a time just ordering out limiting my exposure to people in markets and the outside world which included exercising.

In time I knew what was going to happen to my mental health and my waistline, but I said to myself I will get back on that horse and exercise at my local park and I did but at the same time I was depressed about the situation and the motivation just wasn't there which meant my waistline expanded slowly at first and then over time I was shocked at how much I gained.

When it comes to my mental health, I have seen a direction correlation between a large waistline and my mental health which only made me feel worse. Over the course of my life, I have always struggled with my weight. Bullied for most of my life being the fat kid, embarrassed of my body and my lack of movement when it came to activities like P.E. Part of problem.

I think was that during most of childhood and teens then adult years I lived with a great depression, low esteem and poor self-image which led to me eating more. Mom and Dad who I love where not the best examples for healthy eating and lifestyles, so I learned from them as well. These habits carried with me until today with my love for sweets, fast food and snacks.

For many this is not an usual experience many gained pounds over the course of the year due to the stress of being stuck at home and the stress of no childcare, schools closed for many and having the literal whole family at home driving each other nuts at times, all added to the stress, over eating, lack of exercise and ultimately weight gain. But one of the bigger issues was mental health and the toll it took on many some taking the drastic step of suicide. Although suicide did not cross my mind during this time, I can only imagine what other's have experienced.

This year would be the point of redemption for me as I took a long look at my pudgy self and was frankly disgusted with myself being a role model to my wife and daughter looking, the way I did, It was time for a change.

Losing weight was not uncommon to me, I had done it before as it was going to take time, patience, exercise and eating right. My first problem when I previously tried to lose weight was the amount of effort I was putting into exercise which for me I find running to be the most beneficial to weight loss but I just walk daily I don't tend to see the results I want.

One area I really have to almost eliminate is fast food although I do eat occasionally but unlike a year ago I was eating it almost every day with a lack of what I call real home cooked meals so that definitely contributed to my weight gain.

I also had to drink one think I was not a fan of drinking which was water, now drinking half my weight in ounces for water, eating breakfast, a light lunch and light dinner and eliminating snacks. Now I don't want to make it sounds as if I starve myself because I don't its just that with all the water I brink and certain foods I eat literally make me feel full , foods like oatmeal which take my hunger pangs away.

Since late January I have lost a total of twenty-two pounds, consistent now with losing about two pounds a week which is considered healthy weight loss. My mental health and energy have also improved although we are not out of the pandemic yet, I make it a point to exercise six days a week running for about one hour and that's all it takes for me. My hope is that by July I can lose a total of fifty pounds changing my life and sticking to this lifestyle change.

I believe we all have in us to get healthy if we make the choice and stick with it, be patient with yourself and know there's not quick fix to losing weight. I have literally tried starving myself coming to see that ended severely hurting me physically and in the end did nothing for my weight loss but ultimately led to poorer health by eating more.

As mentioned, this has been a lifelong struggle but I am determined more than ever to get this done right and stick with it for the long haul. For many of you this journey may sound familiar, but I just want to say don't give up. Lastly there is one fictional character I remember everyday in my goals and that is Rocky Balboa ever giving up because anything can happen when you fight for what you want.

Chapter 6

Second Chances are Possible for You and I!

May 14, 2022

Second chances are always appreciated in our lives whether it's a second chance at a relationship or a career or to rebuild. I can honestly say I have gotten a few second chances in life especially after my Suicide attempt in 2007. At that point in my life which I was in my mid-twenties I didn't fully appreciate my life and what I had to offer. I was sucked into a life of self-pity, depression and anxiety. I know that today many live like that of all ages and it's hard and unfortunate when you don't see your true beauty.

My Second Chance in the waiting

It was difficult for me growing up, because I was constantly being told how worthless I was by a grandfather who we lived with most of childhood into an adulthood. This affected my relationships with others especially when it came to making friends as I was also bullied as bullies could smell fear in me which followed me for many years until a few years ago I lived in fear. Fear of failure, fear to never live up to a being a good father and husband. I still care about those things but not to the point where I am stricken with fear I have a healthy understanding of what that should look like. I know I am going to fail, make mistakes and really blow it times but that doesn't take a way from who I am and what I strive to do and who I strive to be because all of us are a work in progress.

After my failed attempt on my life, I rebuilt and attempted to start over by trying to refocus but really it took years to do that. One of the people who encouraged me, pushed me was and is my wife to this day and she is one of the main reasons I believe in second chances, because she allowed me to see the beauty in life.

You see for a good portion of my adult life until my late twenties I was alone, even though I tried to date, meet people I was always rejected, which I account was due to my confidences and my weight which ballooned at times due to my overindulging on the account of my depression and anxiety. I struggled for many years until about a year ago I lost over sixty pounds and feel healthier, happier and more content than I have ever been. Although I have been married since 2010 and have my daughter 2013, I was never truly content with myself and our life because

I seeked more, better job, more money, better living situation and being a better provider.

Today I am not saying life is perfect, but it's much more manageable than it has been in the past and I see life moving very quickly.

As you see I have gotten a few second chances and so can you, but sometimes you need to seek it out and the powers a be will provide them to you.

I guess what triggered this post was a song I was listening to called "Second Chances" by Shinedown, here is music and video below.

Remember that we are going to blow, sometimes really blow it but that's ok, cut yourself a break and begin again and again and again as each day is a redo to be better. It takes work and time, but we can all get there.

Looking Within

Remember to look within you and see your gifts and value even if others don't tell you, you have them but self-reflect often on what those are. I wish these are lesions I would have thought of at those points in my life where I struggled the most and hope those who read this will find comfort in these words.

Chapter 7

The Voices In My Head Won't Stop

July 29, 2023

My dark thoughts continue as I am falling into worry and hopelessness. For many and, I have only not been working for two weeks, but prior to that not working from March to May, which is not a relatively long time.

As of late I have been waking up at 3:56 AM and yes, I know that is a strange time but that is the witching hour. I worry for the financial safety of my family, even though I am working part time teaching, my wife is working PT, I am getting some unemployment benefits and I have some savings but still with the high cost of living in California, the money goes fast.

Each day I search for new opportunities on LinkedIn, Zip recruiter and other sites having had a couple of interviews, one which was a 2nd I am waiting to hear back from soon, one that was not a good fit from the employer and then another one with my old company. I know for many jobs searching is painful, but temporary, but some have longer term unemployment, which is my fear.

Linkedin, more like DepresdIn

Going on LinkedIn can be one of one of most depressing places to be as hundreds and thousands share their stories of pain, hardships, unemployment.

Sadly, my mind is going dark as I think about death, as I think my exit strategy, as I think what life would be like for my daughter and wife if I was no longer around. I also think would my soul stay behind or would I go directly to heaven.

Being someone who has an interest in the paranormal I think if I was to die prematurely before my time, would I still feel the need for a purpose to stay behind to make sure my wife and daughter are ok.

I know my wife and daughter and my sister especially would be quite devastated emotionally and financially although I do have life insurance and before you say well life insurance doesn't cover that it does, but there is a certain amount of time one can't as there are what's called contestability clauses for two years and I also have life and disability insurance on the car. I am worth more dead than alive at this point in my life sorry to say.

I am conflicted at the same time of these thoughts as I am a believer in Christ, as messages have spoken to me about having faith and having faith and that GOD is in control and that he will provide. Of course, I believe because I have seen his power work time and time again right in the nick of time.

As I always tell the LORD I am open to whichever direction you want to send me. I am thinking that yes I will be open to other positions that even pay less for now to get over this hump, something most people don't want to do because we have bills, expenses, rent like anyone else. Each day waiting and waiting and waiting, getting an interview, being declined.

I can never get used to the email declines, some I could care less from companies I have applied with, but the ones that hurt are the companies that I know I want to work for and decline me.

The other painful situations is going through two or three interviews and then the decline, so close almost like stab in the heart questioning what I did wrong, then trying to find comfort to keep trying.

So far, I have applied for over 150 jobs, with a job interview, but each day I will continue to apply, apply and apply.

During this time, I also find comfort in doing my daily exercise, clearing my head and also music, but ill admit the music I listen to sometimes pushes me further in despairs, often songs that have suicidal and depression themes, really, I have been listening to Runway train by Soul Asylum.

I have also listened to Papa Roach, Bad flower and Linkin Park among others, not realizing there were so many songs about depression and suicide, but it makes sense as many artists' struggle.

I will continue to try to remain positive, wait patiently, but I will say that I cannot do anything at this point anyways because it would surely leave my family in dire financial straits if I was to die today.

Lastly television has gave me some comfort as I have seen some of my favorite shows characters go through difficulties, giving me a laugh at times, getting my mind off my troubles, but my mind is still troubled, but writing helps.

Chapter 8

I will never be valuable...

November 7, 2023

I will never be valuable in this world as I look around I often see whose who society has said are the most important and valuable like business gurus like Elon Musk, Jeff Bezos and others. In addition we are constantly be told by society that those in entertainment like Taylor Swift, the Kardashians, musicians, movie stars and even celebrities pastors.

I think about the value of my life each da in some way or fashion, I think about those who are deemed those society can not live without and some of those I mentioned certainly we are told each and every day how important they are.

As a Christian , this goes against what GOD tells us in his word, that he is not a respecter of persons that in GOD's eyes we all have equal access to God's word and to enter heaven or hell and shows no favoritism to man , women or child. But if we look today, there are people who we consider incredibly prosperous with money, wealth , fame, the currency of this world.

I know we should not compare our lives to those around us and in this world, because we are ALL unique and special in GOD's eyes. I have yet to see this in myself and have not for many years and in all honesty I feel like a complete failure, even more so each day and to add to that I truly believe I offer no value to this life and world. I look around even had normal people, so to speak my peers and in my eyes they are so much better off, better fathers, sons, brothers and offer so much more than I do here.

Many will say, but you do have value, you have your family who love you and yes I have a family who loves me, but they deserve so much better than me. I look at other families we have friendships with and I see them so better off than us and they are younger, more successful and happier. I know again some will say well you don't know that, how do you know they are happy, everyone struggles with something.

I can't help but to look at my co-workers each day as I compare my life to theirs, again I Know I do not know their lives, but in my mind, they are far better off then me and just happier. Since I feel I offer no value to this world and probably never will, WHAT is the point? I have often thought of my last days, thinking that it will most likely be in 2025 some time, BUT it depends. It depends on many factors that will determine my state of mind, one of those is stable employment, being able to provide for my family.

Since 2018 I have been laid off/let go 3 out of 4 times putting my family's financial security at risk. Some would think well how you can be so sure, HEY why talk about it, just DO it now. I say that in my heart its not that time, because when I leave I want to be sure my family will be ok financially, I know they will not be well emotionally for a long time, because there will be a whole in their hearts for many years and probably be there for life, but in the end they will have financial security to live a better life than the one I can provide.

In my mind, I will just be forgotten in time, forgotten by my previous co-workers, those interactions I came across in my lifetime, but in the end my family will be affected I know this, but that pain will heal. I have worked and fought to get somewhere in this life and I have FAILED, but its not without trying. I have looked to others for help, to see me as someone of value, but sadly I do not think anyone sees me. Maybe I am not alone in my feelings for validation, to be considered for something more even though I worked hard for it, but NOTHING.

I will say I love my family of course and it pains me to think of these things, because I should want to LIVE, but don't. I should want to see my daughter's life until my last natural breath and I do, but I don't feel I can and maybe won't because I want her to be the best in this life and to this point in my life I have failed her. Yes I have given her everything I can, a home, food, clothes, my time and she is a daddy's girl, never leaving my side from the day she was born, but she deserves better and I tell her that each.

I tell my daughter, there are better fathers and I tell my wife there are better husbands out there and I am going to go find him. I mentioned to them people in our lives who I believe are better fathers then me, better providers, more time to give and more successful in my eyes, in my eyes they deserve so much better and I am a hindrance to their lives.

I hope one day my mindset will change, that one day I will see myself in a better light, but I have not seen it in most of my life. It's difficult being your worst critic and I am, waiting for the rug to be pulled out from under me at all times, because I know it will come again one day.

I do hope, I have a lot of hope in my life as I look to my writing which is what keeps me going, I watch film and music, which gives me some peace of mind as the wheels in mind never stop. I often watch ROCKY for inspiration, and I look to films where people have endured hardships and overcame them with success.

From the looks of my life, one could say, there is nothing wrong with my life, I have jobs, a roof over my head, food, family, love, what more do I want. I want to feel worthy; I want to feel as someone who has value in this life, someone who lives life to the fullest with happiness knowing that life is tough, but life can be beautiful too and sadly I do not see that.

As you can I struggle, at times I feel I am growing more disturbed in my mindset, in my thinking about and my thoughts are not healthy which I equating to self-hate. May be I do hate myself as I am repulsed by my fatness, my body and its hard for me to believe how is it that severely overweight and obese people love themselves, I find it unhealthy physically to have so much weight, unnatural weight putting a lot of pressure on our hearts.

In addition, society tends to hate fat people although we live in very body positive culture, but still I don't want my daughter growing up thinking its ok to be obese and if she does become overweight and obese, she needs to work hard to maintain a healthy body and lifestyle.

I tend to live in regret on a regular basis, thinking of this year which I think I will never forget, but know as more time passes it will fade from memory.

I look for the day that I will truly believe I have value, that I will wake up and say I was living in a big lie of believing I was worthless and truly begin to live, but I don't know if that day will ever come, until then I will do my best to push forward.

Chapter 9

Giving myself the Gift of 5 more years of Life

December 11, 2023

The holidays are certainly a time of self-reflection, what we consider to be the most important. Although one could look at my life and see that I have nothing to be down about, as I have a family wife and daughter whom I Love. But each day I think how much better their life could be. I do try each day to make their lives better but feel over the last ten years I have really failed them.

Heart Felt

The other night my wife and I had a good heartfelt discussion and I let her know how I felt about my failures as a father and husband, working two jobs to work to give them both good things in this life. Yes we have a roof over our head, food, clothes, but no money and haven't had any real money for the most the ten years.

When I look around, I see others who have had great prosperity in their life and marriage but for some reason we have not. We do Not have a house; we do not have lots in the bank. Our health is good, we have a good car, and no one goes without. From our looks of us we appear fine, but when I look around, I see everything I haven't done for my family. When I look around at my peers, I see them as younger with high positions, more money, better family life and great quality of life. When I look at our apartment, the furniture is worn, needs to be replaced.

The Year of Pain and Mistakes

This year has been especially eye opening due to my lay off in March, but quickly landed two opportunities in April. Two attractive offers with two good companies. It was both exciting and nerve-racking, in the end choosing of the positions. Both positions pay me more than 15% of my last salary.

The position I chose was with an international utility company, one of which I had been trying to get into for over 10 years. The interviews both went smoothly, and the jobs offered swiftly accepting both positions but burning one bridge on the position that I turned down. The other role I was excited about, ready to learn and looking forward to turning the page on a difficult season of joblessness and hardship.

It turned out that the job I took was not what it seemed as the person I would be working under turned out to be a micro-managing passive aggressive, egotistical women who worked for the company twenty years refusing to allow me to train and learn, forced to walk away.

GOD opened a door rather quickly with another great company but taking 15% less than the company I was laid off from on account that I was going into an industry with no prior experience but has the skills to do the job. The people at my new company are kind, compassionate, patient and professional who many have been with the company for over ten years, some as long as forty years.

From those reading many have probably experienced similar situations especially with having to walk away from a job and good one at that. The rest is history as I am now in training and looking forward to what comes.

Over the next five years will be a time of evaluation, a time to rebuild, but IF things do not go well, then I will be forced to finish my life. I never understand why people feel the feel to suffer for years, decades, when they make great efforts to live a good life, yet others have so many blessings like a great career, money, loving family, cars, house and so much more.

But when I look at myself personally, yes I have my wife who I love and my daughter, but where is the money, where is the house, were is my prosperity. Many of you reading this may say "Well you have to work for it", "It will come in time, be patient," and not everyone in this life gets to be "Happy".

Filled with Anger

Over the years I have grown angry, jealousy fills my heart everywhere I go almost to the point I hate going out. When I go out, I see the people, I observe them, their body language, their happiness, their joy, their life and I yearn for that life. Many of those I observe are young exuberant, full of life, happy, living their life to the fullest. I can only ask myself at their age, why couldn't I live that life? Why couldn't I have lived, always feeling held back.

I will say that when I look back in my twenties especially, I searched for love often, getting rejected time and time again, NOT good enough. In my late teens, twenties I was in college, had freedom to a certain degree and there were suitors who I thought had interest in me, but I was too blind to see their intentions.

I would have loved to know what Love filled like in high school and my early twenties, but didn't meet my future wife until late twenties, but even then, I made so many mistakes not fully enjoying all the moments. Don't get me wrong, I remember the happiness myself and Delia enjoy going out and spending time together, but it was also a very painful time because we had a friend who did great damage to our relationship getting involved in our relationship, playing each of us, as she was Delias (My wife's) friend first and then I met this friend at work.

I think a lot about...

I think a lot about love, happiness and sorry to say I look at others and their perceived happiness. Now many would say I have no idea if people are happy or not just by looking at them, but I would disagree. I feel I can tell a lot about them based on the energy they exude. I feel I have lost that energy many years ago. Sadly I do not remember the last time I felt the sense of exuberance, happiness, optimism which is why I have decided its going to be time to hang it up in five years.

The signs I will look for before saying goodbye

There will be some milestones I will work to accomplish in five years that may change my plans, one would be making the money I lost this year in the form of my year's salary. I will also look to get promoted at my current job hopefully in five years. I will also like to complete more of my books, blogs, vlogs and podcasts leaving my daughter and wife my life on paper, in word and video so they have something tangible to watch me, to hear me in hopes to bring that some comfort..

I know that me not being there will be devastating to my family, especially my young daughter who would be 16/17 at the time of my passing, but old enough to recover and not let it derail her life. I would also hope to leave behind money to secure both their futures.

I get that money does not matter, that I am the important one, but I think we fail to see at times that Money is what makes this world go round and without we are nothing, we are less than nothing which is the reason I refuse to let my daughter and wife with nothing. With money they can recover, live their life without the fear of being homeless, jobless, money less but will have the means to do much more than I can give them in this life.

Frankly I am worth more dead than alive in my eyes and at least with money to survive they will not have to struggle to not have the things they need. Yes, I get my loss will it will never be a wound they can never recover from and that it may affect their mind over my loss, but in the end they will and can recover over time.

Sadly, I do not know the feeling of losing someone to suicide, but I do know the feeling of loss of a loved one who I loved deeply and remember reach day how much I need them now, like my mother who passed away in 2015, that loss still hurts even though that was a natural death.

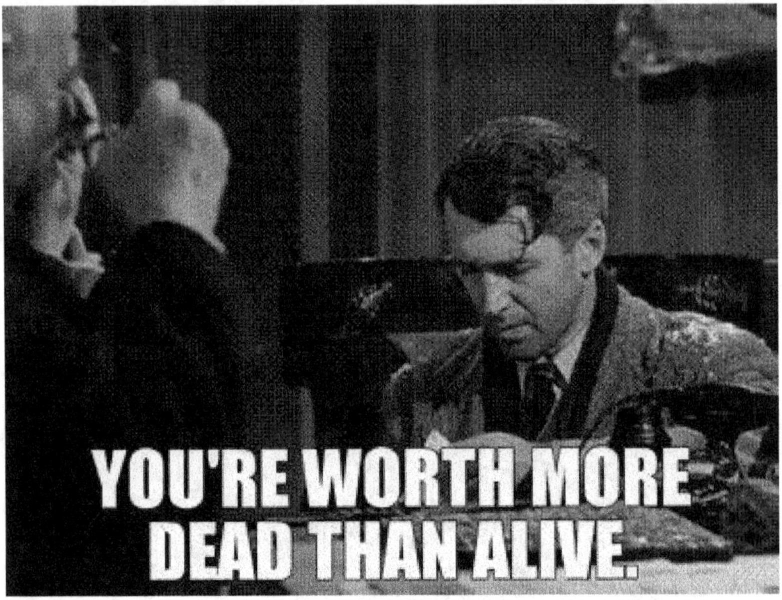

I will of course miss my co-workers if I have the same ones five years from now, but each of those I feel I affect I will leave behind closure letters to each of those individuals in hopes it can help them understand my passing, but unsure how much of a difference that will make.

For many reading this, this is painful to hear and often many will turn away, not listen, not care and I understand for many reading are not those who care about my well being.

I struggle at times as I conflicted over this view and my Christian faith, but understand I am not alone as I have reflected here times that there have been men and women of faith to take their lives, which goes to show you that the human side is weak. As much as we want to say just stick it out, push forward, everything will be ok, but in reality, it may not be so again I ask am I just to live and suffer in silence.

It angers me when I attempt to speak up about it , I am often told to be quiet, don't talk like that instead of someone saying it will be ok, don't feel that way. But often I am told to go seek therapy, get on meds, but that will NOT do anything, tried and done that as I have struggled with this for over twenty years. Death is apart of life and people are forced to recover as people lose friends and loved ones each day, life goes on.

My heart is at war right now as GOD says Joseph, I am here, I will get you through this, depend on me and I say "LORD, give me peace, give me strength, help me another day". I am not heartless to want to leave my family behind but in my mind, I continue to see I have no worth in this world and maybe that is the problem too, I compare the value my life to what society says is valuable.

Only GOD knows the future, only he knows , what the next five years will look like, but I know its up to me to try to have a good state of mind, not let things get to me and go with the flow, but that is hard at times when now I see what I have lost this year trying to get it back. Getting a glimpse is something that I will carry with me any years but will try.

I often watch many supernatural shows, one being supernatural with the adventures of Dean and Sam, and one common theme is fighting good and evil with the devil and angels, but often the soul is talked about. In the soul it talks about the value of the soul and how GOD values are soul more than anything and how valuable are SOUL is and powerful.

I want to believe the soul is more valuable than money and fame and riches and I Know it is because GOD says it is. All I ask in my life is to have peace and to feel OK, to know that I am doing ok but when I look out into the world, I see that I am not. I am just not rich enough, successful enough and clearly feeling I missed something in this life that could have helped me today.

I understand that many struggle with insecurities, being without, some without food, shelter , some in poor health and yet they push forward, I do not know if that is me or not, because I wait for my last days. I am hopeful too that my state of mind will change, that I will want to live and I do.

Each year I will evaluate until year five and it's possible at that time, Life and I will be at a place where I feel no need to end it, I hope.

Chapter 10

The Internal War I Fight Each Day!

September 22, 2023

Did you know **September is Suicide Prevention Month**?

I find this to be important to many out there who are struggling like myself. I often think of suicide and in all honestly, I think of how I will plan my exit in this world. Even when things appear to be ok or well, I think about it. I think in all honestly that I am a failure even though one will see and say you have nothing to be ashamed of, you have education, degrees, and a good career more than most people have, all true.

There is a WAR Within ME!

But deep within me a war is going on, a fight, a struggle to accept myself, to feel content but sadly I have felt this way for many years even when one can say you shouldn't feel this way. I have a family, a wife I love, a daughter, sister, father, brother-in-law, I don't really have friends unfortunately as most friends I have tried to make have recoiled from me, run from me after they get to know me and that is why I have chosen not to try t make friends.

Even at work, I work to keep that part of my life private to prevent employers from cutting me/firing me and coworkers especially since many fear working with me after I disclose how I feel at times, yes depression is stigmatized, those who speak about suicide fear discussing it and I get it.

Even my loving wife when I try to discuss my feelings she fears for me, feels bad and doesn't want to hear that I have these feelings and I get it, you don't want your loved ones to talk about ending their life, it's too painful to think of them not around, but what is scary is I do not fear not being here anymore, because in my mind I am checking out, but not before leaving my family financial secure.

MONEY DOESN'T BUY HAPPINESS BUT IT SURE HELPS

I know money doesn't buy happiness, it cannot replace a person, a person is much more valuable than money. In my mind I see Money as being more valuable because in this world Money talks, if you don't have money, you are nothing, you can not eat, drink and sleep, no shelter, nothing, your nothing.

Many of you have lost someone to suicide and I have read many articles of people who have lost loved ones wondering myself, what does one feel losing someone to suicide, what are the feelings they have. I am sure people are anger, full of guilt, depressed, confused, lost and a flood of other feelings and emotions.

People continue to say Suicide is selfish, but in my mind, I say its selfless, because I would live my family in a better way because they would no longer have to see my suffering, they would be able to live life in peace to have everything I could not provide for them.

I AM A FAILURE!

In my eyes I am a failure, I have failed to be a good provider to my wife and daughter. Yes, we have a roof, we have food, clothes, but we have little money. I know from the sound of what I am saying so many other people live like I do, that is LIFE. Many struggles worse off with health issues, money issues, homelessness yet they continue to push forward, which amazes me and I ask WHY! Why live life like that, why not just take yourself out of the equation, end your suffering, but again many don't feel the need to end their life, they want to live.

You see people in great depression, thoughts of suicide and even performing suicide want to live, but feel they have no choice, their pain is too great, something therapy, medicine will not cure. I continue to go to work each day, try, learn. I continue to teach my students, continue to take care of my family, love my wife and daughter but each day there is that thought that my time is almost going to be finished here and I plan for that day. I even think about how I will do IT.

I would do IT in private away from prying eyes, away from people, but still in a way someone would find me, inform my family. I would leave them last words, my love on paper or video and I would leave them with money to survive of course which in hopes will bring them comfort and move on with their lives not to struggle, to be financially better as I truly believe “I AM WORTH MORE DEAD THAN ALIVE”.

You see I am someone who hopes that these feelings will go away, that the tide will change in my life, that I will have no reason to take this step, but I do not see that happening. As I grow older, I see myself as less valuable to society, to my career and I know my family values me, loves me but If I cannot support, care, provide for them then what good am I.

People say all you need is LOVE, but that is not true, you need love, food, shelter, Money to be truly ok. I think of the love of my wife and daughter, I think if I am not here how would my wife and daughter think of me, would it affect them mentally, would it destroy them emotionally, could they move on, I believe they would, I don't think I am that important.

MY ATTEMPT OF 07

For those who do not know, I did attempt to commit suicide in February 2007, but it just so happens my sister came home at that time, when I was in the middle of act of hanging. I do remember blacking out shortly, then waking up on the floor as my sister had used feats of strength to remove me from the noose around my neck, to this day I know she will never forget that image, even bringing up any memory of that day she immediately freaks out, gets angry and has even cried. Some of you may say well of course who wouldn't want to remember that that is a horrible memory, but I do not remember as I was seconds away from not being in this world.

I LOVE MY FAMILY and ALWAYS WILL

I love my wife, my daughter, my family, sadly I just don't love myself enough to want to be here as I am constantly keeping score to those who are more successful, have more money, have better family lives, who have picture perfect lives. When I look at my family, I see love from my wife and daughter, but myself in despair.

When you look at a picture of me you see my smile, but it's a fake smile at times, not always, but fake because in a picture no one wants to see a sad face. If ever in the future I am not here anymore I would want my family to remember me smiling.

Most days I feel great anger for my mother not being in my life because she died in 2015, I feel great anger my mother cannot see my daughter grow up, care for her, spend time with her. When I see others who have the privilege of being a mother and grandma, I get angry because they have no idea what it means not to have your mother around, often taking them for granted.

I do not wish anyone warm, I do not wish for people not to have their loved ones, mother, grandma, grandpa around but to appreciate them and remember that there are those who do not have the privilege and I believe it is.

THESE DAYS

These days of mine are filled with angst, sadness, depression, thoughts of suicide. But I will say that helps get me through my days not only my family, but my GOD Jesus, listening to his words, reading his words, seeing and feeling his love. I know JESUS doesn't want me to end my life, I know he wants me to live, to be happy and know he is in control of EVERYTHING, and I believe he is.

He is in control, he is in control of my past, present and future. He is in control, he was in control when we lose our jobs, when we get sick, when we encounter trials, but of course we are also given free choice to make decisions that can cause hardships upon ourselves, but GOD will provide for us, clean up our messes and redeem us.

For me, I know if I was ever to take the step to end my life, GOD would forgive me and because I believe in him he would welcome me to heaven, I know not ideal in the sense because I would love to grow old and go in God's time, I do not believe GOD wants us to take our life, but again gives up free will.

For those considering something like this, you should talk to someone of course, but at the end of the day you will decide and must live with leaving your family, friends, and loved ones behind especially if you have significant others and kids especially.

I am thinking of Stephen "Twitch" Boss to end his life last year, the DJ of Ellen who ended his life although he had a beautiful wife, kids and looked like a beautiful life with Money and fame, but even that was not enough.

For those reading this, I know some of you may feel concerned, but please don't be, I am at peace for my thoughts, but maybe I shouldn't be. For now I will continue to push forward, survive, love my family, support them, support others and make attempts to heal my broken mind, heart and spirit in hopes I don't have to consider ending my life prematurely and live a long life until the Good Lord calls me home, that is my hope.

Chapter 11

I should be Happy...

October 29, 2023

I should be happy, but strangely I am not. I should be happy to have a job, which I am and grateful to GOD for providing me a job, but each day I feel unworthy to be there among such incredible people. My co-workers are all different ages and backgrounds, many of them are my age, older and some younger. Some have been with the company five months, a year, 5 years, 10 years, 20 plus years. Since day one I have felt included, accepted, but deep down I do not feel worthy of their presence.

You see over the course of my 20 plus year career, I do not think I have had a company make me feel like I matter. I am truly waiting for the rug to be pulled out from under me, waiting until they call me into the office and let me know they actually made a huge mistake and they were sorry.

I am counting the days when they tell me, I hope I am wrong because frankly I do not think I can take another Lay off, firing, restructuring, although I have no control over it. As I get older it becomes increasingly more difficult to get employed which makes me feel even more useless which in all honestly would probably push me to put an end to my journey here on earth. Some may think I am being dramatic but I can not stop having dark thoughts about my demise.

I plan in my mind how long I would actually wait until I perform the act, would I wait until my daughter is older or younger. I think about what I would say as m last words and yes I would detail why hopefully leaving my family closure, but I doubt that would help.

As the late there have been other factors that have probably contributed to my feelings, one would be my weight as the pounds have begun to creep back. From 2021 – 2022 I lost over forty pounds, which gave me more energy, my clothes fit better and look better than I have in years.

This year has been torturous as I lost my job in March , then on the hunt for a new employer in May, but during that time I tossed and turned, struggled with my choices although there were good choices ending up in July leaving that role due to differences which never in all my years have I have happened, then the job search again all while the bills piled up, rent, car payment, Credit cards and what not adding tons of stress , lack of sleep and constant worry if I and when I would land another position.

The waiting truly hurt me, but what hurt me more is not being able live with my decision of leaving the last position before this one, constantly thinking what would I have done differently, if I made the right choice, how I hurt our family financially and how I hurt myself in the process, thinking why couldn't I just stick with it.

I really wanted to stick with the last position, but I was being pushed and prodded and not given the time to train as I worked with a passive aggressive project manager who I discovered she was not who I thought she was.

Yes I could have ignored her, took her shit, her attitude at the same time hating my life, my role and my choices. I also think was it me, maybe I was the problem as there were others who had my role and seemed fine.

But sadly I did check around and I was not the only one she treated like that , but the one who decided to leave, which shocked my managers. I did not get to say goodbye, because the contractor I worked for was my advocate who spoke on my behalf, letting my managers know I was interested in resigning, unfortunately they did not dispute or fight for me, but allowed me to go on my way.

I feel literately tired each day and its not because of a lack of sleep, its because my mind never stops thinking. When I go into work each day, I see smiling happy faces who welcome me. I have so much to learning which is daunting but exciting at the same time. But currently I am living in regret unable to move forward as I truly can not enjoy my life at this point.

I look around at those around me enjoying their life, their time together as a family and I live each day waiting for my days to end. I feel like I am not allowed to breathe, not allowed to do anything for myself. When I come home each day, I see people at the park enjoying their time, playing, laughing, eating while I have to get home to prepare for my class, work, work , work and what do I get out of it other than a paycheck.

Hours, days, months, and years pass me like nothing looking back at what have I done with my life, what value do I bring to my life. It's hard not to think about my failures in my career and look at my peers on how well they are doing. For example, I have a good friend and family friend who is much younger than me, incredible houses, good family lives, money, cars and happiness. Again, maybe I am being overly dramatic. I hope each day I have peace in my heart, that I can enjoy and appreciate my life and that I can smell the roses, yes maybe one day.

I hope I feel better soon, maybe its just another phase, maybe tomorrow I will wake up appreciating my life more, realizing I have gifts to offer this world, but currently do not.

Chapter 12

What Happened to This Boy?

August 26, 2023

I often go back and look at old pictures of myself and think of myself in the sense of what happened to this little boy. The picture you see here was obviously when I was a young boy, I think I was rather cute. This boy was innocent, a clean mind and heart never wanting to hurt anyone, but often I was the being hurt.

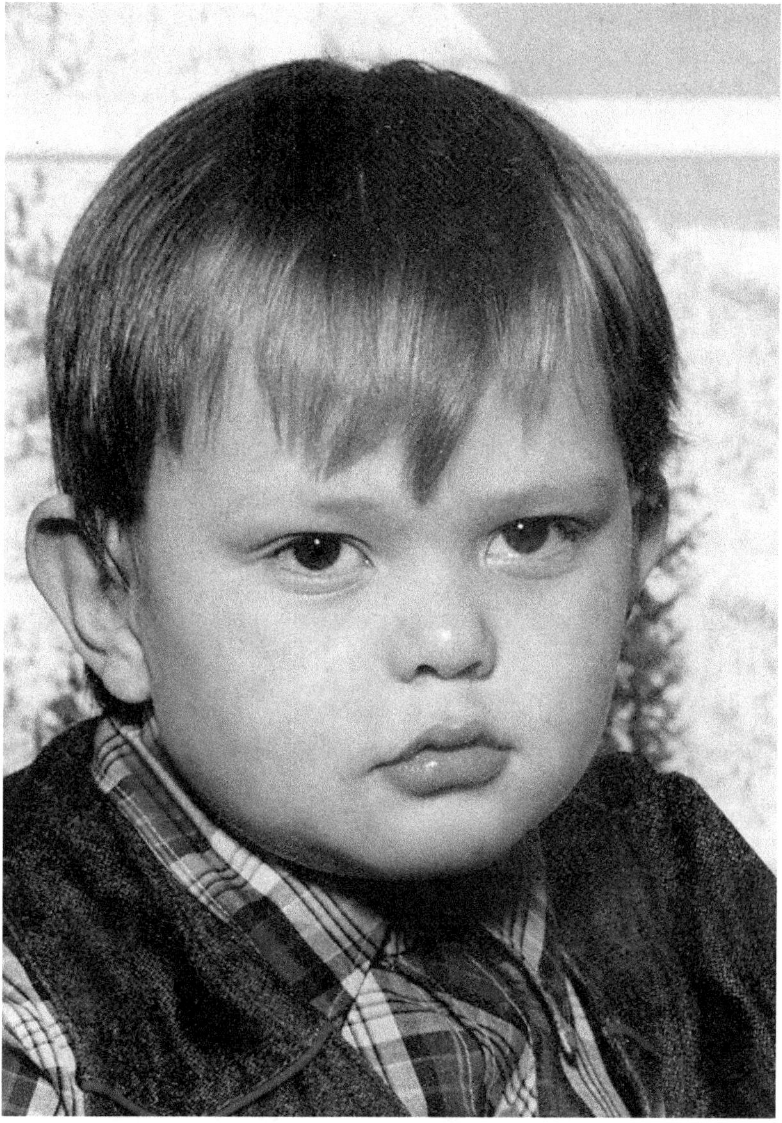

No I was not physically or sexually abused, thank GOD, but sorry for those who were and have been. No my hurt was purely psychologically often ignored and forgotten. Although my mother is no longer around to dispute this. It was my belief my mother did her best trying to raise myself and my sister, although my father was in the picture, he was hands off to raising us, giving us wisdom and even playing with us. My mother who worked for the school district as a teacher's aide but the psychological hurt came from the person I refer to the devil or my grandfather, but he doesn't deserve to be called a grandfather, an unloving, cruel man who would put me down from the age of five until adulthood, using vulgar language against me, my sister and mother each day. One would ask why wouldn't we just leave , live somewhere else, why because my mother frankly didn't have a lot of financial support although I believe she could have done it, I believe she too was emotionally broken from her own life's struggles, but she tried so hard and for the most part raised my sister and I to the best of her abilities, getting us through school, feeding us, dressing us and always having a roof over our head, but this came at a high cost living in a house of hell, tortured each day.

The boy in the picture was a sweet boy, a part of him still exists today, but he is almost gone because of life's struggles, still feeling a sense of worthlessness. Many have said just let go it was in the past, he (The Devil) died in 2016 so why can't I let go because my scars go deep and I don't think I will fully ever let them go.

You see, parents forget and even those around children the powerful influence they have over the wellbeing of them, the effect they can have on their kids by how they treat them and even the people around them.

Children who are innocent grow up but that innocence never truly leaves them until people, parents, teachers, grandparents, friends break their spirit, that was me. My spirit has been broken for too long, although there are people who work to support me today like my wife, sister, daughter and father there is only so much they can do to repair my broken spirit.

I look at this picture and wonder what I would be like if those who were supposed to love me and protect me did just that. I am not referring to my mother but others who took the time to love me, teach me, treat me kindly. Many I would have been a different person, a whole person, but I am don't feel that way.

Children truly are the future and they can do so much in this world when we treat them with love, respect and care, but sadly that is not the case as many kids are raised without care, ignored, forgotten , neglected all in the justification that parents are working, they didn't have the time thinking their kids will be fine, they will grow up to be good people, stable minded and successful but that is not always the case.

In my case I was verbally beaten down told how worthless I was, how I would never amount to anything and of course a child who hears this believes it to be true and I did and have even today.

This boy is a reminder of innocence forgotten and how we need to protect it.

Chapter 13

When Self Sacrifice May be a Good Thing

September 2, 2023

DISCLAIMER : This post is sensitive in nature that discusses self harm and Suicide. If you are feeling suicidal , feelings of self harm and in the U.S. dial 9-8-8 to speak with someone or 9-1-1. These thoughts are my opinions.

I often think about death, a lot. I think about what my last days on earth will be like. Will I die a natural death in old age or will I take matters in my own hands one.

I was recently reading about some you tuber who states that he has great shame that his parents may not have enough for retirement and that It will not be his job to take care of his parents when they get older.

To Each Their Own

Sadly in American culture we are taught to each their own, but in other cultures like Korea they take joy in caring each other as a way to pay back all the years they took care of their children, I wonder why this concept is so hard to comprehend here in the good ole' US.

I was thinking of a controversial thought, why don't people self-sacrifice more in our country, meaning when one gets older or really any age and they become a burden to family and even society that we do not just end life.

I think in today's world people want to live and I know when seem hard to believe that no everyone wants to die unnaturally but either die of old age or of course there are situations when one dies like cancer, sickness, a car accident, basically a death not by our hands.

The Burden On American Families To Care For Their Elders

In U.S. culture people are made to feel burdens on their family when they get older. I will not say everyone feels this way. I personally remember when I was nineteen caring for my grandfather who had Alzheimer's at the time. Although it was very difficult caring for him along with my father, I do not regret it because it was a time, I will always remember being able to see a man who had worked hard in his life, completed his race in life, died and went to JESUS.

Not everyone will have that experience, some simply put their family in homes, but for many its not because they do not love them, but love them enough to give them the care they will need. Taking care of an adult is not for the weak of heart. It's painful, tiring, frustrating and painful to watch over someone you once knew no longer that person.

I truly think more people should self-sacrifice themselves, as a lesson to their loved one about what true sacrifice looks like. As a father myself, I work hard for my wife and daughter, to give them a decent life but at the end of the day when I can no longer do that, I cease to be useful anymore and I am WILL not be an inconvenience to my daughter and wife. I get that when we have a family, we are to love them no matter what, care for them like they care for us, take the good and the bad together like a real family, but sadly it seems real families are rare these days.

I will NOT be a Burden

When my daughter gets of age, has a family of her own and if I am allowed to get older, I would NOT want to be a burden to her and her new family, I refuse. I refuse to be a burden to my wife and Yes I am aware we are married through sickness and health, richer or poorer but as father and husband I am the one needs to keep the family together and when I can no longer do that, what is my purpose, frankly I have none.

I think if more people took it upon themselves to self-sacrifice we might have a better society, a society that may care more when we lose people we fail to care for and appreciate. I know my theory will never materialize as people in general are selfish wanting to live no matter what pain we cause others or ourselves, but it may be worth considering.

I think if more people self-sacrificed people would not have to live lives in poverty, in pain, feeling a burden to those around us. It appears even our own government makes its citizens feel like a burden, since we weigh down the system, take up resources.

Some after reading this may feel I am advocating for Suicide but I am not, my point that often in society people consider their loved ones burdens like parents. I get it maybe you have not had a great childhood, maybe you had terrible parents so this message may not be for you.

If you if you a decent childhood raised by parents who provided for you and did the best they could although you may feel they should have done better which is quite judgmental by the way. Young adults who live at home, who are single without the responsibility of caring for a family does not know what that pressure is. The pressure to hold the finances together, to keep everyone fed, to house everyone, to keep the train going at all times, NOT EASY.

I would self sacrifice myself for my family, if my family was on the verge on homelessness, without food, I would sacrifice myself so they would survive.

Is it a lack of compassion in the U.S. for those who care for us feeling one you reach a certain age you shouldn't be required to care for your loved ones if need be or are generations today much more self centered , selfish about the wellbeing , if that is the case then those individuals would not care if their family, parents self-sacrificed themselves all in the name of not be a burden to them, making those family members happy that they will not be responsible but for themselves.

I am unsure why that youtuber triggered me in this thought today. I watched briefly but could see the contempt for his parents seeing that HE would never take care of his parents if need be, NOT HIS PROBLEM. Some may say well that's his opinion he is entitled to his opinion and you are correct, but should think hard about how much value he and others place on their loved ones and what they are will to give to support them in their times of need. If you are one that says TO EACH THEIR OWN, NOT MY PROBLEM, then you should do some soul searching because frankly you may not have one of love and compassion for others. I get its difficult and may not be fiscally possible but still the question is WOULD YOU and if you can how would feel, would it eat at you each day to find a solution or would you simply just move on. Tough questions and answers I know.

Chapter 14

How anger can help fuel the better you!

July 9, 2022

For most of my adulthood and childhood I can honestly say I was not happy, I was depressed and even at point suicidal. Much of these feeling stems from my childhood and how I was raised. Having a daughter who is now nine years old I relish at being her father and always there for her. But growing up I lived with my mother, Sister and grandfather who verbally abused me since the age of five years old with put downs, curse words and thank goodness no physical violence but it did come close to that.

Childhood was my foundation for today

I marched to what I was told at a young age as my mother tried to provide for us the best she could, but relied on her father for housing and food, although I mother always worked it was still hard. Call it bad luck, but I think its probably deeper than that.

I believe she too suffered from a lack of self-worth because she was brought up in a household of no real love and attention because the father she later searched for and found abandoned her in her childhood. I think of this has a horrible cycle that took years to break, and in all honestly it didn't truly break until my grandfather who in my opinion shouldn't even be call that, but he died in 2016 and my mother passed in 2015.

I vowed when I had children and even my wife to never treat someone subhuman like I was treated growing up as it affects me even today just thinking of it. But life goes on and I still had to live my life and survive and to do that I had to let anger have control of me to push me harder to get out of this mindset of depression and self-loathing.

Many Suffer today and don't have to

I sympathize with many out there who suffer with these types of feelings living in the shadow of people who have hurt us, its not easy to break free. For most of life I really didn't realize the damage it has caused until you look back after twenty years and ask yourself why my life isn't better and its because deep down I truly felt I didn't deserve to have good things in life like a good job, money and even a family at times, but you do deserve it.

Anger is an important feeling that I believe can push us harder to succeed in life. Some of you may not agree with and say anger is not helpful it hurts people. But really, I am not talking about projecting anger on to others, many people do that today and that is why we live in such divisive times. When anger is used properly, we can funnel our energy to see our mistakes and correct that behavior for the better, I know it did for me.

Are you tired of your job, tired of living in a way that doesn't fit how any person should live? Do you have no relationships with friends and family or any relationships for that matter? All of these things we value in this life we can change for the better. We can change our mindset to let go of the past, the hurt and let anger take control for a moment.

Letting go of anger

Today I am no longer angry, but self-reflected on the mistakes I made in life and why I am today, but I am working to correct those mistakes in life, personal, career and how I see myself and others its all possible.

Some of you may not understand where I am coming from because some of you may not have had the hardships I have had. Maybe you grew up in a loving family and home so you have no reason to be angry because you have a healthy understanding of who you are and what you are capable of. For the rest which it seems like there are many out there, this could be a way to release yourself from the pain and get angry and change course now, its never too late.

We do live in world and in a country full of despair, depression and anxiety and some would say well for good reason look at the world. Look at how people are treated today like subhuman with no value. But really in society we all society to view us that way. Take the mindset you are not worthless; you have value regardless of what your bank account says. We all have gifts and talents we can use we just have to see it for ourselves, which means getting angry and opening our minds to those gifts and pushing the limits for ourselves to see what we have in each of us. Once we fully realize that potential let go of the angry, its not meant to be carried like an addiction but be let go of at a certain point.

I know today I have little or no angry within me, but I still get frustrated with my own limitations, but I am only human after all. Never give up trying to be a better version of yourself!

Chapter 15

Failure is not an option, but I am a failure

August 13, 2022

I often reflect on my life from childhood until today recounting those of life's accomplishments and where I am today in my life. I can honestly say I have not accomplished as much as I had hoped but I believe its most due to my upbringing and my own self-destructive attitude at times.

Growing up being the child of divorced parents, I grew up with a Devil of a grandfather, my mother whom I loved and sister and father. Growing up I was always told how stupid I was , how I could do nothing right, this coming from a grandfather who I had the horror of living with most of my life.

Average from the Day I was Born

I was an average student in school from elementary to college never reaching my full potential in those years. I was a shy and quiet child growing up, showing respect towards my instructors at all times never getting out of line but I really stayed in the background never really raising my hand or taking risks in class.

I was bullied, the fat kid as I would regularly get made fun of , pick on , chased around school. Although the bullying wasn't really physical, I was no beat up, but I was spit on once and there was a time in Middle school I attempted to defend myself and tried to kick another student only to be too slow and the other kid forced me to do the splits in front of my class.

I was always searching

I was always looking for someone to spend time with, a girlfriend even at a young age and often fought for the affection of girls getting rejected all the time. These girls were not the most attractive girls in my opinion or with the most sparkling personalities or even popular, but I was rejected. This happened throughout my life, but High school is particularly painful as I tried and tried and tried, failed.

There was one girl who I was very drawn to, her name was Ruth Milton, she hung out with the druggies and smokers, and I followed her. Often, we would hang out at the movies. Ruth was rail thin, blond hair, blues, and crocked teeth, but I didn't care as being her friend was good enough for me, but over time my feelings really grew for her. At one point after high school was finished, I confessed my love for her but again she rejected me and never spoke to her after that.

I failed going to my first college out of high school Cal state Maritime Academy. I didn't bomb out but was bombing my coursework especially college algebra and the failure was too much to handle so I left going back to the horror house and restarting once again at DeVry University, graduating in 2002.

I failed at Love

In college I failed at love too, finding one girl friend out of college who I met on Yahoo Personals, but that last a few months, her name Sylvia Gomez. I met other women in college, but I was too blinded to see what I had in front in me as many of them wanted relationships with me but I didn't pursue for some reason, two I remember in particular Rachel and Liz, two good women, but one I felt just wanted me to get immigration status, both were students like myself at DeVry University.

I do regret not being more opened mind back then as I was in my early twenties, but I was struggling with my own life at those points, failing to see my true self. I am sorry to say my family was not there for me in that sense of providing encouragement as I grew to figure that on my own. Its incredible when there are those in our lives who encourage us, provide advise on how to be successful in life.

I failed at ending it all

Over the course of getting almost committing suicide in 2007 and surviving, then finding my future wife and then my daughter life has changed quite drastically for me over the years. I look back and reflect on those difficult times when I probably would have re-attempted to end it all but didn't because of those now in my life.

I will say the reason I failed to end my life is probably because my sister just happened to be home when I was committing this act and saved my life as she removed the noose from around my neck and getting help right away.

I often don't always talk about those moment as it makes people uncomfortable because many don't take such drastic measures. Today I work, write, Teach, and try to live a life as a devoted family even though its pretty easy to fail today as even society wants to see us fail.

One of the things that keeps me going is my writing, blogging and vlogging now and can't forget my podcast giving me the outlet I need to express myself.

Recently I attempted to express myself on LinkedIn causing alarm with my employer who I removed it. It really wasn't about the company but about my failures and how I feel at times. I know we all walk a different walk, but I look at many even much younger than me and see how incredibly gifted many are today with the help of technology as well. I look at my daughter who is 9 and she even appears more gifted at her young age then I was at her age but that could be because she has a normal childhood unlike mine.

I know that sometimes we may not self-reflect on our lives, the past like I do only looking to the present and the future, but I believe the past is a way to see how and why we failed and if we continue to fail in our lives and if we do we need to change course.

I hard things is can no longer fail just by myself I have a wife and daughter who are affected, so I must be extra careful that my failures don't hurt us.

On Paper I am Not a Failure

On paper I don't look like a failure, but I feel I am, although I have what many want and don't have a loving family. A wife and daughter I love who get to grow with me. Not everyone has that, many are alone thinking about ending it all today because what is the point of living without people in our life. I don't agree with that but that's not my mind or thoughts that yours or maybe someone you know.

I am trying to make up for lost time today focusing on my career more, my writing, building a legacy for my daughter and wife in case I am not longer here anymore.

The wheels in my mind turn constantly I wish I could just turn off my mind for a moment to enjoy life and appreciate what I have, but I can't this me. I am no longer manic depressive, but depression is always apart of me, that is a failure I wish I could shake but can't as I am stuck with it.

We must remember we all fail in life even though we look at others and see great success but maybe those people are failing internally, psychologically, health wise, but on the outside, they appear to have it all together.

Today we live in a visual world where we can crop out sadness and the realities of our life, make us appear happier, thinner living a grand life but its all illusion.

I hope one day, even on my last breath I can appreciate my failures have led me somewhere in this life, somewhere people will learn from my failures and accept their short comings and accept its apart of who they are. I can not accept my short comings but I know I have failed in this life , I've been failed by people in my life and I continue to fail because its pointed out what my failures are like Joseph you talk too much, Joseph your too emotional , Joseph there are far better people in this life then you who have done so much more already and they are much younger then you.

I will keep pushing forward

I will keep pushing the limits of myself, my mind, my career and teaching myself, my family why failures don't have to stop them but force them to push harder against whose who say you CANT DO THAT. FUCK THOSE PEOPLE!

Stop listening to others' opinions who have no value, who have no impact in your life. Opinions of politicians, world leaders, TV hosts who go home to their nice mansions with their fat paychecks acting as prophets to you and I FUCK THEM!

My mind is tired, so tired of trying to live up those who tell us we failed. We failed our companies; we have failed in life in reality they are the failures although society doesn't see them that way because they have money and power to show they did something right in life. They got some poor suckers to believe their bullshit.

Some of you may say why the turn, because this is where we all need to realize that our failures are not always failures but because society , education and those around us don't give a shit about us, never have, never will. We have to realize our own self potential as early as possible so we can go out to prove it to ourselves and the world.

Maybe I am not a failure after all, I just happen to have believe all my life because I trusted those in life like our companies who tell us we failed. STOP LISTENING TO THOSE WHO OPINIONS HAVE NO MEANING! Listen to that inner voice, that is the truth. Better Yet Listen to GOD as he will NEVER Lie to us, I know for a fact he tells me the truth, but that's me.

Chapter 16

What I would tell my younger self

Chapter 40 - What I would tell my younger self as a generation X'er.

September 11, 2022

As a generation X'er born in 1979 and being in the workforce for over twenty years, I have learned a thing or two about what I would have done differently and how my frame of mind may have been different.

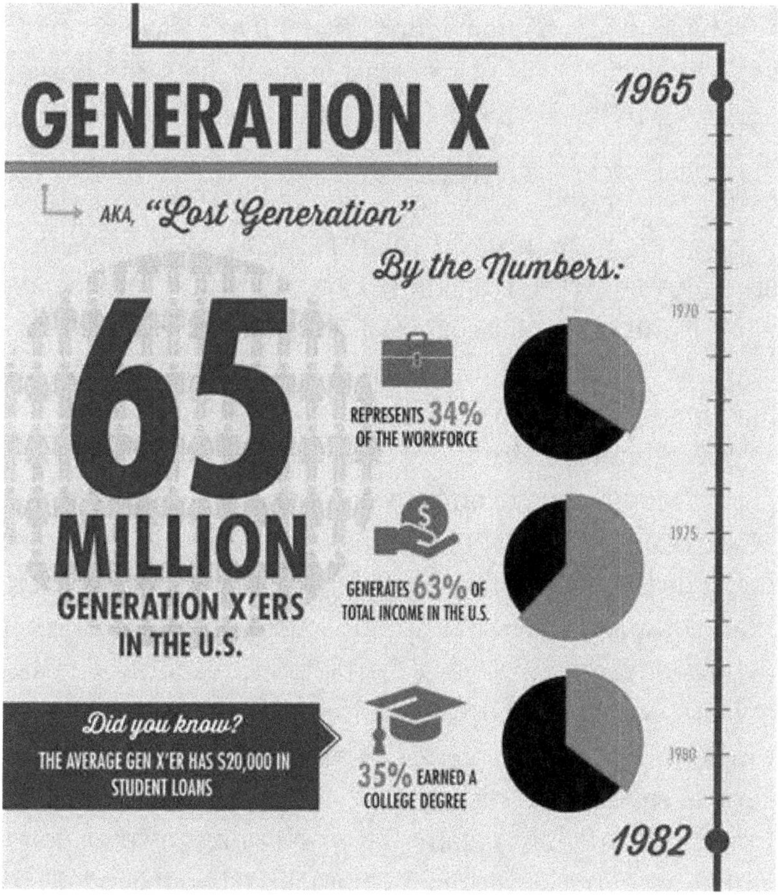

Do Let people situations get to you

Growing up I grew up in a home that verbal abuse was a constant due to my grandfather who we lived with. He would tell me how I wouldn't do something right; how worthless I am and add a daily dose of profanity and vulgar language since the age of five.

This had a direct impact on working to please people. I would constantly want to please my teachers, my bosses and even today I struggle with letting go and not getting situations get to me, things out of my control. But if I could tell myself many years ago is not to sweat those things, we have no control over. Don't let hardships, struggles and everyday life get to you and to appreciate what is important like family, friends, good health knowing that all things may not aways last especially having family and friends around.

Save, save, save

Growing up, my family was considered low income. Mom did her best with the little we had but failed to teach us the importance of savings from a young age. Yes, I did allowances growing up but would often spend it on toys, candy, and waste it. When I got into adulthood with my first real job I did save at first but that was because I lived at home with no real expenses. I had no real concept of saving for a real purpose like a home, a car. When I started my family I really have no savings at that point which were in my thirties. I would also dip into my 401K at times often wiping it out to pay off debt and bills, which to this day I wish I would have done differently.

Watch the debt

Debt is something that can sneak up on you if you are not careful. Most of us carry some debt like a student loan, a car, a home, credit card. We must do our best to live within our means even if that means we go without. Do not subsidize debt like credit cards and loans to live on. I will say I know because I have done this myself when at times I did not make enough money, I would relay on credit to help get by but in the end I ended up owning more then I wanted to causing financial hardship.

Have Fun no matter what

Some would say well doesn't fund cost money and yes it does but doesn't have too. In my twenties I often focused on my job, never really focusing on having fun such as traveling, which I regret not doing more. In those years of your life when you don't have responsibilities like a family to support its important to focus on doing those things that you may not have a chance to do. Its so important to enjoy life no matter what age, but its particularly important to enjoy your twenties and thirties and those may be years that become really foundation to the people we become later in life.

Stop the comparisons

Some of you may not do this, but I often did. I often compared my accomplishments, the money I earned and my lifestyle to my peers who had similar backgrounds to me. In college I remember feeing quite resentful of my peers who made much more money than me and had better positions. Remember our careers and how quickly we get there is not a race although we sometimes feel we need to hurry up to reach a certain level of success early on. At times we will see success comes early for some, later for others and no success for many. But we all have a different journey in this life. You will see in life we all have success and failures, and we all are here to play the long game in life, so enjoy the ride and remember you have your own unique gifs and talents.

Everything happens for a reason

I have had many failures in my life in pursuing a career. I have taken jobs that have failed me, and I have failed on the job for not being a good fit. It's important to remember that not every situation is meant to hurt us, but it's meant to be a lesson. Often when we work for others like a company, we will experience layoffs and even firings which can be hard to take for many because we tend to take that as a personal attack on our abilities and us as people. Its not personal and we have to remember in work its only business. I know that is hard to grasp at first because we care about our work, its our livelihood but we to remember there are other opportunities for us and everything happens for a reason.

Be Kind

Being someone who has suffered with manic depression and being bi-polar I have experienced a great deal of unkindness from people who frankly do not understand someone like me. I can be incredibly sensitive at times to feedback, criticism easy to take personal. I have gotten better and know in a way I have right to be angry if I choose too. But kindness is a choice we can all make, one that will allow us to be content in this life. We live in a culture that has the tendency to be very angry. Especially since 9/11 I believe our culture has changed drastically and even today its easy to be angry and unkind to others, but don't. I feel we will all live , longer , happier lives if we choose to be kinder, happier to everyone.

Don't be too trusting of people, organizations and government

Growing up I always felt people did not and could not have bad intentions that people really do want to just help one another. But as I got older, I could see that people are often out for themselves. I tried to live a life of ethics, of kindness and trustworthiness. I think its so important not to take anything at face value especially what you read and watch.

Take Risks

I often felt afraid to take risks in life especially my career. I wish I would have taken on more entrepreneurial risks to make it out on my own early in life instead of relaying on an organization to make money. Today we happen to live more in world that encourages independence in work because of the gig economy. I encourage you to take leaps of faith on your own, I feel the fear is real, but we may see its not as bad as we all make it out to be. In the end we may find ourselves more successful in our career and life when we take risks.

Never give Up

This life gets tough its easy to want to give up. I did almost give up, attempting to take my life in 2007 but failed (thank goodness) I am still here. I let life get to me, I let worries get to me, I let people get to me. I should have realized that I am enough and not let others like friends, family, bosses place value on me. We all have value, but we have to see if for ourselves and believe in our value never letting anyone tell us otherwise. Keep pushing for your dreams no matter what stands in your way. Live your best life for you.

You're not alone

It often feels in this big world we are alone, even when we may not have friends or loved ones, but we need to reach out and connect with others, seek help. I have mostly kept everything in which caused harm to myself. We do live in a very connected world with social media but that is not the same of actually reaching out to people physically. Social media is a great tool but its no substitute for having a real conversation and building good relationships, focus on those and you will live a happier life.

Journalling is so important

I find documenting one's life and legacy is so important as there are people in our life who should know how incredible you are. Sadly, many my loved ones have passed on and I have lost that history of their life, who they were and how they lived. Now one could say why live in the past, but I have found we learn from the past especially those people from our past. That is one reasons I blog, Vlog and podcast so my future generations like my daughter can look back and know who I am, how I lived, my thoughts, beliefs and values.

Don't live in regret

We all have regrets from choices we have made or not made, failures and mistakes in life. We all have them big and small. Living in regret does nothing for us to move forward. Yes, we can learn from our mistakes, but don't dwell on them move on and forward no matter what and never look back.

Cut yourself a break

Cut yourself on slack, don't be so hard on yourself it does no good but harm. I am not saying don't care. I am saying those things in our life like work we tend to take very personal. There is nothing wrong with having a mission and doing well in life but when you have failures in life, move on and remember your only human but being so hard on yourself only harms your wellbeing and mental state, its simply not worth it.

Create goals

Goals will give you focus which will help fend off procrastination, fear and fear of failure. Goals will allow you to create a plan for your life that you can focus on each day. Whether its to save money, get an education, getting healthy or any kind of goal close to your heart, make it happen and put it in action.

Get Healthy

Growing up, I was often overweight and obese from a young age. I would say I was probably at my heaviest starting around age twelve. I was bullied at school and lived in a home full of aggression, vulgar language, and verbal abuse from my grandfather. Its important to start with the basics like exercise, eating right and consciously thinking about our bodies and keep ourselves at a healthy weight. I understand we are all different, sizes and shapes but we all can shed the extra weight at times for those who struggle. For those who don't struggle with weight issues, finding ways to live a healthier lifestyle which would only prolong our life. Letting go of drugs and alcohol. Today I am a healthier weight, eating better and feeling better. I am not talking about getting on a diet or starvation but focusing daily on our wellbeing, total self -care.

CEO'S are not more important than you or more valuable

Often growing up we were told to look up and value the CEO, business letter and politician equating them to be more important, more intelligent and more valuable today but not true. Yes, they do have important positions but their value as a person as a human is no more value then you and I. Lets stop placing those individuals with such high importance, they are no. What matters is you, your story and path.

Chapter 17

My Dark Thoughts In My Time of Joblessness

March 20, 2023

My dark thoughts have already been in overload since losing my primary job March 2nd. I am working to be positive but its not easy for someone who has the tendency to think of the worst case scenario. I tend to dream about an escape out of this situation as this type of situation brings me trauma. Although I understand that many are struggling through this exact experience but for someone who has struggled with depression and anxiety and thoughts of escape.

The other night I dreamt what my family wife and daughter would be like If I was not in the picture, if I decided to just end my life. They would be ok financially, but they would suffer emotional pain of me not being there. I know many don't like to think about that or even make it a topic because we should all want to live even in the toughest situations but each of us are created differently. Some have that bold spirit to keep pushing forward no matter what. Although adversity happens to all of us, many of us think of just today, something years ahead and how their lives will be affected and how they can prevent collapse of one's livelihood.

Each day I look at LinkedIn and see the despair people are going through the job loss, but put in perspective its not every industry, its been primarily in tech, which is exactly the industry I was in as an implementation consultant, just a title, more like a project manager. In the last five years I have gone through 3 layoffs. Part of the reason my mind has shifted dark could be related to that I am viewing on television and online, which can have a negative affect over my thinking, and I tend to carry that into my sleep.

One of the darkest thoughts I have is why do as society stigmatize suicide and euthanasia, that when people are suffering and we all suffer differently cant people just be allowed to die in their own way. Why is it that we as society try to hard to stop people from ending their lives. I get we shouldn't encourage people to do that, but if people make a choice and even have support from their family and friends, why is that so wrong.

The conflicting side of this is ones belief system as a believer in Christ, I know its morally wrong to do such an act. But I know we also have a loving god who is also forgiving. Sadly I have seen and heard about many pastors who have committed this act. They are human, they suffer and as much as I would like to believe they are stronger in their faith, they human side of them is weak like all of us.

My mind races to the men especially who have committed this act like Chris Cornell (which is debatable per his spouse), Chester Bennington of Linkin Park, Johnathan Brandis and others.

I truly believe people should have a choice, yet I understand the morality of taking one's life especially from an eternal perspective. Being a believer in JESUS, I know he would want me to live, relying on him during those challenging times, those trials. Often listening to the word of GOD especially messages on dealing with adversity and trials,

James 1:2, comes to mind:
My brethren, count it all joy when you fall into various trials.

When I have dark thoughts especially during times like these, I often remember those times, although they were each under different circumstances, I was a different person each of those times. For example, in my last job lay off in October 2019, that was particularly difficult because it was during the holiday season I was left jobless, Before that it was in January/February 2018, so as you still three changes in employment not by choice in the last five years. I can hear employers now, "WELL IT LOOKS LIKE YOU HAVE BEEN JOB HOBBING A LOT". I hate those words as I have heard employers say them often to me, even in my twenties when its expected to figure out what you want to do in your life.

I truly believe GOD is in control, that what we go through is appointed to our growth and we mostly overcome those things in our life like a loss of a job. A job where we as people slave for an employer to pay us so we can live and eat and have health insurance.

I search for ways to alleviate the stress of job loss, my racing mind, my worries, anxieties and my thinking of escape from this situation. There are moments of levity when I read a positive story of someone who has also struggle with finding a position to be hired and hear their excitement.

I want to believe what I am struggling with is normal, that people go through this all the time and in reality, is true, since many of us rely on organizations for employment, but I think there must be another way.

As of late I have been deep in nostalgia watching my comfort television shows and movies remembering those times and I would say even simpler times. When I say simpler times, I would say pre cellphones and social media. Currently I am binge watching Buffy the Vampire Slayer and Night court, the new version and the 80's version and finishing off with Rocky, all of them and lets add Cinderella man, love that movie.

During these times, I tend to self-reflect on my life, my mistakes in career choices, my choice in positions and overall, my choices. I know I should not dwell in the past, but its difficult when decisions of the past really affect me today such as the first college I attend out of high school , Cal State Maritime Academy, but left after a few months due to my depression and struggling academically, ending up completing my studies at DeVry University and Keller Graduate School for my masters. Although I am happy I went for higher education, now that I think of it I should have made better school choices.

I am trying not to let the voices in my head get to me, they are not literal yet, but a constant voice of telling me about failures and then usually ending with my way out of this life.

This piece I have been contemplating over two weeks, because these feelings are not just going to go away, yes I am hurting. But trying to put things in perspective, that it's a job and a job is not me, I am me. I am unique, I have skills, I have lots to offer that another company will want. Yes this self-doubt is getting to me and I need to stop.

I hope in time my mind will shift once I start to get employers to see what I have to offer and even better if a new opportunity comes along soon.

In the meantime I am hopeful for today, but tomorrow is a new day and hopeful the weeks don't bleed into the next.

For those going through times like these, looking for work, going through financial difficulties, health struggles we all have to believe it will be ok. It may not be today, but it may be. Let's keep our head up, that includes myself.

This rant was made possible by a man in desperate need to work soon, who supports a family, has rent, bills like many, but is also going through challenging times and I am not alone.

Lastly , a late addition to resources that I was provided in responses to those who are considering using anti-depressants , which I will say help , but like anything else there are risks you should be aware of.

Chapter 18

Preparing my Heart to say Goodbye

August 6, 2023

As of late, I am under great distress over searching for a new job after my last role did not work out. My mind is living in regret, as I replay my career and personal failures over and over again never resting. For many losing a job is traumatic enough because of the stress of lack of income, lack of health insurance, lack of job purpose.

My Despair Begins

For me being someone who is the main support of the family, I have rent, food, bills quite overwhelming add to that the constant rejection especially those when I go above and beyond to make myself stand out in the job interview only to get rejected.

I think over and over again about my last role which I really like the position, but unfortunately, I wasn't being allowed to learn, the person who I support the Project Manager was passive aggressive to me, threatening my job and sadly no one could do anything, because I was considered a contractor, not regular employee up against a 20 year employee. Adding insult to injury, I took this role in place of a role I now highly regret, no longer available.

It probably would have been fine, if the other role I had properly given up that role, instead of kept changing my mind as I told the employer I was going to take the role, then not take it and then take it and then finally giving it up, I blew it. I know it's a learning experience, but It was a great role and the role I gave up was a good role, it was a position that I felt was an opportunity of a lifetime for me.

I guess I could have stuck it out, but the company put a nail in the coffin when they wanted to place me on a PIP plan (performance improvement plan) after only 5 weeks on the job, I hadn't even been fully trained yet, I was still learning, yet the PM was reporting me to my manager and supervisor on what she didn't like about my performance.

For many this would not be a reason to leave, many would stick with the position, work to deal with the people who are not allowing you to do your job and ignore the person, but I was not able to just ignore the person, I was basically like her support to the projects, she was not someone I couldn't just ignore. Its been painful for me as one of my most memorable failures adding to that I was laid off in March.

My Depression and Anxiety

As of late my depression and anxiety has taken a toll on me, as I am unable to be at peace, unable to rest and sleep in a constant state of worry. I have truly contemplated end of life, but I am unable to do that right now as I would leave my wife and daughter practically penniless as my life insurance is not fully vested past two years as there are clauses that would prevent payment before two years. Many would think that I shouldn't be thinking about this, that everything will be ok, I will get a job, be patient, give yourself a break.

In my mind I think about losing our apartment, unable to support my wife and daughter as my mind falls in despair as I think about how I would leave this world. I think about what would happen to my wife and daughter, would they be ok. In my mind I can't help thinking they would be better off no longer needing to worry about me as they each could have a real chance at happiness, to be financially free to a long time not to worry about the financial matters of this world.

Deep down I'd like to think that this world is not about money, that's its about living, running the race of life, getting to the natural finish line of life when we take our natural last breath on our death bed well into our older age. I think about all of those in my life family and some friends who may miss me but in time they would move on , the years would pass and I would soon be forgotten.

Most I don't believe think about their last days or the value of their life, but truthfully I do as the old phrase in my mind sticks "Your worth more dead than alive". Sadly these thoughts are nothing new to me as I have attempted to take my life before but many years ago in 2007 well before my wife and daughter were in my life.

My attempt was by hanging and I almost would have succeeded except my sister had come home just as I was hanging, and she pulled me down and from there the rest is history you can say.

I would imagine if I was to go out again, I would probably go in the same fashion as I remember the rope put me out in a matter of seconds as I remember darkness, stars and then I was out, then suddenly conscious again.

Another strange thought I have if I decide to take this fateful step, is my spirit, will it directly go to heaven or will my spirit stay earth bound. As many of you are aware I have an interest in paranormal thinking its possible my spirit may wish to stay behind to make sure my wife and daughter will be ok, protecting them the best I could from the afterlife.

My mind not well right now as I feel very conflicted right now as I am a man of faith, a man who believes in GOD and I know God wants me to have faith in him that everything will be worked out to his glory. Its not that I don't have faith, although It may seem like I don't but I am scared, my mind and heart are not well right now.

I am confident in where my soul is going if I was to attempt what I am thinking, although Christians may believe that if one was to take their life, they would immediately go to hell, but that is not something I believe because our GOD is a loving, forgiving and merciful GOD and my soul goes to eternity for believing in him and I have to believe as many who love GOD especially those who were pastors have sadly struggle with mental health and have taken that course, in heaven now.

I truly do have a lot to do if that day comes, such write and finish any remaining books, create more blogs and vlogs which are all meant to leave behind my words, my thoughts, who I was for those who once knew me especially for my daughter. It saddens me to think of not being able to see her grow up, attend her firsts of everything, missing graduations, first dates, major milestones. One can say well you can be there, you don't have to do anything.

At this point although I have a great deal of many skills and can find another role, its look bleak out there as many in tech are also looking, although I am not specifically looking for jobs in tech, I am open. I have had a few interviews and although good positions pay well below what I have been making for years, making it difficult to survive on those wages.

The Search Continues

I will continue to apply for jobs, interview, take care of the family the best of my ability, but I feel my mental health will continue to deteriorate, my feelings of worthlessness will continue until I get back on my feet. Some may say well maybe you should see a therapist, speak to something. Being that I have struggled with mental health for many years, I honestly do not believe a therapist will help me with the fundamentals of getting a job, providing for my family.

For those who are going through joblessness right now, depression and anxiety my hope is it will get better, but until then I am planning my exit strategy, leaving behind no questions about why and if I did what I plan to do.

For now I will keep fighting, pushing forward and trying to stay positive, but right now that will be tough.

Chapter 19

Unfocused and Becoming Unhinged slowly

March 4, 2023

It was October 13th, 2019 when I was last unemployed , similar to this time around, but looking back my feelings at the time have not all the changed that much, but back in 2019 was in a much different place mentally and physically.

For those going through it due to being laid off or fired, this is for you. I was actually apart of the Tech Layoffs.

2019 Lay off/Firing

Since be unemployed something that many of us or most of us have experienced, I have been taking it harder then usual because I have a family to support. I am trying to take it day by day, some days are better then others.

I keep replaying and feeling as a complete failure right now, as I search for work knowing ageism is kicking in soon and getting remarks from interviewers that I am "Too Qualified" for the jobs I apply for, like I don't need to work, eat and pay bills.

I think all too often we look at a single piece of paper a resume and already assume the person would not be happy. I am perfectly content just working, although its great to have a career direction such as if your accountant, a lawyer , doctor you get the the point.

I take these situations even more personal now then lets say 10 years ago when I did have a wife and daughter to support and have my daughter who looks up to me as an example of stability.

I can't sleep at times, luckily haven't lost my hunger but that may be next, I feel myself slowly slipping back into a depression state at times, my anxiety beginning to take hold of me, the negative voices coming back.

I equate much of my success and happiness to having a job, being a provider for my family and society and if I cant do that I feel useless. I have thought what choices I have I can continue looking for work which is what I do, I can become a consultant, learn new skills, finish my novel and edit the damn thing, so there is a lot I can do, but with this life bump in the road I feel at a standstill.

I am thankful my wife is working almost full time which helps, but I am the breadwinner of the family, its my role to care for the family and provide. I know that sounds old fashioned, but I take great pride in being the provider.

Right now I feel lost, unworthy, hopefully those feelings will change soon. I have a strong support system but there is only so much they can do, aside from be positive , you will get a job, don't worry. What many don't understand about me is I need stability like most and this really throws me for a loop.

For those out there, following me keep me in your thoughts and if you pray, pray for me during this time. I know its something we all experience from time to time, but that doesn't mean its easy to overcome. I am applying for jobs each day, trying to take care of my mental health by exercising, eating right and trying to get enough rest and trying to be positive for the future.

I am sorry I have been away from my normal scheduled programming of my short stories I have some still, hopefully we will get back on schedule for all of you to enjoy.

Take care and thank you!

Chapter 20

I'm Only Happy When it Rains

October 16, 2022

I often think about what the world would look like without me it. It's a hard question to ask ourselves at times because we are here sometimes fighting life, trying to survive. Some go through life with a silver spoon in their mouth, some are raised by parents that frankly shouldn't even have kids and those have children, who are good parents but cannot fully provide for them. Just kids and we as people have a roof over our head, food on the table, clothes, transportation.

Life in LA

Growing up in Los Angeles it was a real shit hole, yes there are nice parts of the LA but I grew up in south central predominately Hispanic and black neighborhoods. My family having lived there most of our lives growing up in Los Angeles, Bell Gardens, Huntington Park and Downey.

Growing up you don't always realize what a shit hole is even when you look around it appears this is how people live, its normal. Not everyone is rich or will rich, many just hope you live a middle class life style with the ability to do normal things like go to the movies, go on vacation, eat out, have decent clothes. I did have those things with a side of verbal abuse from the devil incarnate my grandfather who we lived with most of our lives, mother, sister and myself.

I'd like to think my upbringing wasn't unusual, that there are others who probably had far worse upbringings with abuse, living in poverty.

Deep down I am never happy

Why do I think about these things, because I am sorry to say even today, even with my college degrees and the time I put into my career, I guess I was not smart enough, good enough to have real success which some would ask what real success is. There are obliviously different forms of success to have a nice home, lots of money in the bank, a nice job title and the respect of whose you work with being somewhat of a leader, but I am none of those things. I have attempted to push

my way up the latter often pushed back down, not allowed to prosper to move forward, but those in power keep me down. Those in power feel I am unworthy. The difficult thing is why do I care so much. Its starts from childhood, trying to be a pleaser of people. Throughout my life I have tried to please teachers, Bosses, Family members, friends, colleagues, co-workers, customers you name it.

I ask myself the question is this life worth it and yes, their people that I love like my wife, daughter, sister, father, Brother-in-law and others. But I often wonder what life would be like to be a spirit and to wonder never to die.

Why Death is on my Mind

I think about death more these days, it could be what I watch, I watch a great deal of paranormal shows like Ghost adventures and the dead files. In the dead files Amy Allan who is a psychic speaks with the dead and Steve her partner a retired NYPD detective.

Something I found interesting is the dead stick around, their spirits, their souls whatever you wish to call it. But what I find interesting too is that there are those who pass, who are followers of Jesus, and their spirit stays here on earth. I guess I find it strange because often when Steve is interviewing the families or people who these hauntings happen, the families often state their loved ones loved Jesus and God but wonder why they are not at peace.

I am a believer, and I am a believer that we can't be at rest if we feel we have not finished something here on earth like after death you still have a purpose and must stay and then you can move. Such as staying behind to look after a loved one. I have seen many times in Dead files loved ones stay behind to watch over a child, family member and then once the family member told them it was ok, their work was done then they moved on apparently.

Some do not even know they are dead, because their life is taken from them to live in a state of acting as if they are alive. I wonder If they continue to go to work each day, make breakfast, go to sleep. I am sure they will notice that they can not be seen. I am now thinking of the film "The Others" with Nicole Kidman. One of the most eerie films around. I will not spoil it for you if you've never watched.

I also think about the film Thirteen ghosts and imagining all the tortured souls that wander around us, those who live in our homes maybe even watching us as we sleep, bathe and go about our day. We live in a world of spirits. I do believe all spirits will make their way to wherever they need to go whether its Heaven or hell.

What is the point of what I am saying, I am saying that I am in a form of despair and looking for a way out. Although I will not do anything, I am always searching for something in this life. Yes, I search for wealth, materialism, financial stability, mental stability, a sense of being ok, but I have not felt like that for a very long time. That is no reflection on my family, its not their fault, its me I am broken. I am sure many may feel this way.

In today's world we live in a world of consumerism, a world where if you don't live in a mansion or a nice home then you are nothing, you have failed and you are a failure. I am a failure and have been for many years since my teens and It has only gotten worse.

I think of myself as a failure of a father and husband because I can not provide what they deserve, I truly believe that my family deserves better. Some may say well money isn't everything. Lots of people have money who are miserable, who hate life. Yes that is very true but at the end of the day they have choices with money, they can go to school, they can purchase what they need to feel better.

I hate feeling this way and often think if I was a spirt or ghost would I cease to exist and move on to heaven or stay here until I have peace. I am sure one day I will have peace but sadly I think I would have peace not being here anymore, but my family would be torment of not having me in their lives. I ask myself what worse living in torment at times is and being a good provider to my family or leaving them in need and torment of me not being around although they would eventually move on from seeing me in torment and grow to be happy themselves.

I know these are hard questions without a lot of answers. Many will say just live your life, talk to someone, get medicated but don't do anything or think about doing anything, you are loved.

I hate having these feelings, they affect all areas of my life in my personal life, my work and teaching that these feelings get projected as sadness, anger, and fear.

For many of us we work to severely hide these feelings from people, even our family out of not trying to concern them , co-workers and friends. Even today those who don't suffer with these thoughts could never fully understand why we get these thoughts. I am honestly happy that those people don't feel the way I do , that I know they probably struggle like everyone else, but can truly cope better and move on. With myself I can not always move on so quickly.

Suicide Continues to Haunt me

Not sure why I am think about this , but recently or even now its Suicide Prevention month and - was reading this article on Garbage's front women : Garbage's Shirley Manson opens up about mental health, menopause, suicide and survival: 'I understand how somebody is driven to the point where they feel they need to escape' (yahoo.com)

Amazingly she is 56 years old and I feel quite old now, as I grew up with this women, singing her songs and I believe I saw her in concert at one point.

Its hard not to live in the past when I think of the 90's and early 2000's, times that really shaped a person. Times that should have shaped me better in life but didn't because of my depression, my anxieties and my contempt for life.

That is LIFE

Even today I feel I can not fully be content with my life, although one would say well you have everything you need, a roof over your head, food, some money, good jobs, what MORE do you want. What I want is to provide for my family and not feel like I am on a hamster wheel that I can not get off and enjoy the fruits of my labor. In California it feels like that, WORK, WORK , WORK, PAY , PAY,

PAY, RENT, RENT, RENT, PAY , PAY , PAY, NEVER SLEEP, NEVER REST , then WORK, WORK, WORK.

Some of you may say well that's life isn't it. NO that is not all to life is working for the MAN. The MAN could care less about you and I although they say we are valued, we matter but we do Not. We are only as good as the value we bring to the company. The moment we stop to bring value, $$$$$ then we no good to the company any more. Living in the U.S , a capitalist society that is engrained in the fabric of who we are.

At times when I write I know I write incoherently or in some type of rage, which I am at times because certain things burn within me. I imagine those of you who read this and are like what is this guy on and I assure you on I am not anything.

I guess will say that there are times I am happy for some reason. I happy to see my family prosper , having money in the bank, pay the bills which I can at the moment, feed my family and be able to take a decent vacation at least once a year to recharge. I don't get to take a vacation often or on a year.

I guess one could say I'm only happy when it rains, because the weather matches to how I am feeling at time, or gloom. I have works to look on the brighter side of things, I really have, especially during those times in my life when I was searching for a better life, better career and so on.

This particular piece I am writing now I have been writing for weeks now, thinking maybe I will feel completely different, but I do not. I don't want my family to suffer, to go without and as a father and husband it breaks my heart to see them go without.

From the looks of our life, we live like any other, have an apartment, good car, three jobs and a daughter who is nine.

I will work to calm my nerves, have peace, let go of the past, but that's not easy. Its hard not to think back on my life, the wrong turns. Most if not all of make wrong turns in life. But what I have seen that many who make wrong turns often make those corrections to correct their life. Some work so hard to build a life but fail, have hardships and can never move forward in ways, that is how I feel and felt at times.

I will say it was not from lack from trying. I honestly had good intentions of having a career but my choices now that think of them were not the best, although not out of ordinary. Today I work to be content with my life, what I have but know that life is a give and take. Although I would love to have more in life like money and possessions, I know deep down that is not important. Family and Love is what is important in this life but I know it does have some importance.

I love the rain, the lightning and thunder because I am only happy when it rains. The rain washes away the bad and allows the good, which is what I hope for my life and anyone's life. Let the bad wash away and the good stay.

My Faith Sustains Me

Last where my faith comes into this discussion as a man who believes in GOD, in Jesus Christ, I am conflicted at times. Not for my love of GOD or following what the bible says but really listening to GOD's words and following them and going against my own nature.

Today I was listening to a message online from one of my home churches Calvary Chapel Downey and pastor Reyes talked about not living in the past and how often we live in the past and that is not what GOD wants and that often we worry about tomorrow.

I am thinking of this scripture:

Thank you for listening to my rants, my insecurities, my feelings of uncertainties, my flaws. I think its so important to know we are all flawed, and I know at times we may say well at least I am not as flawed as that other person, but in reality its not a competition we are just flawed differently. Some appear not be flawed but perfect. Perfect life, money, wealth, Family, beauty, good health, great career everything many of us crave but in reality, they are not perfect, they are broken people who are so good at showing the world a mask. Is that you, if it is stop hiding, show your true self. Don't be afraid to show your flaws, be proud of them, they are what make you perfect.

Chapter 21

A New You is Just Around The Corner for 2023

January 15, 2023

What the new year means to me, to you, to the world. It means something different for everyone. Some create resolutions for the new year to be new person, new goals. I am often reminded of when I would attend my local gym, a 24-hour fitness which by the way is no longer open 24 hours since the pandemic. After each new year I would see a new crop of those who joined to kick off a year of health only to see that many no longer there a few weeks after. Some may say well what is wrong with that, people are trying to get healthy. The problem with that many of those who joined never intended on being serious and you know sadly many of us are like that.

Change is right around the corner

We all want to change for the better and a new year gives each of us a fresh start. One of the best years of health was in January 2021 when I looked at myself in the mirror, at pictures and actually hated myself. Maybe I have always hated myself, but I said to myself I can change, I need to change for myself and my family and have lost about sixty pounds, some of the weight has come back but in the form on muscle. I look at before and after pictures of myself from last year and attempt to remember that time in my life. Although a year is not that long ago sometimes, we forget how much we have grown in a year.

Maybe not physically but maybe mentally, maybe spiritually, maybe more mature in our thinking. I often self-reflect on the man I am today, feeling a sense of regret that I was not the man I am today many years ago. Many years ago, I was full of self-hate, full of self-doubt, someone who didn't see my true value thinking and waiting for the validation of others to tell me I was valuable. But when I had my family wife and daughter I in time could see my value, appreciate my value as I raise my daughter and see her growing, changing and maturing and it's a real gift.

Don't Worry, Be Happy!

Today I try not to worry like I once did as I have vowed to not let things get to me like they once did, things I had no control over. I have learned that life is messy and as much as many of us like to make life fit into a nice box we can't. We are bound to fail daily, sometimes royally because as human beings we are imperfect.

After last year when I unfortunately contracted Covid, something within me changed like a switch in me when off as if I was once blind could see. That all the things I worried about didn't really matter. I started to see that I made it this far in life and I shouldn't fear any more, asking myself what am I fearing. For years I stood ideally by , year after year as life passed me by, not always enjoying and appreciating what I had.

My wife often reminds me of my unhappiness, even during the times that should have been the happiness like my daughter but she is right. Often I was angry, depressed, dissatisfied with my life and what and how I was providing to my family, although I worked hard, slaving to get ahead but always in the same place.

In the new year, I hope you be stronger but physically and mentally, be wiser and more cunning in this life as I am now 43 years old, years away from a new milestone, mid-life.

Whatever Stage your Life, you can make your life Count!

Maybe your beginning your life, maybe you are a teen, a child, an adult and maybe you are an elder who has life a long life already. None the less we can all take this new year and grow in news ways I never thought possible. I am someone who tries to believe there are new possibilities, we just have to try , put in the effort and see what takes place.

Laugh more, enjoy life more, appreciate life more, because life truly is short. I am often reminded of that daily as there is always someone who passes this life, often the young who are full of hope that leave this earth by their own hand or some other way, death is inevitable.

Love more, appreciate those in our life more, family, friends, co-workers and even the stranger on the street as we are all in this together, all human for the most part. We all have a choice to make in how we treat ourselves, how we see others and our perspective.

Create your Own Perspective

My new perspective is to not worry about what I can not control, almost not to care but deep down like most of us we care but I have seen worry take over my life for years and for what.

Make 2023 a banner year of self-growth, of love and know that you can choose to be happy and not let this world bring you down. The world today is not always full of love, but of hate, of anger but we do not have to choose to partake in this behavior.

Live each day like its your last, hopefully its not your last but if it is go out appreciating life, because life is messy and complex but we do not have to make that way, especially on yourself.

New years resolutions are ok, but remember that they often fade within weeks or months, choose to live each day anew make goals every day.

Chapter 22

Hey Stoopid, Shut Up!

March 6, 2022

For many who read this you may be able to relate to this, but for some you are part of the problem by feeling it necessary to tell those in your workplace to be quiet, not speak and even to shut your mouth. Sad to say I have been told this and even quite recently.

For most my career I have been told to be quiet, you are not speaking unless spoken too and this came from co-workers and even managers. I remember one time on a call with a client I was told by an equal co-worker non manager that I was not speak and she didn't want to hear me to keep mute.

This piece is not to point fingers but to bring awareness that this still happens today in companies across the globe, especially in our culture here in the U.S. It is in our culture we are told companies are all knowing, especially managers, but sad to say this far from true, many managers don't know anything but put in positions they have no place being but are put there because someone felt they deserved the position.

Thinking back on the past

I can go back to most my career and I had a few employers each unique in their own right but I often was told to put my head down, don't rock the boat and I listened. Part of the reason I did this was because this is what I was told as a child growing up by an verbally abusive grandfather who many times people justified by saying that he acted that way because he was old school and just to accept this behavior. This acceptance of his behavior which still affects me today because it was done to me from the age of five until adulthood and although he has passed on those behaviors still haunt me.

First and foremost, employers and any employers are not all knowing, but they do a lot, but we have to remember they are run by people who are very much flawed in many ways like myself but we certainty try our best not to be flawed. Going to the best schools, getting top education does not make those who manage us or run companies better than us, many just had better opportunities and had privileges that many of us don't have. I will not take away the fact that they probably worked hard to get where they are at today, but so have I and many ways when the odds were against me.

Culture of part of the problem in the workplace

Sadly, our culture is taught that we must be go getters, burn the wick on both ends and do what it takes to get ahead even if that means stepping on a few necks to the top. I know not all of us do this but many do.

For all my employers I have the best intentions of working hard, being a good employee and being a productive member of the team. But in that process of being a good solider I was often disrespected, lied too, and treated invaluable. Today although I love my role and the company I am apart of I too have had the best of two worlds, a manager who affirmed me, encouraged me and supported me and I also have had a manager who treats me like I just started my career and not as a professional but as someone doesn't know how to do my job although history has proven I am good , even great at my job. Being that I work with clients, they survey my performance putting me at 96-100% satisfaction rate, but sad to say that is still not good enough.

Today my approach is to keep trucking, do my job and in all honestly if the company feels I am not valuable enough to them they can of course let me go and another employer will hopefully see my value. But we all need to see our value for ourselves.

I have value from a professional standpoint having worked with clients and customers over twenty years, I have a bachelors and an MBA along with lots of skillsets. As you see I am not an idiot, but there is one problem many employers have with me, I talk to much.

Shut up or else

Yes, I am a talker, and I am not afraid to say I love to communicate, its who I am. I love to explain how I feel, be vulnerable, emotional. I have been told recently I am too emotional and to stop being so emotional, that clients do not care about what I have to say and to stick to the script, basically to shut up and do your job. My job is to talk to clients, communicate, teach them and train them which is what makes me great because I also teach students to be the best version of themselves and not fall the for the same traps, I have been apart of.

I will not be quiet anymore, for most of my life and career I have kept my head down doubting my value , self-worth and even me as a professional, but no more and we as people must stop allowing others to dictate and tell us what our value is to them, Who cares what a manger or co-worker thinks of your value, their opinions are worthless unless they help to build you up and not tear you down.

I know that managers and co-workers will give us feedback and even criticism that we all must take. When this is provided to you, accept it but don't accept it. What I mean by is to think if the feedback is meant to help you be better or is some ideology /methodology that only that person believes because they were told from a company standpoint everyone must believe. We do not all have to believe the ideology of any company, we are not robots, we are not soldiers, we are people all striving in many cases to bring profitability to a company and many times we don't even see the financial rewards of our productivity. Yes, we get a paycheck, benefits but for most that is not enough, we all want more. We all want to be valued, trusted, and respected in the workplace but often we are not, but taken for granted.

Working for others is a business relationship

We must all remember working for any employer it's a business relationship, we work and in return we get paid. But its not one sided, we work and produce for an employer but often that is still not good enough, but companies want robots at times, but be good little boys and girls and just act and do what we are told.

I do my job, I do it well, but even today I am told in not so many words I am still not doing what I am supposed to, so when is it enough. For many we keep going, working, and going on business as usual while employers mistreat, disrespect the worker.

I understand no employer is perfect and all of have a choice to leave and go somewhere else, but really should we have to if employers and even co-workers/managers followed suit. I believe if we work for an organization we can have longevity there, support the company mission and be productive members of the company and many of us do. But again, how much must one give and wait for the respect to reciprocated and often times doesn't come but we take it anyways.

Each of us are unique, have value which often times we forget and listen to what employers tell us what value are is but we shouldn't. Let stop believing the lies we are fed whether intentional or not and realize that we must stop putting our head down, stop being quiet and told to just shut up because like many you still grow to an age and for me it's been over twenty years I have accepted this behavior and cringe it took me this long to realize my value.

If I could speak with the young Me

If I could go back to the young Joseph, I would tell myself to cut my own path, don't depend on a company to form our path in life and career because often times employers are one sided, which is what we can do for them and not what they can do for us.

Again, for many out there you many disagree but I would seriously look yourself in the mirror and think long and hard, was it hard work that got you where you are today or was it because you bowed to the employer/ coworker to their expectations. Some may not care how they go where they got today, and many don't realize their privilege whether its their education and or even their race that got them where they are today.

I have nothing to be ashamed of but often feel shame for the college I went too, my background and even my race made to feel that I don't meet a manager's expectation for what they want me to be. I am not playing the race card but understand all characteristics of who we are matter and play a role in how we are treated, regardless of if a person says they are not racist and treat everyone equally, but really don't.

Ageism exists and many will experience a lack of respect

I have come an age where I am over 40 and ageism has begun to affect me and my career because I am no longer youthful and because I am made to feel like I am going to retire tomorrow which I am not, but again another form of valuable in our culture today.

What this have to do with this piece, basically that it's another form of worth employer's places on us due to age and something that I can not change but exist today.

We can all do better in life, for ourselves and especially in the workplace to really treat everyone with respect, be slow to criticize and disguise it as feedback which many employers do.

I have a voice and will use it

Stop tell works to shut it, that our voice has no place with the customer, the client, our voice matters. The reason I feel I was told my voice doesn't matter is because it won't make the company profitable anymore then its already being made. Our voices, what we have to say of course as a place, but I have always used my voice to affirm and make a client, a customer better which is how it should be used.

I will continue to read the room in my career and in life to speak when I feel it will help and not bring down someone which many are quick to do today. I will continue to bring positivity to the classroom, to my clients and customers because frankly that is who I am not. I will not be told to shut up any longer and NONE of us should be accepting this, lets all stop living in fear of how our employers view us and remember how we view ourselves.

My legacy will know better

On a positive note, here is my daughter Mikaylah, she is nine years old, my future generation. I will not let her repeat my mistakes of feeling worthless in your life and work. I will teach her to make her own path and not rely on companies to tell her what path they see for her; they are unqualified to do so anyways. I will teach her not to put too much stock in people's opinions of her because those are worthless to value herself, respect herself and if a company doesn't see her true value go somewhere else.

Let's do better

I would like to think companies, co-workers and managers can all change for better, but often times will ignore what I am saying, its ok I am used to it by name. I know many of you will not agree with what I am saying and many of you will justify the employer's position that they are just too busy, focused on the bottom line and that its up to us individually to change and accept the way things are. I am certainty not the problem, but I have no issues in being better, growing and taking feedback and applying to my work and life, but will employers do the same.

Many of you will say I should just keep my head down, don't rock the boat and things will get better in time, something I hope for but rarely happens. I have my faults like anyone else, but not to the point where I should be told to shut up. Organizations have their flaws, sometimes major ones they are unwilling to recognize and correct so who is the culprit of the problems and where does it begin and end. It will take both parties working together to get better, but as we have seen today organizations see their side only and want to enforce their side on those who work under them instead of creating partnerships within the organization.

Hopefully this enlightens some of you to look within and see how you can grow and not let anything or one stand in your way, because you have the power. Currently I am working towards studying and eventually taking the PMP exam to get my project management certification, another milestone I hope to accomplish this year. I will never stop being a better me and I am unwilling to let anyone tell me or make feel I am worthless because I am not.

Keep striving being a better version of you and don't let those in your workplace deter you or slow you down, you owe it to yourself.

Be joyous, spread cheer, be positive in your life and workplace because that will make all the difference in your life and those around you, I stand by this in my life today.

Godspeed everyone!

Chapter 23

Tis the season for Suicides

December 27, 2022

During this time of year, the holidays. I often think about the amount of grief and sadness people are going through. I believe that this is time when suicides are at the highest levels as many go through this time of year feeling lonely as they look around who appear to be happy, have happy lives.

I tend to go through this today, as I begrudgingly go to the mall or the store for Christmas shopping I look at the people, their faces, their body language, how they spend, what they buy. Looking at their faces I see happiness, sadness, frustration, worry. I wonder what some of these individuals go through, if they will be alive in future years.

During this time of year, people are spending, giving and going to debt, some more then others, put themselves in financial harm. Now I get that many spend this time of year because frankly this is this the time when people tend to spend making up for the year. In the United States we are full of consumerism, spend, spend, spend and then in January we feel the effects. Now some may prepare for this time of year, but many cannot.

Many will attempt to get past this month, many have not been able to and have called it quits, finding that there is no reason to tis the season to be Merry, even if watching all the Christmas classics may help but usually wont. One of films I find great solace in is Charles Dickens A Christmas Carol. Having watched the films, story a true reminder of how the human spirit struggles and how there have been no shortness of people who go without as Crachit and Scrooge display that perfectly. Another film that displays the importance of life especially during the holidays is Its Wonderful Life.

Although I have been provided for in my childhood and into my adulthood, I know what It means to want and need, although not to the extreme of others who are homeless and without food.

Money doesn't buy happiness which is true, but it does give you options to get help like seek therapy, get proper medication and eat and live better, this all helps.

Recently there have been some very public suicides in the media, one specifically is Stephen Boss, Ellen DeGeneres DJ died by suicide on December 13th, 2022.

A man I had no knowledge of prior to his death but that is simply because I do not watch Ellen and or follow the dance world. This man appeared to have money, fame, a family who loved him and was in film and Television. Just today saw an article that Cmdr. Robert Ramirez III, 47 died by suicide, who was decorated navy seal commander.

Lastly recently in a nearby town of Anaheim, California, a suicide at the Disneyland parking structure by the name of Christopher Christensen.

These are just a couple examples but per the CDC are is 1 death per 11 minutes due to suicide. Here is where this information is from : Suicide Data and Statistics | Suicide | CDC. This number is astounding and very sad.

I personally know what it means to have attempted many years ago, I obliviously did not succeed, it just so happens my sister came home at that exact moment, saying she was feeling ill. I was hospitalized for about two weeks after my 72 hour hold was done. I believe these feelings of depression developed over childhood, a childhood filled with verbal abuse from my grandfather, divorced parents and being overweight and bullied. Over years my self esteem stay low, feeling I could and would never amount to anything .

After graduating college I was lost, had no direction of where I wanted my life to go and received no guidance from family and friends, I really was alone although I lived at home seeking help. Over the course of my life since 02/07/07, I have gotten married , had a child, live and work, pay bills like anyone else.

I still struggle with depression at times, question my self-worth in my job and just my life. I know I am loved and not contemplating anything so no worries. But for those struggling with negative thoughts, thoughts of suicide, one should speak with someone, you are not alone.

This is where the story takes a turn, I often ask myself why is Suicide stigmatized in the media and by people. I get that we are taking our lives, a life I believe doesn't truly belong to us but GOD. A life we had not choice in but God gave us life and we are taking it. As a follower of Jesus, I struggle with this, because I truly believe GOD does not want us to suffer, but in a way he does.

Frankly the people who truly love those who die and complete this act are their family and friends. In the end we all die. In the end time passes by , years go by and eventually that loved one you lost is almost forgotten, but people move on with their lives.

Should people live in agony and one's agony may be nothing to most of us but something for someone else, like finding love. Its amazing how many people are searching for a loving companion, a boyfriend/Girlfriend, even a future husband and wife spending years searching. I know that was me, because honestly I just wanted someone to spend time with me, love me and accept me for who I was, but many years ago I found no one, just rejection.

There are those who suffer to get somewhere in life career wise and don't get where they wish to go, eventually it becomes too much. Others have unrealistic ideas about money and wealth , feeling their life amounts to nothing without those zero's in their bank account.

Thinking of those people, we look at those who have everything we want, money, wealth, fame, attractiveness , a so to speak beautiful life, but often items in the end those who have that don't appreciate and value what they truly have. Often you will find those who have nothing sometimes literally the happiest. We all have and want things that make us personally happy in this life.

One the relationship I have today that has kept me going is GOD, more specifically Jesus. But sadly I have seen today is Pastors who should have the strongest relationship with Jesus die by suicide, like Jarrid Wilson a Harvest Church Pastor who also led a minister on mental health.

In addition a lead pastor by the name of Andrew Stoecklien. No man or women is immune to depression, to anxiety to committing such acts, its all tragic.

Know life is not perfect, most will not live a life of a celebrity, life of a millionaire and billionaire, remember there are around 8 billion people on this earth. 8 Billion souls who are searching for meaning, the meaning lies with those in our life like family and friends. You may say well I don't have any friends or family, I am alone. You are never truly alone, GOD is there, he has not forgotten you, he loves you. You may say well I am not really a church person, I don't believe in the politics of church, the hypocrisy of those followers. The truth is most if not all of people are hypocrites, no man or women is perfect. Despite the look of a persons perfection, they are not perfect, Only GOD is perfect.

During this time of year, if you are feeling down and out, worthless, remember you are not, you have value even if people are not around to tell you. But if you decide to take the dreadful act of suicide , I just want to say I am sorry your soul is so sad, that humanity has failed you in showing you kindness and love.

If you do decide to take this act, please let others know why, especially those you live behind, don't leave leaving loved ones in despair blaming themselves. Those who are left behind may truly not know why, if they are to blame or if you suffered in silence which you shouldn't.

I get we live in a rotten world and its only getting worse especially if you look at the politics of our countries today, the greed, the hate and hypocrisy but at the end of the day our government, our jobs, our co-workers could care less about our wellbeing, they have no skin in the game of our lives, but our mothers, fathers, brothers and sisters, sons and daughters, they have real skin on our lives, the ones who love us, who love you.

We truly don't know what others struggle with, be kind, be generous to those around us. We are all just trying to get by this life. Give yourself a break and know that everything it will be ok, not perfect, but you have control to do things in your life.

Don't allow those around you to bring you down, bring down your spirit but know you are unique and special with your own set of talents and gifts unlike anyone else.

Lastly if you are having thoughts of suicide and self-harm please speak with someone, in the U.S. you can dial 988 and or 911 for emergency.

Have a blessed and safe new year, Don't drink and drive, call a ride share if you are going out. May you have a blessed 2023.

Chapter 24

Being Thankful even in Thankless times!

November 22, 2022

Being thankful can be challenging. There are certainty times when I think and forget to be thankful for life , for breathing, for good health, a job, some money, food, a roof over my head. Yes I have a lot to be thankful for. We live in thankless times and times where people fail to be grateful for what they do have. I get that many don't have a warm bed, food, good health, but many decide and choose to be grateful for life. I often this is in children who teach us valuable lessons on being grateful.

Today I see so much division, hate, anger that people just wish to place the blame on society, government and anything they feel justifies their feelings. But at the end of the day we have control and make choices that lead us to today. Yes may not have made good choices for ourselves and family and playing the consequences.

GOD is always there and in my family we are thankful for everything we have although like many we want more. More money, better living situations, better health, although our health is good. Often many of us will look at others who have more, more riches, nicer homes, fancier cars and compare that to our lives, disappointed and ungrateful for what we do have.

Let's stop focusing on what others do have and what we do not have , but thankful for those in our life that love us and those we love ourselves. Thankful that you are not living on the street, but if you do live on the street as in homeless that is a brighter day for even those individuals.

I look around today and see ungratefulness, a society of ME, ME, ME. What do I get , who is going to give me this in life, Why do I have to work for this and that. Now there are those who look around and say, its ok if I do not get everything I want in life. Its ok if I don't get married, have kids, have the perfect job or career, but I have good health, I have a roof over my head, I have a mind to do things and the will to do things in my life.

There are many who do not have the will to do things for themselves, who lay in bed all day, who drink to ease their pain or take drugs. There are who have just given up because they forgot what It means to be thankful for what you do have.

I certainty try to life my life according to the word of God and scripture says such as :

- 1 Thessalonians 5:16-18 Rejoice always, pray continually, give thanks in all circumstances; for this is God's will for you in Christ Jesus.
- Colossians 3:17 says, *"and whatever you do, in word or deed, do everything in the name of the Lord Jesus, giving thanks to God the Father through Him."*

There are many scriptures about being thankful, why is that well because GOD knows that we as being have the tendency to be ungrateful. I am sorry to say often when our eyes are opened is when tragedy affects us, not that I wish that on anyone.

A few years ago on Thanksgiving , we almost lost our daughter, as in she almost died. We were visiting my sister for thanksgiving dinner, we were happy, thankful but on this day, our daughter was hit by a car. Our daughter who was around 6 at the time attempt to cross the parking lot when at that moment a car was carelessly driving fast and I believe when Our daughter attempted to cross she ran into the car. The impact of the moving car threw her a few feet away from the car. Her store coming off and get some scraps and bruises, no broken bones , but was taken to the hospital for observation. The police and fire men were wonderful and caring from what I remember, but sadly no apology from the driver. One could say well who was watching our daughter and your right that was our fault, I guess we had trust she would say put, but she ran towards us, something I will always remember. It was one of the scariest moments of our life, unforgettable but thankful to have our daughter with us today.

Through my life I have grown to be thankful for my life, my literal life as many , many years ago I attempted to end my life, but was saved. Saved to share future thanksgivings, Christmases, holidays, getting married, the birth of my daughter. I know what I means to feel hopeless, ungrateful, Thankless and I truly know deep in my gut that is not who I want to be, because I do have lots to be thankful for. Although my mother who passed away in 2015 is no longer here, I have my father, sister, brother in law , wife and daughter.

For those who believe in GOD and JESUS, because God is in control of your life. Give thanks because GOD will work all things together for good to those who love him and are called according to his purpose (Romans 8:28).

In this time of season remember to give thanks, tell those in your life, your thankful for them, love more, be kinder.

Chapter 25

My Time of Trials and Brokenness

July 16, 2023

I am broken once again as the devastation of another job loss is such a short period of time. It just happened on recently but deep down I can say I felt that this job would lead to this for some reason.

My dream became a Nightmare

This job was especially personal to me because it was a place, I had wanted to be apart of for so very long, like over 10 years. It was exciting to get the opportunity, but in the end the opportunity was not what I expected it to be.

I was part of the project management department, and I was what is called a project specialist, which is a support role. Like most roles that start off everything is good, you meet new people, new duties, new responsibilities, ready and willing to learn.

For those interested I was a Senior Project Specialist for SCE (Southern California Edison) in the Major Projects Organization and more specifically in the Licensure division meaning I get the opportunity to work on complex projects in Electrical Transmission and Distribution. The projects I am apart of take years to complete anywhere from 5 to 10 years or more. Part of the reason the projects take so long is due to our role of getting proper permits and licensures with local , state and federal agencies, one being the California Public Utilities Commission and other agencies like California Department of Fish and Wildlife. I work each day with many within legal , regulatory and environmental fields working together to make sure we dot every I and cross every T meeting strict guidelines before construction can begin.

I would be entering a new industry, the utilities industry, having been in the software industry and personal finance and banking industry. For the first few weeks I was assigned to a colleague who would train me until she was moved to her new role with the company, having only 3 weeks with her and then I would on my own. For many this is plenty of time, but for some we need more support.

Not that I can not work independently, self-develop myself, I can and will but still need support, but most importantly I need those who I work closest with, I need patience to learn and to work with me, something I soon saw would not be possible. I worked directly under the Project Manager (PM), a woman who has been with the company in her role over twenty years.

Respected, but More Than Met The Eye

A women very different then I have worked with before, older than me, an immigrant with a strong Spanish accent, confident and capable, but ultimately not a trainer, not someone who was going to or willing to teach me, but allow me to observe her, learn from her but having never been a specialist herself.

Over the course of weeks, naturally I made mistakes along the way and at FIRST she was ok with my mistakes and understood, but slowly lost patience with me , starting to make comments about my future with the company, more specifically telling me "You need to get your act together or this job will not work out for you".

It is my view that when someone goes out their way to make and say this, they have already made up their mind on my future and would no longer be supported. After this I was shook and that evening, I was different from my family, angry but said to myself that I would change, change my mindset, be different. Going in with a different mindset, a mindset of coldness, a mindset NOT to be myself with my kind nature.

She e-mailed me asking me a question, I was straight to the point no pleasantries. She noticed my change in demeanor and shortly asked to speak with me, bringing me into an empty conference room. She asked if I was ok, and she could see that I wasn't and I told her I was not ok based on yesterdays events.

I advised her I was not sleeping as of late, thinking about my position, how I could be better and improve and she assured me that it will take time, coming off as caring and compassionate, trying to soothe my feelings feeling we had come to an understanding, but I was wrong.

Her behavior appeared to get worse, she now becoming passive aggressive with me as worked to ignore her but starting to see that she essentially was becoming a bully to me. Something interesting I learned about her was that this behavior was not uncommon, that the person who was had trained me also had a complicated relationship with the women and in fact that is why she was going to a different PM and after speaking with her, she confirmed the behavior. Others I worked with were especially open about her without me even asking.

The Final Straw

As a contractor I do not have all the inherent rights that a regular employee has, I do get health benefits, but ultimately my standing in the company is not the same as I do not get the same resources like HR like a normal employee does and in essence I can easily be gotten rid of, fired and from my own observation I am not as valued as a regular employee.

This last week the main contact with the contracting company reached out to me, an incredible nice gentleman who has been the person who worked with me to arrange the interview, negotiate pay and onboard me. This gentleman is an agent of a larger organization who works to employee this company with contractors where I worked for him, and the company was apart of is his client/customer.

He brought to my attention his meeting with the manager, supervisor and the PM I was supporting, and the comments being made by her about my performance. The comments were outrageous, mentioned my poor performance, my writing skills, my failure to use technology, all lies.

Yes, there were areas I struggled with at first but completely one sided. Then I was present with a plan he wanted me to take part in, a PIP (Performance Improvement Plan) which is basically putting me on probation for 60 days, I found offensive and just wrong having only been there a short time. I inquired about placing me with another PM, but deep down I knew that I may not be possible, which led me to giving my two-week notice.

In my gut I knew if I entertained this PIP plan, her behavior would only get worse putting me in a horrible mental state for the next 60 days. Yes, I would still have a job for sixty days and my contactor/Employer encouraged me to be part of the PIP plan and to fight for my position. I have NEVER is over my twenty-year career have ever been on a PIP plan and never have experience this before.

I admit like anyone else I am human and need time to learn, that does not take away from my professionalism, I am someone who has skillsets, knowledge and know how in projects and complex systems, I am not someone who just graduated college yesterday and I am not someone who is just starting out in life.

It's painful because this is my dream company and in no way did, I want to just walk away and I could have stayed stuck it out, took more abuse for the sake of seeing if things would get better. But I have lived in torment for months now, not at peace and unable to sleep.

It has been hard enough being laid off in March, trying to recover as bills, rent continued to pile up. I am trying to maintain my mental health, be positive but It has been difficult and this is nail in the coffin I know I will not be able to forget this failure, but I must move on.

I do feel shame that I could not just accept the behavior, but I don't feel I should have too. Being that the company I worked for prides itself on treating its people with respect, in valuing its employees and contractors. I would think that the manager and supervisor would have fought for me, but deep down I know I have no standing and that the 20-year employee has more value than me and they are unwilling to have her change because they know she will NOT.

In today's corporate America, there is what is written and then there's true action. I am someone who chooses to treat others with respect, grow, adapt and change, but others are unwilling.

This is certainly a lesson, I never thought I would learn but did, hopefully a lesson for us all.

I pray GOD will open new doors, in the meantime GOD only knows what the future holds and what he has planned, but I will have faith in new doors being opened.

For those who have struggled with a difficult decision, it may be simple for many to say to stick with bad behavior, ignore those people, speak up, FIGHT, its not easy. Its not that I am unwilling to fight, but if I felt I had a chance to win the battle then I would fight. Ultimately I felt I was not Fully supported and although there were people who wanted to support me, the ONE person I really support from to do my job was not going to support me, in the long run continue her abusive behavior.

Deep down I feel GOD attempted to warn me about this role, but I did not listen and this was the end result, GOD knew what was going to happen but gives us CHOICE and we have to deal with the consequences. GOD is all knowing and has a plan, now I must continue to do my part and just apply myself again.

Chapter 26

Being Thankful Period.

November 18, 2023

Being thankful can be difficult at times as we look at our own lives, often comparing what we do not have, whether it's a job, Money, a house, nice cars and I Know these are materialistic things and one can easy say well those things DON'T matter.

Of course, a matter, because we live in a world where possessions are proof of our existence, proof we did good things with our life and ultimately are successful. I know we can lose it all in a blink of an eye and often people do, especially with our possessions. We lose jobs, we lose money, we lose cars, possessions and homes leaving us with the most important thing OUR LIVES.

I'll admit I don't always appreciate my life and many of you have read my blogs about just ending my life. Within myself I look for the good in life still such as my family, loved ones, friends and coworkers. Yes my co-workers have a significant importance to me although they are often temporarily because people leave jobs, move on to other jobs and they are out of our life.

But I have found having a good co-worker makes work worth it, no longer a dreaded task, but a place where one feels comfortable and people you can call friends. I will say I have not had too many experiences like this although I have been in the workforce for over twenty years.

To me relationships are important and I often strive to create meaningful relationships with each person but its difficult because I will not get to know everyone and there are obliviously people who do not wish to know me in that way.

This has been a year that I truly have tried to see the brighter side of things, to be truly thankful and I am but along the way I became angry, bitter about my own failures this year and I am often consumed thinking of my own mistakes this year with my career after being laid off back in March. I truly say that I will not fully get over this year until I have gone one full year with a job and no issues, which I am hopeful for 2024 not to have any disturbances of having to search for a long time.

This year my finances went through the ringer, my weight loss gains were loss , my mental health deteriorated , my self esteem shot and then the dark voice in my head that was dormant for a very long time came back telling me to prepare myself for the end (The voice still speaks to me daily).

I look around now at being employed with a great company, a company I have strived to be apart of for seven years. A company that is so big it has over fifty thousand employees across the globe, The largest company I have ever worked for.

But within the confines of my department, we are small and mighty with about fourteen of us, all different ages, races, ethnicities and backgrounds. I found it so refreshing to have coworkers who looked happy and spoke together as we are in cubicles hearing and seeing everything. I am hopeful to be here for many years giving me the choice to leave if I ever decide too instead of being laid off.

I find I have a hard time letting of the past, letting go of how I felt years past. Like last year it seemed everything was great, I had a job I liked, customers I liked, co-workers I like I was comfortable. There is probably where a problem lies, I was comfortable.

When I get comfortable, I get bored, but there is something I hate getting in job as I get antsy looking to see what is out there, searching for a new opportunity to grow, which is probably why I have not stayed at a company more than three years, but I hope that changes.

I think we can all be thankful for something, although I know some may disagree. How can one be thankful for a life of pain, of abuse, of severe adversity. I can only imagine what some go through today, much worse than I could imagine such as health issues, some would say financial and trust me I have had my fair share of financial even today, but I have learned to cope, to a have a different perspective with money. Yes I look around I have my wife, my daughter, sister, father , brother in law, friends and lots I do not see.

Each day we must remember there is beauty in life too, yes there are hardships, life is painful at times, but we can learn so much because each day as long as we have breath we can start anew.

This Thanksgiving let's try to be thankful for what we have. For myself as a believer in JESUS, he commands us to be thankful. As I look through all the Thanksgivings in my life, yes it was filled with food, so many turkeys I can't even count, but I remember those years with those who are no longer here like my mother, those with my wife, daughter and sister too. Those were good days and I had bad days when the devil himself was alive and made thanksgiving miserable.

I know it's hard to be thankful at times, but we must. Life is so much better than we are thankful for each breath, for what we have and know for the things we do not have in this life we can grow to live without it and still be thankful, thankful to GOD.

May each out there have a blessed Thanksgiving. Be Safe. Be Happy. Be Blessed!

Here are wise words from our lords in remembering to give thanks.

- 1 Thessalonians 5:16-18 Rejoice always, pray continually, give thanks in all circumstances; for this is God's will for you in Christ Jesus.
- Colossians 3:17 says, *"and whatever you do, in word or deed, do everything in the name of the Lord Jesus, giving thanks to God the Father through Him."*

Part II – Social Causes

Chapter 27

Getting Radical and No Longer Giving a Sh*T

January 30, 2022

The year is now 2022 and over the course of the years especially since 2010 and then in 2013, which is the year I got married and had my daughter. I can honestly say for most of life although I have been provided everything I need, a roof, clothes, food and of course those things I didn't need. But once I got to my teenage years which can be tough for anyone, that is where my depression truly started to affect me and especially until late twenties and mid-twenties when I unfortunately decided to end it all, but did not succeed.

Hardships are a way of life for me

Since starting my family it has been tough, I have struggled to make it although I am educated man with a bachelors and master's degree I had no street smarts. Over the years I have accepted everything that has been provided to me especially in my career, never questioning my worth of what a company said I was worth. Of course, many of us take jobs accepting the companies are just paying us fairly but in reality they are not because deep down its about their needs not ours.

Some of hardships I have been endured include being a good provider, not struggling for years financially but be a support to my wife and daughter which I have been, but I have also brought them through hell to make my career better.

For most my childhood and adult I felt worthless, because for most of childhood my grandfather who I live with told me I was worthless and a piece of shit who couldn't do anything right and I believed it.

Over the course of years due to hardship I have changed, which most of us do. My heart was once soft, kind and tender has grown hard and at times filled with hate for mankind all at the same time supporting my family , loving them.

The Pandemic and My Change

Over the course of these last two years in the pandemic, I have grown harder, less patient and at times angrier. I feel myself slowly becoming radicalized and its not because I am watching Fox news or being on social media, but in reality, seeing what this world truly for what it is. We live in a world that is filled with greed, a world about getting what's yours while stepping on your fellow man, women and child to get there. All the Rich can contest to this , as I believe many did not become rich or wealthy by being Intelligent and kind but really taking advantage of the weak and disadvantaged.

I have lived under the man's thumb for all my life, living and serving others while the company gains wealth at my expense. Some would say well that is most of us and it is true, but when will we wake up to see we are only making others rich.

I often think of movies that reflect this and I am reminded of one of favorite films Metropolis, a film made in the 1930's that depicts an under world of workers that keep society going as people slave away for the rich.

What has been eye opening for me is how easy it has been to take advantage of people and even more so during the last two years. People have lived in fear and continue to live in fear for good reason due to Covid as many have died and gotten sick over this Virius that I believe was purposely created to inflict pain on the world, Yes I believe the Chinese are the culprits. I know this may not be an opinion people will agree with as many continue to feel it was done on accident. But history will show Chinese hate the west and many other countries looking to destroy our way of life and they succeeded by stopping us in our tracks and the world for that matter.

But we have our own problems in the good Ole U.S as we have failed to control the Virus and help people be safe as many feel the government has forced its agenda on mask wearing, Vaccines and straight up fear. Ill admit the virus is real and can be deadly, as I got COVID weeks ago and to be honest I don't feel the same. I feel as though I have lost a bit of myself, and I truly do not remember the month of January as I got sick early January.

Society Eats its Own Young

I have watched as I have seen society eat itself from within and even look to eat its young as we have all lost any sense of reality. As a man who believes in GOD, I see the writing on the wall to where we are headed and its not like I wasn't warned to this earth and our country and the state of California going to hell as we speak, not state is immune to what is happening.

Yes the pandemic has changed our culture forever and continues to change it. We in society preach kindness but in reality, hate is what is protect to others. A sense of self righteousness rules society now, but deep down it has always been us versus them, The rich versus the poor, white versus black or brown and ultimately always thinking that those who make more are more important to society because society says the CEO is more valuable then the janitor or the mechanic.

When will we wake up truly to see we are all equal in this world, we are all human for the most part and in the end we all die and some either go to heaven or hell, but ultimately we die.

I truly worry for my 9 year old daughter, what this world will be like in 9 years when she is 18, hell I cringe at what will life be like in 5 years.

I think for 2022 maybe its time to get radical, change our thinking and belief in how we feel people treat us and our value and put more value in ourselves and off relying on companies and society to tell us our worth.

Love one another, especially your family they are truly the most important people in our lives, friends, co-workers, bosses are last on the list.

I grew up poor most of life, didn't know I was poor until I realized what others around me had and that I didn't have that like a nice, fancy rides, better clothes. Some may say those things are not important, but they matter.

Even today I am what you would consider middle class, we live in a good neighborhood apartment, daughter goes to a good school and district and I work in a profession many would consider decent, I work in software and I teach college part time.

My eyes continue to open as I see myself manifest into a new Joseph, its strange to see myself at times as I look in the mirror and see myself growing less concerned about what others think of me, defending my voice, speaking up more.

I often reflect on today through what I watch on TV and I love my TV and movies as this is sometime I reality I live in and some of my favorite movies include Rocky, Breaking Bad, Rambo, Expendables and others to name a few. We live in a world of violence to take what's yours and don't take shit from no one, that is what where I am headed. Not headed t

owards being violence of course, I am going to go out and do something crazy to myself or others but will start a war from within and protect that to people around me by my change in attitude and tone. Some of you may say but why, why change. We all need to change, because the world is going getting harder and we need to be a little harder ourselves.

This blog may not make a whole lota sense but it makes sense to me, but hopefully you see I am changing for better or worse unsure as this journey is taking me somewhere.

God Bless.

Chapter 28

We are a nation bully's

April 25, 2022

Recently my wife came home upset from work due to bullying taking place at her work. My wife who is a little older than me has had to deal with bullying and discrimination at a major fast food corporation, you can only guess which one it is, but they have been in the news before and are represented by a famous clown: McDonald's settles discrimination lawsuit with Herb Washington (cnbc.com)

Devoted Mother and Wife

For five years my wife devoted taking care of our daughter full time while I worked and supported our family. After our daughter started attending kindergarten, she went back to work in 2018. From the moment she arrived she has been treated like a second-class citizen. At first she work tirelessly the graveyard shift for a year and then evenings but the culture of the company never changed but go worse.

It was only recently she was made a trainer which she fully deserves, why she stood around as the store made 18 year old's managers who have done nothing but make her life hard with put downs, derogatory generalizations due to her nationality as a Salvadorian.

This employer is not a so-called equal opportunity employer as she has been made the official dishwasher and floor cleaner instead of working with customers, cashiering.

Generation Z's and Millennials are a problem

Some of may say well what's the big deal, it's a job deal with it. The problem is there are about ten other lazy generation Z's and Millennials who work with her, and they are not told to wash dishes, clean the floor.

Now some of you may take offense to me singling out certain generation and feel that every generation is a fault. But the reality is that those generations are known to be lazy, rude and disrespectful although many of you would say my generation X is just as guilty.

Unfortunately, we live in a world of bullies and worse yet we live in a country where division is caused by these bullies who feel their opinions override the rest of society but that is untrue. One could say well I wife could just speak up and she does but is considered and called difficult to defending herself.

I advise my wife we will find her another position soon to hang tight that all not employers allow bullying and discrimination like this one, but it does exist.

We are a country of bullies

We live a country of bullies that I believe will only get worse as we treat those who have immigrated and born here from different nations. I know many will say we are NOT a nation of hate, but I believe we built this country on a continue of Love and hate and its in our history that we hate those who are different, whether it's a person's skin color, sex, creed, religion and other differences.

We should NEVER stand for hate, discrimination and bullying in life and the workplace as corporations and businesses allow this terrible behavior to take place.

My wife has told other managers especially and she has been told to stay quiet, don't say anything to the younger generation of workers and I have told her NEVER to be quiet, never just accept that treatment

This a message to bullies

This is message for you bullies to stop your bullshit and those who are affected by these bullies you should stand up to them. Fear not them nor the employer and stop allowing this behavior to take place in your life and workplace.

Workplace Bullying 101

Know the subtle signs: *excerpted from* http://www.workplacebullying.org/ercs/

1. **Deceit.** Repeatedly lying, not telling the truth, concealing the truth, deceiving others to get one's way.
2. **Removal of responsibility.** Removing someone's responsibilities, changing their role, or replacing aspects of their job without cause
3. **Projection of blame.** Shifting blame to others and using them as a scapegoat; not taking responsibility for problems or issues
4. **Withholding information.** Intentionally withholding information from someone or giving them the wrong information
5. **Intimidation.** Overt or veiled threats; fear-inducing communication and behavior
6. **Rationalization.** Constantly justifying or defending behavior or making excuses for acting in a particular manner
7. **Undermining work.** Deliberately delaying and blocking an employee's work, progress on a project or assignment, or success; repeated betrayal
8. **Impossible or changing expectations.** Setting nearly impossible expectations and work guidelines; changing those expectations to set up employees to fail
9. **Constant change and inconsistency.** Constantly changing expectations, guidelines, and scope of assignments; constant inconsistency of word and action (e.g. not following through on things said)
10. **Criticism.** Constantly criticizing someone's work or behavior, usually for unwarranted reasons

Know the obvious signs? *These behaviors undermine everyone's success*

11. **Aggression.** Yelling or shouting at an employee; exhibiting anger or aggression verbally or non-verbally
12. **Coercion.** Aggressively forcing or persuading someone to say or do things against their will or better judgment
13. **Punishment.** Undeservedly punishing an employee with physical discipline, psychologically through passive aggression, or emotionally through isolation
14. **Belittling.** Persistently disparaging someone or their opinions, ideas, work, or personal circumstances in an undeserving manner
15. **Embarrassment.** Embarrassing, degrading, or humiliating an employee publically in front of others
16. **Revenge.** Acting vindictive towards someone; seeking unfair revenge when a mistake happens; retaliating against an employee
17. **Threats.** Threatening unwarranted punishment, discipline, termination, and/or physical, emotional, or psychological abuse
18. **Offensive communication.** Communicating offensively by using profanity, demeaning jokes, untrue rumors or gossip, or harassment
19. **Campaigning.** Launching an overt or underhanded campaign to "oust" a person out of their job or the organization
20. **Blocking advancement or growth.** Impeding an employee's progression, growth, and/or advancement in the organization unfairly

Obstructionism: Deliberate delays and preventing a process or change for the purpose of advancing power and control.

Deliberate Deception: Lying about a person or their performance to achieve a goal. The goal is not for the greater good – but to advance power and control.

Scapegoating: Placing blame on a person as a substitute for someone else. Sometimes because the person you are really targeting has more power. As a means to hurt them, you target people close to them or their appointees.

Bullying is not a leadership style - These behaviors are toxic and undermine the fabric of our democracy. True leadership that benefits everyone allows processes to work.

It's not what you say it's what you do that matters

Name it to change it

Some of you may fear the other person but you shouldn't fear them. I personally have dealt with bullies most of life in school and a grandfather who bullied me every day. Bullies are weak despicable people who don't deserve our respect and admiration.

I myself will never allow bullies to take advantage of me, mistreat me, disrespect me or my family and neither should any of you.

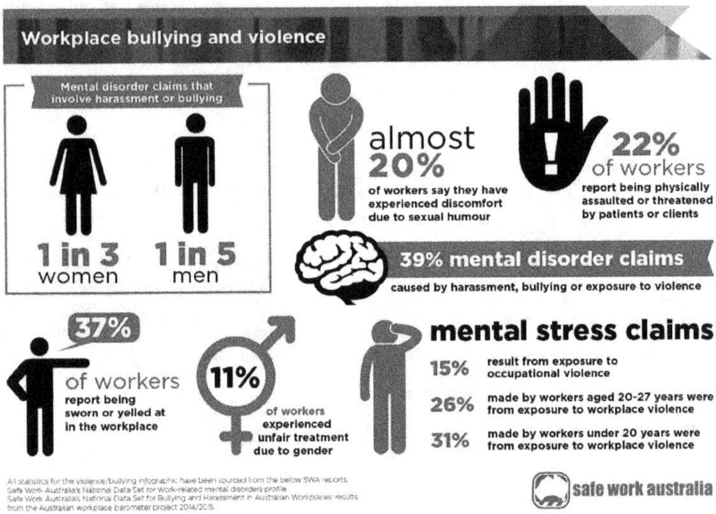

Chapter 29

In Amerika, is it ok to Lie, Cheat and Steal

September 3, 2022

I often think about what is acceptable in today's society. Growing up in the 80's and 90's times were different or at least I think they were. Before social media existed and even phones we had conversations with people, played outside.

Rage over the state of our country

I reflect on my life to this point and often I can be filled with rage over our country as business leaders and politicians work to destroy the norms of how we should live taking rights away, favoring the rich while poor and middleclass are left with very little without an afterthought.

I don't believe the lie that companies and those in politics care about the people, its really about self-interest, what they can get out of the people whether its money or more power.

Its even more infuriating that we continue to follow the former guy as if he is GOD, holding on to his words like they are pure truth but they just pure lies and every word he has ever spoken has been lies yet people choose to eat them up.

I'd like to think we are an intelligent society, but I severely doubt that as he are being led by stupid, immoral people.

I think how we as society finds it ok to act in a manner to be violent, spread hate, lie, cheat, steal and even murder our fellow man, women and child.

is good and good is evil

We are coming to a point where people are justifying wrong behavior when some else murders another person coping to "Self-defense". That those who decide to shoot up a school and kill innocent kids are treated as martyrs. How the right tries to own the left and the left tries to own the right and how we are no longer a country but a divided country who live to terrorize each other whether its in social media or in our every day lives.

We live in a world of debauchery where its ok to mistreat children and abuse them and who is going to stop them. We live in a world where drugs and money rule and again its perfectly fine that we live in a country that allows that to infest our country killing it from within. I believe we allow drugs in this country, and this may be a bold statement but I believe our government allows drugs to enter our country so that we can try to catch the bigger fish at the same time killing those were should be protecting.

Drugs, prostitution, and child endangerment continue to happen today and who is protecting us as many of us must now protect ourselves.

I would like to believe in a world where police are there to protect us but have seen its very easy for them to become corrupt without any accountability. Again, a big lie that we as people are important. I won't say there are no good police in the world there are who really do try to make a difference, but in time those in those fields start to see what they can get away and who's going to stop them.

Who is going to stop me if I decide to go out an hurt someone. I believe we live in a world where there are two justices in this country , one for the rich and one for the poor. If you have money, power and decide that want to go out and murder, lie , cheat and steal you will be allowed to do so because you lawyers who will defend you and bill to keep your life and stay out of prison.

But for the rest of us there are really no choices. You can say that judges and the law will be followed for every one of us, but again that's a big lie too. Because I would surely be put in prison for life, raped, abused where the only good option is death. But rich never have to experience that, even those who do horrible acts get pampered with the luxuries of protection from gen pop.

Society is not equal, nothing equal about it

We don't live in an equal society but in a world made for those who have money and power as the rest of us suffer. Its nice to believe in the illusion we all matter and make a difference but really, we do not unless you have power and wealth.

As Christian man its difficult to realize this as Jesus has already told us in advance what this world will turn into as this is not new. As in Jesus time, this was also seen as the rich and powerful ruled making those who were just trying to survive slaves to labor.

Although there was no technology in the times of Jesus, there were rulers, people of influence and power who made it their mission to make it difficult for others, regular folk to live, nothing has changed. Today we have still had slavery but in a different form, slave to debt and working for companies who pay measly wages all at the same time forcing you and I to make them money, become wealthier.

There is no trickledown economics, but just those who become wealthier. Those who become wealthy and powerful don't get there by good old fashioned hard work but by those give them power or those who take power but pushing down others to get there, that is the world we live in today.

Stepping on people is the way of life

In today's world its easy to push people down, get what you want by lying, cheating and stealing and if you think you don't have to do that, you're lying to yourself.

In the U.S. there are those who have privileges just for being a certain ethnicity or skin color, we are not an equal nation everyone is afforded the same opportunities that is one big lie. I have personally seen this in my own life as I have worked hard to educate myself with degrees and years of experience, but did that get the position, the power in companies I worked, NO. I 've watched those around me with less education get the job all on the account of the skin color, race and ethnicity favor.

I ask you what the point is to live life like this to always work towards something when you never fully get there. But its all possible to lie, cheat and steal and really make it. I know many of you will say I don't want to live like that. I want to live an honest, hard-working life and I can say good for you. Live in love and kindness for fellow man, women and child. You'll be happier for that as I have witnessed that we are in a country where hate is considered ok and even encourage by those political leaders who are supposed to be representatives of people, people you and I elect.

Spreading hate is the new norm

I never elected anything to spread hate and even if I didn't vote for them, they should be representative of the values of the people, but I don't even see that today as many of those in power spread hate to the masses and people eat up, act on that hate and its considered ok.

The times we live in will only get worse as we are the modern-day Rome, self-destructing from within every day.

Today this was in my heart, coming out of frustration of seeing Amerika turn into something none of think we would ever see as our country gets worse as anarchy continues and in time, I am sure we will have purge by those who want to act on their hate in a legal way.

Our days are numbered.

Chapter 30

Should I care about Abortion?

June 25, 2022

I often look at the times today and see how I can adjust my perspective for myself and guide my family in having a realistic view of what is happening in society. Society is shit in all honestly as much as I hope for the better in humanity, I know its only getting worse.

The future of my child

I fear for my nine year old daughter who will one day be an adult in this rotten world , but hope that I train her right to have the right mindset for this world.

Growing up as a generation X'er I was taught to shut up and just do it as far as work, family and the alike. But the newer generations like Millennials and generation Z's are taught differently. Actually most of these new generals are offspring of my generation I just happen to have had my daughter later in my life instead of early two thousands.

I could never be a parent in early two thousands, I felt I was a still a child myself, needing to mature into the man I am today. I didn't want to be forced to grow up like so many have to do due to those kinds of responsibilities. Scary to think during those years I was going to my mental health issues and to bring a child in the world at that time would have pushed me over the edge and further broken me mentally and financially.

Current events

I guess what brings up this topic in a way if the recent supreme court ruling of Roe Vs. Wade and how now states can choose how they wish to offer abortions in their states. Abortions will NEVER be eliminated as much as I would hope as a Christian, they didn't exist they do. Even before abortions existed, women would take dangerous steps to eliminate a pregnancy themselves putting their own lives at risk, some I have heard would stick a metal hanger inside them to remove the fetus and cause an abortion. I don't agree with abortions and certainty GOD doesn't believe in them either because its his life created and its ended without coming to full term.

This is not a topic I talk about regular and in all honestly, I don't feel I have a right to tell women how treat her body, its her choice. Just like I wouldn't want to be told you have get a procedure or do something with my body I didn't agree with like cut off an important appendage.

Women are Angry and Rightfully so

Women are upset, angry and rightfully so because we live in a country that allows men and women to choose our fate and how we should live our lives, but that is wrong, our country is wrong. I wont go as far as saying that I hate America, because I don't but we are on the wrong side of history that will have a huge ripple affect over our country and world.

These times that we live shouldn't be a surprise to someone who believes in GOD, actually he already foretold this kind of thing would happen and it just means he is coming back again soon.

I look at my life today and think would I be here today if my Mom decided to terminate me and in all honestly would I blame her. My mother whom I love dearly had a very difficult life financially, personally and felt could have had a more fulfilling life maybe if she didn't have me so young, which she was twenty years old. I know she loved he and she had me out of love , I am unsure of her religious beliefs that that time in her life but glad I am here today to experience and love my own family.

Abortions in Society and Culture

But I observed that abortions come off as being a all too casual event in our country that you can just go to a doctor and suck out the fetus. Other countries don't have this ability and in some countries abortions are illegal.

I can not speak to why women do it, it could be because they are not ready for a child, yet if they made a choice to have sex unprotected then actually that unwanted baby is their fault and should have used protection. In cases of incest and or Rape that is completely different because women didn't have a choice. Again those are horrible situations I cant even imagine what that must be like for that women, but does that make abortion ok, Honestly I don't know.

I often think of the show Law and Order SVU and Olivia Benson who was a product of her mother's rape was given life. She has struggled knowing her mother was raped and she was the result, but I think ultimately appreciates not being aborted and be allowed to live her life today with her own son.

Fictional reality

I know this is fiction and a TV show, but many women probably go through this today seeing the value in that child's life and although it would be difficult to have a child being raped, I think a women should give birth to the child and just give it up for adoption as so many men and women want to have a child. Again I know it's a personal choice for women to decide that and I can never imagine the fear they must be going through thinking about giving birth, but what if that women is surprised and wants to keep that beautiful child and raise him or her.

I can imagine that many of children aborted today and, in the past, maybe could have been something amazing. In my eyes those potential children were all amazing. What I mean is that they could have had a choice to do great things in this world but were not given the chance to.

These are things I think about during these times but know that in the United States I will continue to see the supreme courts decision in the news. I will continue to see the downward spiral of society and just the continuation and manifestation of anger and hate grow in this country. I choose to be positive, live in the reality of what is happening in our world as Men and Women decide each of fates in this world and country.

Gloom and Doom upon us

Don't mean to so gloom and doom but that is how I see the world today as we allow men and women to choose our fate.

I am waiting for the day when what I right today will be considered illegal and that I can have no voice, similar to what I have seen and read in George Orwell's "1984".

Difficult times are upon, even though we do see a lot of fear mongering going on in the media and Television to scare society into submission and we mustn't submit to society and the culture. Yes powerful men control things and that is by design as we have allowed it, as the ruling of Roe Vs. Wade is one example.

Keep the good fight up and never give up!

Chapter 31

Rage Against the Machine!

July 16, 2022

The machine, when you think of this term what does it mean to you. When I think of the machine I think of a repressive system, society filled with greed, hate and angry. We as world are supposed to be intelligent. But as I go through life at still the young age of 42 , I see how stupid we are as human beings. We pride ourselves on doing great things. Some of you will say well yeah we as humans have done sound great things or I can rephrase that to say we have done some pretty great horrible things.

Recently I was watching a Netflix documentary called "How to be a Tyrant". The truth is that anyone can be tyrant. Despite our laws and rules in place anyone can become one and nothing is really stopping them. We look at those horrible humans like Hitler, Mussolini, Leni, and many others. People fail to understand that in our country (U.S) we are ripe for a takeover into dictatorship. We have had close calls already, but we live in country that is ruled by the elite and powerful who truly wish to suppress those without a voice like the poor, immigrants, people of color to name a few.

Control is already here!

It may come to a surprised, but many people want to be ruled even dominated to be told how to live your life. Its especially scary how even in our country politicians wish to rule over you and I dictating how you and I should live and what we can do with our own bodies. I am not necessarily talking about the abortion discussion and recent supreme court ruling, but generally government wants to control our moves along with big tech like Facebook, twitter and other companies who collect information on all of us every single minute of the day.

Some may not know this, but everything is being track, your keystrokes, the websites you visit, how long to spend on those websites and where you shop, EVERYTHING. For some that may not be a surprise since we willfully gave control to these companies.

Westworld is here

I was recently binge watching Westworld, having never read the book. I found some scary similarities to today and how big corporations look to control us. We continue to build our world on AI looking to eliminate humans from the equation to how things are done. Corporations would gladly eliminate humans in exchange for androids that can do the exact same job you and I do and to a certain degree that has already happened with automation.

We haven't fully gone into robotics and human looking robotics, but we are close and will be there one day. I know it sounds very sci-fi. It appears art imitates life in many ways and I reliance on technology and its only getting worse.

What does the future hold for each of us, who knows? We could break out in a civil war one day, AI, robotics and androids could take over every aspect of our lives eliminating the use of humans. Some of you may not believe that will ever happen, but I guarantee some billionaire works on making this reality because frankly they have all the resources and wealth to survive while others would suffer justifying that this would make things easier for everyone, but how would it if people lose their livelihoods, jobs and money to survive as a machine takes over.

The Machine never sleeps

The machine is society, running at all times. The machine includes the bypass of people allowing automation to take control of our decision making. The machine never sleeps as those who run the machine work to find ways to control you and I. Control our thoughts, our minds, our actions, who we support and love and even our race, ethnicity, how many kids you have, who you marry and how you live your life. This machine is not going to stop until it knows it has you and I under control. The people who we think are meant to help us actually want to control you and I to comply with their demands, it stay quiet.

We as society have allowed this, have encouraged this and will pay the consequences of allowing the machine to rule our lives. How do we stop the machine you may ask, well it's a little too late for that as people are counting on the machine running every minute of every day.

What we can do is rage against the machine, never grow tired of what its trying to do. Never allowing your minds to be warped, to be taken control over. Unfortunately, many are ruled today by social media and media alone from Facebook, Twitter and TikTok working to engage you, change your frame of mind slowly in time accepting compliance and finding it ok that you are controlled by society, big tech and government.

The rewriting of history is happening as speak

You may say well Ill never be controlled and I hope that is true, but open your eyes to what is around you, who is around you working to indoctrinate you and your loved ones. I choose not to fall for this trap, I must rage against the machine and will never comply.

I find the biggest offenders to humanity seems to be corporations. Although they are not the full problem, they are big part especially corporate greed. I am not against a company making money and a company being profitable, because we are afforded the ability to make money in this world and country legitimately and illegitimately. The problem is corporations have chosen to identify themselves politically funding causes that go against the peoples wishes. For example, the supreme court bought and paid for by corporate America and lobbyists.

Each day our world does appear to be looking like Orwellian 1984 which many feel that is some type of joke. Some of may not live long enough to see that world but sure enough our future generations are, and they are lost. The Machine is alive and well and demands your pound of flesh as payment.

Welcome to one world order. Some of you may think I sound unhinged, but I am perfectly hinged, eyes opened, maybe you should open yours too or we will all to resemble this.

Chapter 32

What the great resignation has taught us

August 6, 2022

Are we as valued as our employers say we are? For some they would say Yes my employer values me and treats me as such. But for most I don't think this is true as I have seen firsthand "The Great Resignation" take place in our country and possibly even globally. Having lived in the U.S. all my life I have seen how the job market has changed over the years.

I will say I am a generation X and I will say from my perspective we were taught differently then younger generations today. For one I do believe we did grow up at a time that social media did not exist which may or may not have been a good thing. We were taught to be independent, self-reliant but I believe we were taught to accept what was given to us in the workplace such and expected to comply with what was told of us. We were taught that we should go to college because that is how we will make something of ourselves and be successful, essentially, we were taught to just be quiet and respect authority whether it was our bosses, managers and respect that know what they are talking about.

What different generations have taught us

Generation Z's and millennials where I see taught different and many of those in these generations of children of generation Xer's as we tried to teach those generations from our mistakes as workers. I too look to teach my nine-year-old different lessons to the workforce encouraging her to take her career into her own hands and not depend on an employer to give her things. Although there is nothing wrong with working for an employer independent owning your work and working for yourself givers one more freedom to make your own choices.

I too look to be an example when I start my independent consultancy and show my daughter it can be done. Even today I go to work each day and I teach part time for a vocational college but at the end of the day I want more. I no longer want to feel the pressure of catering to a company and making them profitable and rich anymore when I myself can probably do that for myself.

Truly I am tired of feeling that a company will just let me go just because. I have dedicated my life and time to making other companies better within my own right. I am in no way a manager or executive. Like many I am a worker bee do what I do, in my case projects and project management.

What is the point of this piece, its really to open your eyes to employers and how much value they place in you and often times they say we value you, your important, but its all a rouse , a lie. Some of may not agree with my perspective and all I can say is that has been my experience.

The great resignation is here and this is why

The great resignation is real and continues to shape our workforce. Some of the important reasons why the following:

- *No Work-life balance*
- *Underpaid Staff*
- *Lack of Recognition*
- *Toxic work environment*
- *Poor management and leadership*
- These are just some of the reasons as you can probably add your own to this list, but these were some of the main culprits of the great resignation.
- So where do we go from here? We continue to keep our options open to work, change our mindset to stop expecting companies to care. This message is not anti-corporation, or about greed although there are elements of todays work force that is strictly that. Companies want

> us to make them money giving us peanuts at times and that is why we need to work towards to independently making it one our own and it can be done. I know that idea may scare many of you, but I believe the reason we fear striking it out on our own is fear of the unknown.

We need to trust ourselves, our abilities and our gifts which I believe we all have, we just need to realize those gifts and stop allowing companies to smother them, making us believe we don't have the abilities, we all do. I see that now and now its time to take actions.

I hope his piece has enlightened you, but if you would like more information on the great resignation here is some sources:

Chapter 33

Is Free Speech Really Free?

October 30, 2022

Is free speech truly free? Before you turn the page, this is not someone spread right wing Rhetoric about your freedoms being stripped from us. No this is about how in America we have a right to speak , but there are consequences and being held accountable for spreading hate and this goes for other countries outside the U.S.

The connected world

We truly live in a connected world via social media and the internet, which is wonderful thing but it has lead to the most divisive times as people sit behind their websites, their blogs, their social media handles and make choices to spread hate and spew misinformation and in essence they have that right. But why do we as a civilized society listen intently to those who lie to us knowing they are lying only wishing to get a reaction from us, get more followers, likes and reposts. We are all not innocent but culpable. You may say well I am not doing anything just liking a comment, but liking a comment seen by your followers and the world in a way.

We live in what I believe to be the most divisive times in history. For Many who are older than me, maybe you would say and see that differently. But growing up in 80's, 90's and today. I have seen society change in such a drastic way. Yes, there was always violence, murders, and the mistreatment of each other, but it appears to be getting worse.

Social Media has been the destruction of us!

I unfortunately blame social media as a main culprit as I do not believe we had these times like today before social media. I don't want to say well back in my day things were simpler, but in reality they were.

I know each generation will have a series of their own problems that they will have to deal with from both an international and national level.

Over time I have seen myself grow angrier over what I have seen and have seen the softness of myself change over time, part of that is growing up. Now I will say I do not hate anyone but I can see how someone who constantly is in social media especially platforms like Twitter and Facebook can go down the rabbit hole of hate finding it in many places.

If you have been following the news, the world now knows the Elon Musk is in control of Twitter having purchased the platform for forty-four billion dollars. He truly believes and many others that our free speech is at risk but is it really.

There is Never a reason to be Hateful

I believe now it just gives many a reason to be hateful, racist without being blocked, banned and suspended. There are of course other platforms like YouTube that monitors its content, many hate that people get blocked for saying racist hateful things. What is sad that people are so comfortable saying those things. Now you may say well I don't say those things on those sites, I go just to connect with friends and family, I go to get my news, I got to build my brand. All good reasons to go, but many go to spread disinformation, spread hate and division and its allowed at times.

I will say I have NO society media accounts, I even removed LinkedIn because I started to see the site grow into another Facebook and no longer a professional networking site.

Some of you may feel I am taking these sites too seriously and I don't have to read the comments, read the posts or even engage. You are right I don't have to, so what is the true point of having them. I personally only have my blog now and you folks and that is enough.

I think that we have grown into a society that is no longer governed by decency and civility. Ill admit that people need to respect others much more, but it starts with all of us. It starts with accepting people's views and beliefs especially political beliefs which in the U.S. is almost impossible. I am made to feel like some monster by just speaking about political views like I am some baby killer, murderer which I am not, Not saying which way I lean because I really have no political beliefs, I could care less about politics, but I know many people do and its important.

We Live in a celebrity culture and it's a mess

We have already seen the impact celebrities like "Ye" have on speech and Donald Trump and others who find antisemitism perfect ok actually making excuses that the man is mentally ill and we should excuse his behavior and to just move along.

For most of us who are not celebrities If we were even act in a small fashion like "YE" we would be fired from our jobs, but many today act in those manner even proudly.

Hate of any kind is wrong and we should not be falling for it, disengage from it. That does not mean don't care, but we MUST defend civility in our societies. Often many are find it acceptable in society when it should never be acceptable. The sad fact is that we have dealt with this type of hate before especially during World War II and the Holocaust.

Some of you may be thinking what the point of this is to tell us what we already know, YES. It's because we know not to Hate, discriminate, spread lies and disinformation, but many do and do it with impunity, STOP IT.

My Faith Sustains me to be Better each day, But I am not Perfect

As a man of faith and with a strong belief in GOD, it's hard because you see it so often with whose who preach to be good Christians, yet they spread hate against their fellow man, women and child its disgusting forming the opinion people who have strong faiths cannot be trusted or believed, but that is a part of the lie today. There are other lies and conspiracies that continue to do farm in QAnon which I have never felt the need to learn about because I honestly feel that would just destroy my brain cells, not literally.

As for myself I go to my two jobs, work and teach part time, take care of the family, learn to be a better man of GOD and take care of my god given family. I choose not to involve myself with lies, spreading them, but trying to speak a truth in my Joe Meyer Creatives , Just Talk with Joe Meyer Podcast and Just Talk with Joe Meyer Vlog.

I often believe Art imitates life as I think of the masterpiece book "1984" by George Orwell, how relative it is to today's times. But in general, that people just need to read more, stay offline and get back to basics.

I know this piece may seem like I am ranting on things many of us know about, but we choose not to. I think it's important to self-reflect on our choices and actions each day. How we speak to one another, how we think of others and show respect. I know not everyone will show us respect and that is ok, its important to be the better person by showing kindness and respect. If others do not respect your way of life, your beliefs, your values then pay them no attention and move on, to each their own.

Let's all be Better versions of ourselves each day

Let's continue to be better each day, despite what is going on in the world, because frankly life is short and who wants to spend life hating others because we never know when our last day will be here on earth. Love one another and live in peace.

As many of us try to navigate this changing country and world lets remember we have a choice. A choice to speak kindness to those around us. A choice to live a life to focus on the good like friends and family and a choice not to engage in the rhetoric of today.

Chapter 34

Working from Home for the First Time

February 5, 2022

Working at home can be both a blessing and a curse as I am officially allowed to work from home due to our world pandemic. I guess I can say I always wanted to know what it was like to work from home, as I was aware there are many fields that offer opportunities to work from home, like computer programmers and sales to name a few. This is my first experience working from home on a full-time basis and I will say if you work from home or have you known there are definitely pros and cons to each.

I am not sure how long I will be required to work from home, but I will say that at the moment I live in a two-bedroom apartment with my wife and daughter with my mother in law visiting for a couple of months. The word challenge comes to mind right now, but I am doing everything in my power to make it work for the time being.

From a personal standpoint, I will say that's it is great it gets to spend time with my family in a way I never thought possible. I will mention that I am home like many who work from home due to countrywide quarantine due to the Corona Virus or COVID-19, which at this point could have me working from one to three months at home maybe even longer.

It's important to know that working from home is not for everyone, I personally like working in an office with less distractions without the luxury of having an extra room to work out of like so many who may work from home. My home office is right in our living room/kitchen dining area so I have to be sure to put down some ground rules when working from home, but I understand I have to be flexible too, this is still a home.

I am not the type to prevent my family from enjoying the home because in essence, I am infringing on their territory too, so I have to learn to adjust. Some may have a hard time mixing family and work together at times and I would say it can depend on the type of personality to have to make it work. I tend to have a very lack attitude, refusing to nitpick over every little thing my family says or does, as long as I am not disturbed when I am speaking with co-workers or clients I am ok.

If this the first time you are working from home too, here are some tips that may help during this time.

Make a Space

Your workspace is one of the most important aspects of working from home and it will be different for everyone. It's great if you can have separate working quarters, like an extra room, but not everyone has the ability as many times shared space is how it's done by many. Having a spot that you feel organized with all the tools you need to get work done. It should not be a kitchen table. The doesn't mean you can't get good work done there, but it means you should have at least one place that set apart from work. Find that place, it can be a challenge but it can be done.

Shut the door

Speaking of having space, it should be one with a door that can shut. Just like in an office, remote working has plenty of interruptions-often from family. Again not always possible depending on where you live. I have found that in today's day and age many tend to work out of a Starbucks and seem fine. Due to many times, you may have meetings and call using via some type of teleconferencing you definitely don't want family walking in the background or kids playing in your workplace.

Don't lose contact

When you aren't working in physical proximity to your team, it takes a little creative thinking to stay connected.

Tools like Zoom, slack and basecamp make that relatively easy. Create a plan and tools in place so that you and your team know how you're going to communicate.

Organize your day

One of the challenges of working form home is that you are far more responsible for managing your workload. That means creating a plan each day. Depending on you, you can plan the day before or plan the morning before you get on the clock. I will say it also depends on your work as it may be hard to plan in advance, but do your best so each day will be as if your in the office.

Walk around

Being at home it can be easy to plop down in your chair, go to work and never really leave your seat. I find its important to get up, take a walk, take breaks, take a lunch break. I can be unhealthy just to keep working thinking well I am in the comfort of my home is it is like I am at home but really it is not. You are work and should mimic some normalcy to working. There is no shame in taking breaks, spend a few moments with family and do the best you can with the situation.

Try to get dressed

Working from home can literally be you rolling out of bed and going straight to your computer, no shower, no brushed teeth in your Pajama's, don't do it. I find its very important to get dressed, shower, brush your teeth, comb your hair. Now I am not saying you have to dress up, wear a suit and tie unless you feel you need too, but look presentable for those times you will be video conferencing with co-workers, clients and such. I believe this allows us to have more respect for our roles as we do our job from home.

Punch out on time

Working from home it can be easy to work long hours when it may not be necessary to just because you are in the comfort of your home. Keep a schedule of normal working hours, clock off and log off for the day. It's so important to have a balance in working from home which means hours I work. Pretty simple but can be hard to follow.

Check-in with co-workers and the boss several times a day

Working for a large company I telecommunicate multiple times a day so it's a natural part of my job, but it can be just as easy to go radio silent when we are working. For some like myself, I am introvert so it's easy to stick by myself, but I actually don't wish to, I need human contact daily. I think it's important to keep that contact regularly even a simple hello Boss how are you? I think it will be important to one's sanity at times having that contact.

My Work from Home Journey continues

There are probably hundreds of tips of those who are pros at working at home that I could offer, but now these are my tips to help get you started. You will create your own tips as you become a work from home pro. For those working from home due to our current world situation and will be going back to office eventually then take this time to appreciate how capable you are to work from home, be disciplined and get things done. In the end, we will be stronger for these new skills we are learning to be more organized in creating an environment at home to allow us to be productive.

I would love to hear some of your tips as you work from home as we are all in this together and lastly we should all feel thankful we can work from home, many canno

Chapter 35

How Getting Covid Awakened Me To My Gifts

January 23, 2022

The start of 2022, did not start out as planned, having caught COVID in early January. Not thinking I was immune and couldn't catch it, I knew it was a possibility. I was very careful to follow the rules, keep my distance, wear my mask and I was vaccinated. Again, I know vaccination is by no means a total prevention but getting sick really changed me. I was out of commission for a week and to be honest I don't even remember that week as I was in bed sick, sleeping and also experiencing flu like symptoms like fever, cough and vomiting. Thankful I did not have to be hospitalized, because in all honestly, I have heard and read that once you are placed on a ventilator many tend to don't recover.

My Post COVID Awakening

What was most difficult is I was coming off my two-week holiday vacation ready to get back to work and suddenly this happens. After getting back to work I honestly did not feel the same, I still don't as I appear to have brain fog, fatigue and shortness of breath at times.

I think what eye was quite opening to me is how precious life is and how many in this world have lost the battle to COVID and have died. This is certainty strange times and even though this pandemic has been happening since early 2020 it did not truly affect me until recently. Thankfully my nine-year-old daughter was ok, but my wife did test positive and experience similar symptoms.

What was eye opening to me as well is my professional life and having an understanding that this may be a moment in history to not hold back and wait but to truly go for the job of my dreams. I say that because since early 2020 I feel many have lived in fear to move to progress because we are told to stay indoors, don't get COVID, keep your distance and basically keep your head down. For many you may not see this, living in the U.S. fear is rampant and for good reason.

Change in Workforce Culture

I have seen our culture change in the last two years basically especially in the workforce as we are experiencing what is called the great resignation as employees are having an awaking to better opportunities, more money and realizing that many employers do not care about them as much as we want to believe, that we are all expendable and this is the moment we can all move forward. Employers also see this as an opportunity to get a new employee force and the market is more competitive now which is a good thing. I too am considering the move to and looking for other opportunities although I am happy with the company and position, I am at now, I believe there could be better opportunities out there no harm in seeking them. Over the course of this pandemic, I have worked from home which has been great because of the flexibility to be with the family, but I am not opposed to working in an office again, but I would prefer keeping to working from home.

You Have Gifts

During this period in history, I encourage all of you to look within at your gifts, your talents and who you can offer the workforce. Maybe you feel you cannot accomplish anything right now because we are stuck at home, but you can and should keep moving forward in life and your career. I feel this year will be enlighten year like none other and hopefully it will be for. I feel this pandemic has opened my eyes to the possibilities and to remember how short life is and how we must seize the moment for better things, take risks in your career and apply for the opportunity, go back to school , but ultimately create some great goals in 2022, surprise yourself.

Covid and the pandemic is not over, and it will probably not be over for some time, but that should not stop us from succeeding, reaching our goals and going against the tide of not living in fear, because it appears this is a moment in history especially in the workforce that employers are looking for you and so you should look for them.

This article is unique in itself, because of my new perspective and hope you see it that way. Thank you and have a great 2022, be safe and reach for your dreams, this is your year.

Part III - Bigfoot, Monsters and Films

Chapter 36

How Films and Television Speak the Truth

February 21, 2022

I often think of bad men and women who are mother's and father's and raise children. Watching certain show's and movies like the Sopranos, Good Fellas, even your typical Narco or drug pusher. These men and women go against everything most of us stand for, they are straight out murders.

Was Tony Soprano a Good Man?

I think of Tony Soprano, a family man who was raised in the family of Italian mafia, Cosa nostra. If you didn't know Tony he looks like a regular Joe, but is far from regular. He would do anything to protect his family and does living in his posh New Jersey mansion with his wife and two kids.

Each member of the Soprano family is flawed in their own way, but deep down you root for them or at least I did. Tony is an adulterer and murderer but justifies it to keep the family busy going, but in the end he meets his fate.

I often wonder how a man like this justifies who he murders and his actions. I also think about your typical Narco, usually coming from Mexico or Columbia. I get this to a certain degree these are just shows, but I believe they are based in reality. One of the films I think of films like Sicario, Traffic, Blow and savages among the films I have watched.

Are these men and women just a product of growing up in the Mafia and cartel not really have a choice but force to live that life, that could be the case.

Do we live in the age of Narcos and Mafia?

I think about even our own society, do we live in that kind of attitude of a Narco and Mafia where many of us are forced to act out against society, spewing hate and anger. I see our society as very angry, which could be the biproduct of what Covid and the pandemic have done to us.

I also see that things like murder are becoming a natural part of life, although I would never do that society has made it clear its becoming acceptable as long as you doing get caught and in all honest even films have taught us what to do not to get caught by the PO-PO.

Yes we are governed by laws that are met to deter people from doing bad things, but unfortunately that hasn't stopped people because people are getting wiser and using technology and even television and movies to skirt the law and get away with things. Its sad that it as simple if you want to get rid of someone who put them in some concrete boots and drop them in the ocean forever lost.

Oh come to think of it another show I have seen is Dexter who on the outside lives a pretty normal life, but on his free time murders those bad people justification for murder one could say.

Jesus and Bible in relation to Murder

As a Christian and believer in the bible and Jesus murder was a common theme in biblical times even corporate punishment crucifixions to name one form of punishment and I would recommend watching the Passion to give you a better picture.

God himself has even smote who people in anger for their behavior and acts against GOD. But as a believer in Jesus we are taught not to hate or murder people and even the tongue and heart has the ability to murder when we hate a person and shouldn't.

I have seen our society crumble fill itself with hate and justification for murder and hate which continues to grow each day , where a civil society will no longer exists. Many of you will not follow but many of you will if allowed to go out in society and have your own Purge which can resemble the films where government may allow society to kill and murder thinning out society just because.

Films have told us the future of society

Looking back now as film and television displays the future, just like other film favorites of mine like George Orwell's 1984 and the 1930's film Metropolis. The rich and wealthy rule our society as they call the shots to those who shall survive as they plunder society under the guise of trying to make it better.

If there is one thing this pandemic has shown me is our ability to allow corporate America to take advantage, become richer and society becomes poorer. We are not in control, but allowed to thing we are because we have already given up control to our lives in the forms of technology such as social media and the internet.

We are partially in the age of big brother like in 1984, maybe not into the point of complete government control but as we speak there are cites, counties and states and even the federal government creating ways to control us lawfully. So in the end what makes what localities do right but other forms of bad acts are still bad is it because government says its ok.

The film 1984 speaks truth to what is happening today

The truth is like in 1984 the education of facts and history has begun as government attempts to rewrite history such as Slavery and the holocaust like it didn't exist but did. Even slavery exists today in the form of corporations forcing society to take its meager wages and government assistance just to make it while other societies prosper. People live in the illusion the U.S. is still the greatest country on earth and although I am thankful to be an American, its anything but the greatest because we allow the acceptance of hate and murder to be seen as ok and all in the name of business at times.

In the end we are all sheep to the slaughter by all trying to be good little boys and girls , not murdering, killing and not being uncivil, but uncivility is here to stay. As a Christian I know GOD's in control and there will be point Jesus will come back and take me home, but for much of society many will die and end in Hell. In the meantime I live on earth waiting, attempting to understand what good is hate and murder and in all honestly there is no good as people will eat each other up in time and that has already begun.

When we look at television and movies for examples, remember that some is based in reality to real things happening today and some are based on what many want to see into today's society like many of Dystopian books and movies.

Enjoy your life and don't take it for granted

Enjoy your life for the time being, remember not to give unnecessary power to those who we think want to help us. No one wants to help you and I, except GOD to open your eyes.

I imagine what I am writing if I lived in Orwellian times like 1984, I would take taken by the thought police right now, that is the age we are working towards that ideas and free thinking are bad. If the thought police were to come today Word press would be gone, newspapers would disappear, books would be burned like in Fahrenheit 451, and we would rely on government to give us everything even the truth.

This blog may not make sense to many of you but makes sense to me because these thoughts are running in my head as we speak, and I needed to get them on paper to cement that for all of you to remember today.

God Bless all and thank you for listening.

Chapter 37

Should We Feel Bad For The Candy Man

September 16, 2023

As we get into September, let the horror fests begin as films start creeping into each of the streaming services, most of my favorites from Nightmare on Elm Street, Halloween's (Except the Rob Zombie) versions, Exorcist and Exorcist III and many others.

One that I found great interest in as far the story is Candy Man, another favorite having watched all the versions and of course I will throw in all the Saw's, Insidious and the list goes on with too many too count forgive me if I do not mention your favorite.

But Candy Man, having watched the original film when I was about twenty years old and didn't really see two and three until years ago and then of course the most recent adaptation.

I find that many will consider Candy Man the villain as yes, he kills people who say his name five times. CANDY MAN, CANDY MAN, CANDY MAN, CANDY MAN, CAN-, sorry I can not do it frankly I don't want to meet my maker with the Candy Man.

What I find interesting about his story is it is a story of Love ending in violence. First, I love how this story was written by Clive Barker with his short story "The Forbidden". Having not read the original story but feel I must read.

As the original story was actually a Caucasian male having long blonde hair with an unruly red beard, Pale skin that is yellow and eyes that looked like rubies. I find this version quite frightful. In the film version he is played by the incredible Tony Todd, who is black but plays an incredible Candyman less.

Granville T Candyman or Daniel Robitaille was a part of a rich black family in 1870's Chicago. Having gained fame for his portraits and music he commissioned to paint Helen, the daughter of a wealthy landowner. Demanding that Helen poses in the nude as Venus and soon their relationship turns to love.

The forbidden affair brings the city's wrath down to Granville. Cutting his right painting hand off with a rusty blade, covering his naked body with Honey and watching as the bees sting him to death. Lastly the lynch mob chants Candyman five times before he dies. In the short story, the character describes his existence as an urban legend: "I am rumor. It's a blessed condition, believe me. To live in people's dreams; to be whispered at street-corners; but not have to be."

The story revolves around the needs to keep the legacy alive, killing those who doubt his existence. Based on the legend, Candy man was wrong, seeking his revenge through the ages, keeping his legacy alive. Did the town need to lynch the man, cut his hand off, insert a hook, cover with honey, and let bees sting him to death. Some would say just move on, don't take your revenge, revenge is wrong. It's hard because as a man who believes in GOD, I know GOD say's vengeance is his and it is, but when will people just learn probably never. Even today people continue to take their vengeance, harm the innocent and yet at times there seems to be no accountability.

What is interesting is there are other films that despite ideas about those who do harm getting what we think they deserve like SAW or Jigsaw who attempted to teach those who wrong others to learn and seek repentance for their acts.

I wonder do we need more Candyman's in the world, more Jigsaws, hard to say because then maybe one day we might be on the other end paying for our crimes, our sins. Again, a follower of Christ my sins are forgiven that doesn't mean we don't pay for them in some way.

I do feel bad for the Candyman at times, because why can't people just let people be, mind their own business, but again even today people continue to act terrible towards their fellow man, woman and even child.

I think there are certainly lessons we can learn from some of these films, although I do not people to die, I do wish people to learn to be kinder to each other, stop the hate, the violence, the smearing , the bullying but I doubt that will ever happen because frankly we live in a fallen , rotten world that will not be changed until Christ comes back.

Like any story, idea there is a lesson behind it, a lesson the writer is trying to teach their audience that we often overlook, but Candy Man I think has a clear message, but I may be mistaken.

I would encourage you all to watch and even read about the Candyman who knows what this story may tell you about yourself, your views.

Chapter 38

I want to Believe! The truth is Out There

May 14, 2022

I have believed in the paranormal for many years as at times my interest is consumed in knowing about what exist that I have not seen like Bigfoot, UFO's and Aliens in addition to the world of ghosts and spirits. For most the unknown is intriguing that somethings exist that are so different then our human life but I believe are possible.

I have recently been watching the X-Files a show I know existed but really never understood what the big commotion was about when it was on Television until I began to watch as I was sucked into each episode of Scully and Mulder. Now I see why this show has such an incredible following until today.

In all honestly I even watched the most recent film a year ago but didn't have a complete understanding of what it was about until now watching the show and I will surely rewatch the films again once finished.

One of the main themes of the show is alien abduction, something I never truly believed in thinking that just wasn't possible, but MAYBE it is. I do believe the government especially the U.S government is aware of flying saucers and aliens and its possible they even have alien bodies stored somewhere. I know many of you may think that is one big conspiracy aliens don't exist, its just the government trying to make us believe they exists for their own sinister reasons. But how can anyone be so sure as like with Bigfoot there is actual footage especially the Patterson-Gimlin film:

There is certainly a huge interest today even with shows like Finding Bigfoot and Ghost adventures among many the explore the unknown. As you can see I am a believer especially in certain creatures that may not seem possible like the Moth Man which I have written about :

There have been accounts of people who have said they were abducted by aliens and what they did to them as far as experiments. The X-files tends to take it a step further with implants and impregnation. There is some debate over what an actual alien looks like some say there are grayish in color, some green, some even human looking. I believe they are probably grayish looking with large heads and domes, black eyes and tall, thin bodies.

The media continues to speculate what an alien looks like even create shows like Resident Alien that has the alien look human. Our fascination is endless and so are our imaginations, but I believe in certain cases there is some truth. The hard thing is that many are unwilling to talk about these subjects on the account that people will not believe and consider those people real nuts. For instance, one of the films is "Independence Day" with Will Smith. Films have often portrayed aliens as hostile looking to destroy us but I think they are just interested in how we live and have no interest in really living here but maybe some do as their intellect far surpasses our intellect especially with their technology.

Its difficult also as a Christian, one has to think would GOD really create these types of beings and for what purpose is hard to say. If you ask may Christians, they will deny any existence of these beings that that you probably watch too much television that GOD would NEVER create such things. But GOD is our creator he has a purpose for every living creature from inspects to humans, why is it so impassible to believe he would create aliens.

I do pray one day when I no longer here I can ask Jesus if they do exist, and I know he would be truthful in answering my questions about the existence of things I have never seen. In all Honestly as a believer in Jesus whom Ive never touched and seen, I believe he is real and was a real human being thousands of years of go because history states he was and his life was documented in the Bible.

When it comes to aliens, bigfoot and even the moth man they are very possible because of accounts from those who have seen them, and we are talking thousands of witnesses.

I will continue to investigate the unknown and attempt gather facts and data but unwilling to let these interests change me and consume me like others. I too fear telling people I believe because I automatically considered unstable nut, but why I have yet to find out.

I believe the truth is out if we look to seek it out, I think we just need more who are willing and those who have knowledge to share it like the Governments of the world who have knowledge and even real evidence of existence.

One thing is for sure, the interest in films, television and media will not go away as that will continue has Hollyweird will work to make money from it even making a mockery of the subject, but that is Hollyweird.

In the meantime, I will continue to keep an open mind because the Truth is out there, and I want to believe. I don't expect anyone who reads this post to just automatically believe, but research on your own and seek answers you may be surprised what you find.

Chapter 39

Stranger Things was eh, But a step in time for me

July 23, 2022

Stranger Things, a television phenomenon that has attracted the likes of new generations. My daughter who is 9 years asked to watch this show because many of her friends have seen it. In all honestly I have heard about this show but never really had any interest in seeing it for some reason. I think I watched the first episode when it first came out and moved on.

Having just binged watched all four seasons I can see the attraction and as a writer give credit where credit is due to the Duffer brothers who created the show. What is so infuriating is that much of the show's ideas are really taken from films and television from the 80's. I love the 80's soundtracks taking me back in time to my childhood.

The main characters are likeable in which you want to see them safe and be successful in whatever endeavor they encounter from fighting evil to finding love. Eleven is the main character or one of them as a group of friends work to fight evil that has not existed for thousands of years but more like decades manifesting into pure evil.

I respect that there will be writers , content creators who will regurgitate story lines, ideas from the past and I guess I can say I am used to it as many content to as just put in new packaging.

I am angry at the fact that even I probably could have created something of this nature but I am not in television or movies and I am did not go to film school like the Duffer Brothers did. Aside from the mega successful show, I don't see that the brothers have created anything to this magnitude like before, but again I give credit where its due.

The brothers are a few years younger then me and I can only imagine if at the young age put my time into story teller, being more a writer and even going to film school where I would be today.

Anyways that is beside the point. The point is that I loved how Stranger Things has introduced 80's music and themes to a new generation who have no idea of times were like in the 80's and even the 90's before social media and the internet. Yes I believe times were simpler back in the 80's and 90's when the internet didn't exist at the point. Although in the 80's the internet was just beginning.

I will of course watch the last and final season when it comes out and see how the story concludes.

Overall many of you may say well I am just jealous of the success and you would be correct. I am Jealous of the fact that I didn't think of this. I am Jealous for the young actors who are now super successful and well known at such a young age. I am Jealous that I look back at my life in a wife before I becoming married with my daughter that I completely wasted my youth when I could have been more, Yes I am Jealous.

I can also say I am a fan of the show too, I don't completely hate it or anything. Looking back when I was twelve years old when writing was very much an important part of my I would write stories about monsters, murders, also innocent subjects about dogs and animal, I was very fluid in my writing style like am today.

This topic is on my mind, so look out for probably a podcast and vlog on the subject since there are many out there who may listen or watch me instead of reading my writing.

Lets continue to keep things strange, as a fan of the strange , weird and unknown.

Chapter 40

Thirteen Ghost and Their Back Stories

September 17, 2022

I have often had an interest in the paranormal especially the spiritual world. Growing up as a child I had experiences with the spiritual world. I truly believe to this day that an evil entity attempted to take my life back in 2007 causing me to attempt to take my life. An earlier experience, I was probably around ten years old, I remember I would attend 1st Baptist church with my grandparents and father.

Often, I would not go to Sunday school but wander the church while the service was going on. I would go up to the second-floor office when it was empty, look around and play. I would play in the baptism pool it was empty of course, but one time was particularly frightening.

My sister and I was walking around, and she was about seven years at the time and I was looking up at the second floor window when I stated as a joke "I Love the devil". Lo and behold I looked up and could see a demon as clear as day standing at the window looking down at me smiling. It did appear as the devil that many of us are used to as having long horns, red, ugly. With a blink of the eye he was gone.

My other experiences included when I lived with my wife and daughter in my fathers' old home. This home was our family home purchased by my grandparents.

I lived with my family a few year ago but experienced many activities such as footsteps, sounds and even a loud pounding on our bedroom door in the middle of the night. I would often be angry, and my wife would experience great illnesses there along with a shadow figure which would cause sleep paralysis to my wife.

My wife would hear whispers of conversations going on, a phantom baby crying at night. Often the smoke detectors would go off and on randomly, Televisions would turn off by itself and there were knocks, usually in threes.

I am fascinated by paranormal shows like Ghost Adventures and Dead files. I have recent discovered Dead Files. What is particularly interesting about Dead Files is the two investigators medium Amy Allan and retired detective Steve DiSchiavi.

The two investigators mostly investigate homes of those who are experiencing extreme activity similar to what we went through and often worse. What really has got me thinking is what lurks in the night or day , in the shadows that we cannot see. I believe we live in a spiritual world that exists.

I believe spirits pretty much just want to be left alone but that can be difficult because they dwell in places occupied by people like homes, businesses and others places.

There are also other forms of media like movies as I think of the film "The Others" and "13 Ghosts" which surprisingly came out in 2001 around the same time. As a child I watch movies like the Craft and other films. I know films are not always realistic, but they do get one thinking.

I am thinking about 13 Ghosts and the evil spirts that made up the film. The movie which is a remake of a 1960's film tells the story of a ghost hunter Cyrus Kriticos and his psychic assistant Dennis Rafkin lead a team on a mission to capture a spirit called Juggernaut.

Several men, including Cyrus are killed while the team is able to catch the ghost. Cryus's nephew Arthur a widower, informed that he has inherited his uncle's estate. At a point of financial ruin moves his family to the home which is a mansion. The home entirely made of glass. Within the house are twelve angry ghosts imprisoned in the house. A mechanism within the home triggers and seals the home and releases the ghosts. The twelve ghosts and their back stories include the following ghost.

The First-Born Son (Young Billy)

As a ghost , Billy is still in his cowboy outfit, with an Indian feather on his head and holding a tomahawk, the arrow that killed him still protruding from his head. He is always heard whispering "I want to play" when he's nearby.

Billy was the first ghost captured by Cryrus and the first ghost in the Black Zodiac.

The Bound Women (Susan LeGrow)

Susan had a privileged life and was a member of her school's cheerleading squad. Her parents were the richest in town, thus making her the most popular.

During her senior year, Susan dated the captain of school football team, Chet Walters. When Chet caught Susan with another boy on Prom night, he clubbed the boy to death before tying Susan up and strangling her with his tie, breaking her neck. He buried her body under the 50-yard line of the school football field.

Susan's buried corpse was discovered two weeks after her death. Susan's spirit remained bound to earth and later captured by Cyrus.

The Angry Princess (Dana Newman)

An incredibly beautiful women but was unable to recognize her beauty. Her self-loathing and low self-esteem from which doctors tried to save her from was only fueled by a series of abusive boyfriends and led her to having breast implants, nose jobs and other unnecessary procedures.

One night, while Dana was alone in a clinic where she worked, she tried to perform surgery on herself due to imaginary imperfection on her face, but the procedure goes wrong, leaving her blind in one eye. She then gave up on beauty and committed suicide in her bathtub by slashing herself with a butchers knife until she bled to death.

Following her death, Dana's spirit is bound to earth with a hatred of people. Soon captured by Cyrus to become the angry princess.

The Torso (Jimmy Gambino)

Jimmy Gambino was obsessed with gambling and would spend his days at the track instead of at school and his nights gambling in seedy bars. Jimmy eventually opened his own booking business, although he was barely to make his payoffs because of his compulsive gambling. Jimmies inability to turn down a bet eventually caught the attention of mobster and "made man" Larry "Finger" Vatelo, who bet heavily on a boxing match. Jimmy agreed and sealed his fate. When Jimmy's fighter was defeated, he fainted.

When he awakened, Larry and his gang arrived to collect Larry's winning from Jimmy. But because Jimmy was cleaned out, instead they cut Jimmy's body

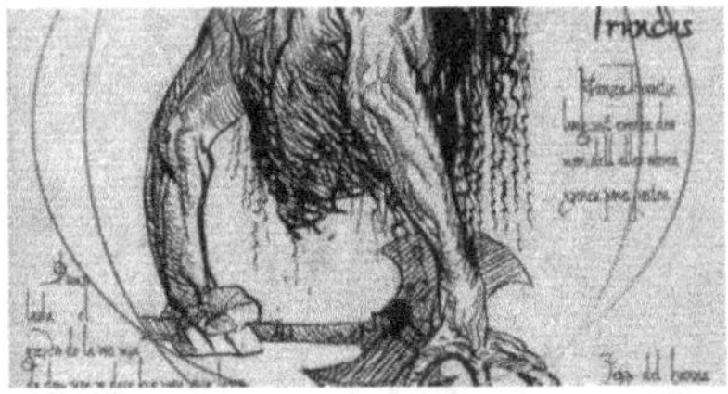

up wrapped in pieces of cellophane and dumped the body in the ocean.

Following his death, Jimmy's spirit remained bound to earth and was captured by Cyrus.

The Jackal (Ryan Kuhn)

Born to a prostitute at some point in 1887. Growing up to develop a sick, uncontrollable taste for women. As he a result he became wild and cunning, sexual predator, attacking, raping and murdering strays and prostitutes in the dead of night like a wild animal.

Seeking treatment, Ryan committed himself to Borinwood Asylum, where he eventually went insane. Scratching his cells walls violently, tearing off his fingernails completely off, making his hands claw like.

When Ryan attacked a nurse , the doctors decided to put him in a straitjacket and tightened it whenever Ryan acted out, contorting his limbs horribly. However Ryan gnawed through it, so the doctors locked Ryan's head in a cage-type helmet and locked him in the dark basement cell. This is where he grew to hate any human contact, cowering and screaming madly whenever anyone approached.

When a fire broke out at the asylum, while everyone escaped, Ryan choose to stay behind and meet his deserved fate, dying in the fire.

After death, Ryan Spirt bound to earth, captured by Cyrus.

The Hammer (George Markley)

An Honest, hardworking blacksmith, until a racist man named Nathan wrongfully accused George of theft and threatened to banish him from the town they lived in . Knowing he was innocent, George stood up to Nathan and refused to move, causing Nathan and his gang to one day beat George's wife and children to death to send him the cruel message to move or else he would suffer the same fate as his family.

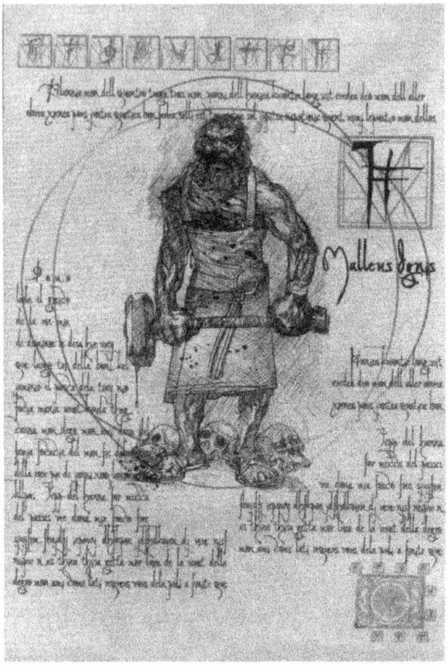

Enraged, George tracked down Nathan and his friends brutally beating him to death with his sledgehammer. When the town discovered what George had done, they dragged him back to his shop where they tied him to a tree and drove railroad spikes into his body with his own sledgehammer slowly killing him.

Then as a finishing touch, sadistically racist townsfolks cut off George's hand and fixed George's sledgehammer in its place.

The Torn Prince (Royce Clayton)

Born in 1940 discovered to be a gifted baseball player in high school, despite his attitude problems and superiority complex. As a destine, all star player, he was offered first-class scholarships from various colleges, all of them offering the best opportunities to leave his small-town life.

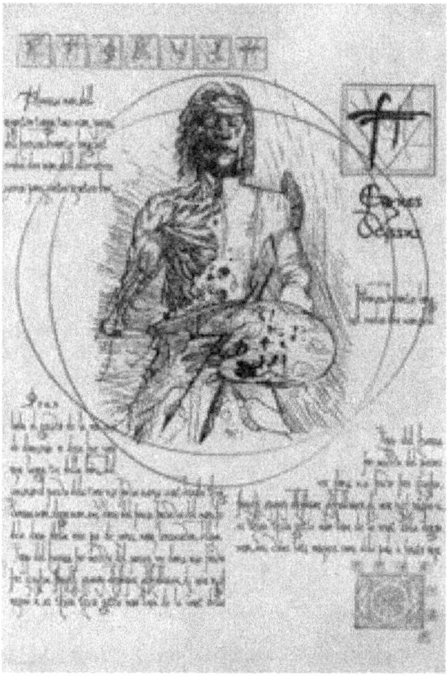

At 17 years old, a greaser named Johnny challenged Royce to a drag race, but unbeknownst to Royce, had cut the brake line in his car prior to the event. This of course caused Royce to lose control of the car, resulting in an accident tearing a large amount of flesh off his chest as well as the right side of his face. This incident quickly ended Royce's life.

After death

Royce's body was buried in a plot of earth overlooking the local baseball diamond where he played. Following his death, his spirit bound to earth, later captured by Cyrus to become the Torn Prince.

The Pilgrimess

During the Colonial times Isabella Smith sailed across the Atlantic Ocean to New England in search of a better life, but the tight-knit townsfolk didn't trust outsiders and Isabella became isolated from the rest of the town.

When the town's livestock began to die mysteriously, shortly after her arrival , Isabella was accused by the local preacher of witchcraft. She denied the claim, but when the preacher fell ill, the town quickly turned against her and corned her in a barn. They lit the structure on fire, But Isabella emerged unharmed.

Instead of a quick death, Isabella was sentenced to a slow, painful death in stocks, where kids stoned her, women cursed at her and men spat at her until she eventually died of starvation weeks later.

Following her death, Isabella's spirit was bound to earth and her spirit was later captured by Cyrus to become the Pilgrimess.

The Great Child and Dire Mother

Born to Margaret Shelburne as a result of rape by the Tall Man. Harold was raised in a carnival as an attraction and his mother's protector. Because Margaret never stopped spoiling him, Harold not only weighed 300 pounds by his later years, but somehow retained his child-like mindset his entire life to the point that he never grew out of diapers. Harold and Margaret were taunted and teased at every turn.

One day, some circus workers kidnapped Margaret as a cruel joke on Harold. In a rage-fueled search for his mother, Harold ransacked most of the carnival, but when he found her , she had already suffocated in the bag the works had kept her in. Enraged Harold kills the circus workers responsible for Margarets death, killing them with an axe as well as some of other freaks, not knowing they weren't actually responsible and put their remains on display for paying customers.

When the carnival broker Jimbo found out of what Harold had done, he ordered an angry mob to confront and execute Harold.

Following Margaret and Harold's death, both bound to earth and later captured by Cyrus.

The Dire Mother

Margaret grew up to be a mere three feet in height and sometimes her own mother would dress her up like a doll. She could never stand up for herself because of her pint size and was constantly stared at and picked on as a result. Seeking acceptance, Margaret joined Jimbo's carnival, but found this life as an attraction for people to google at just as horrible.

While Margaret was sweeping up a donkey pen one night, another freak called the Tall man and raped her, causing her to become pregnant and give birth to her son Harold. Margaret never stopped spoiling Harold keeping him in diapers his entire life and retaining his infant mindset, but Margaret didn't care.

Margaret was kidnapped by carnival workers as a cruel joke suffocating in the sack they kept her in.

The Juggernaut

Horace was abandoned by his mother, almost immediately after birth, raised by his father. As a child Horace grew to such a grotesque height and appearance was constantly ostracized and spend his childhood as an outcast.

Mr. Mahoney put Horace to work in his junkyard chopping and crushing up old cars. When Mr. Mahoney died, Horace was left alone and finally with no one to guide him, went insane as a result. He became a serial killer picking up hitchhikers and stranded motorist to take back to his junkyard. There he would rip them apart with his bare hands and feed their remains to his dogs. This preferred method of murder was what earned him the nickname "The Breaker".

Horace's seventh to be victim turned out to be an undercover police officer, who had swat team surround the junkyard and arrest Horace. However Horace was able to break free of his handcuffs and killed three police officers before he was gunned down by five SWAT officers. They then added one final volley of shots into him, "Just to be sure" that he was dead.

After death, Horace's spirit was bound to earth and haunted the junkyard, brutally killing anyone who would enter. The caused the junkyards death toll to rise to over forty by 2001.

Cyrus and his team including Dennis arrived at the junkyard sometime in 2001 to capture Horace's ghost to become the juggernaut. They use blood and a tape recorded latin chant played across a megaphone to successfully draw the juggernaut into his containment cube. But not before he kills much of Cyrus's team.

The Withered Lover (Jean Kriticios)

Jean was the loving wife of Arthur Kriticos and the mother of their children , Bobby and Kathy Kriticos. Jean loved her family deeply, but tragically lost her one night when she and Arthur were sleeping in front of the fire-place , a stray log rolled out and set the Christmas tree on fire; quickly starting a house fire. Arthur unintentionally left Jean to save Bobby and Kathy assuming Kathy was outside but was actually inside Jeans left side of her face burned and body horribly burnt by the fire. Taken to St. Luke's hospital where she died from her burns.

Six months following her death, Jean's spirit remained bound to earth , later captured by Cyrus. In spite of being burned alive, Jean was the only ghost out of the twelve quite innocent and kind.

Although fictional, looking at these twelve ghosts the back stories seem plausible think of these souls who were very much like you and I. Some seemed only wanting to live their lives, but some were not even allowed to do that. Some of these souls were unstable, crazy, insane and downright murderous.

I think about the Dead file and how there are spirits that literally lurk outside our doors, inside our homes who look to do incredible harm to you and I even getting us to the point of harm ourselves and other people.

Many who have never had any experience with the dead would understand and I think that is a good thing. The spiritual world is not something to mess with but often people attempt to contact the dead, using spirit boards and seances which tends to bring spirits that wish to only do harm, even demons.

Films tend to sensationalize demons, ghosts, aliens and spirits, but this is truly no joke. The reason I wrote this piece is because I truly always wondered the back stories to these ghosts, having seen the film in 2001 and having watched it over a hundred times.

I believe all spirits should be moved on to not torment the living and either go to Heaven or hell Some do belong in hell.

Hopefully these backstories allow you to have more appreciation for the dead and those stories because no matter what we all will die at one point, hopefully you are not one of those who haunt people and can move on in death.

Part IV – On Writing

Chapter 41

New Paranormal WIP

July 24, 2023

For years I devoted my time and energy to the POX, my first novel which I began to write in June 2019 and finally publishing June 2023, Father's Day to be exact. My next book is well under way as I am already at 70k words and I anticipate this book will be a lot of shorter then my first book that started at about at over 340 pages, taking a couple of years to wattle it down. Its out and now available on Amazon and Barnes and Noble but looking to make it a physical book later this year.

As of late I have been working on my newest book with the hopes of finishing the 1st draft soon currently being called "The Menagerie" . I would label this book as a paranormal mystery that takes place in an circus. There is

urder, mayhem, demons, Mysticism. This book is very much more personal to me because of my love for the circus, but also having it take place in Los Angeles in the 70s and 80's. You could say what inspired this piece was my love for the forgotten circus and when the circus was an actual circus and add there are freaks galore.

For those who have read my "Life in the Circus" Series you will see that profiles on freaks originated. Although this novel is not specifically focused on the freaks, it does have them, but there are other origins of this story especially when it comes to the paranormal, dealing with spirits, demons, Native American mysticism.

At this point I am unsure of what the ending will be, but I often think about that, especially when I spend time alone, walking ideas come, storylines are created as I write this story in pieces with no predefined storylines.

I will keep you all up to date on my deeper dive into the paranormal, hopefully bringing some originality to my new novel. Stay tuned.

Chapter 42

The POX is Coming - Debut Novel

May 28, 2023

It gives me incredible joy to announce that my debut novel is coming out June 18th, yes Fathers day. A Novel that I have been working on since 2019 and although it did not take me four years to write it, Over years I have edited and edited and edited. I do not wish to keep editing it as before I know it this book would be out in ten years.

This booking will be available on Amazon and Barnes and Noble as an e-book with the hope of the physical book later this year, but I wanted to get out there.

This book is something I know is not perfect and many writers strive for perfection going as far as spending thousands on professional editing, which is something I did not do, because frankly I do not have thousands of dollars to edit a 266 page book.

I hope people buy and read it, but honestly I find it to be an accomplishment in itself to self publish and put it out there.

More news to come on when it will be officially available for sale.

Chapter 43

My next chapter of Writing and Beyond!

July 2, 2022

This week I have begun the long and ardious process of querying my finished novel Helix 2029. This piece of work which I began in 2018 and for a the past few years have whittled it down from a monsterous over one hundred and seventy thousand words to around one hundred thousand words now. I know for first time novels it should be around eighty thousand and I am suppose I could cut down further, but I think that would diminish the novel to some of the most important parts.

Today I submitted two queries to begin this process knowning that not every agent will want to see my writing or even present me but thats ok, I will work take this process as far as I can most likely querying 80-100 agents and at that point if not bites I will take the next steps possibly self publish who knows.

In addition to quering I have begun my next book which will be story the revolves around the circus. I found the circus to be a great comfort to me although I have not been to one in years and they really dont exist anymore in the traditional sense. P.T. Barnum and Bailey and Circus Vargas were both circuses I grew up with including Lions , Tigers and Bears and Elephants oh My! Until the animal activist decided to do everything in their power to eliminate the circus.

I get that many of you may say that the circus should be obsolete due to how animals are treated and no animal should be made to do tricks. For the most part I agree but I also believe that many if not all the animals were cared for.

What really sparked me writing this next novel is great books and films I have read and seen especially "Water for Elephants" by Sara Gruen which I am reading now.

The other main reason I choose this as my next book is because the circus and its history tends to get forgotton especially with the so call freaks which will be a big part of my book.

I am hopeful to finish the first draft in a few months, but that depends on my time, but I have started this weekend writing three pages setting the stage. I hope to turn this book into some sort of fictional orgins book detailing each character which there will be many. If you've read my circus series you will know I have alot to go off of.

I honestly can not forget the other incredible movie example about the circus is "The Greatest Showman".

The circus may be alive and well at times but not enough today. I truly miss the circus and it hurts my daughter will not be able to experience it like I did.

I will keep everyone up to date on my writing journey. Despite the fact there are tons of novels already about the circus I can not get the deter me from writing this as its deep in my soul to get out on paper.

Thank you for being on this journey with me!

Chapter 44

How Writing Can Help Un-Tap Your Creative Side

June 25, 2022

Being a writer is one of the most important passions in my life today and as I get older, I grow to love other creative ways to express myself. To stick with writing for a moment, I have considered myself a writer then probably the age of twelve.

Growing up I will say I did not live with the happiest childhood and I used writing as an escape to an imaginary world I would create. Much of my influence came from my own imagination but I had sources of inspiration like movies.

Youth Writing Started It For Me

All At that age I wrote a series of works which I will include from a link to my personal blog where you can see my stories that I reincarnated recently. Funny story is that I thought many of stories you will see from my childhood I completely forgot about and found them when I was going through my family's home as they were moving out.

Writing is different for everyone for some who are reading this you may say well big deal I write every day, but if you write stories, novels, journaling then we definitely see eye to eye because you know how writing helps you mentally each day. Currently I make it a habit to write regularly and currently editing a long novel at my first attempt as we speak. Along with blogging for my personal blog and this blog fulfills my urge and need to write in addition I just added podcasting.

For whose who wish to grow your writing skills and it's something I feel we should all strive to do is we must write and read regularly. Reading plays just as an important part in my writing as I am able to learn new styles of writing, attempt to look into the mind of other writers and see areas I can add to my own personal writing style.

The Benefits of Writing

I have seen how writing in particular has helped my mental health at times as I struggled to keep my thoughts within as I didn't want to express those feelings to those around so I wrote and began to selfheal myself. Like mentioned earlier I had a difficult childhood and even as a young adult, so I feel I had lost many years and to be honest I do not remember much of my childhood even happy moments.

Growing up I lived in a home with verbal abuse from a grandparent who constantly put me down and treated me as the hired help putting me to work and I am not talking about typical chores. I grew up with my mother, sister, and one abusive grandfather. So because of this I dived into writing and if you decide to read any of my "Stories from a Child's Past" Series you will see many of the stories I wrote were very dark and about the need to run away.

From scientific standpoint there have been studies to show the affects of writing when it comes to heal and I will reference American Medical Association (Vol 281, No. 14), a study lead by Smyth, 107 asthma and rheumatoid arthritis patients wrote for twenty minutes on each of three consecutive days-71 of them about the most stressful event of their lives and the rest about the emotionally neutral subject of their daily plans.

Four months after the writing exercise, 70 patients in the stressful writing group showed improvement on objective, clinical evaluations compared to 37 of the control patients.

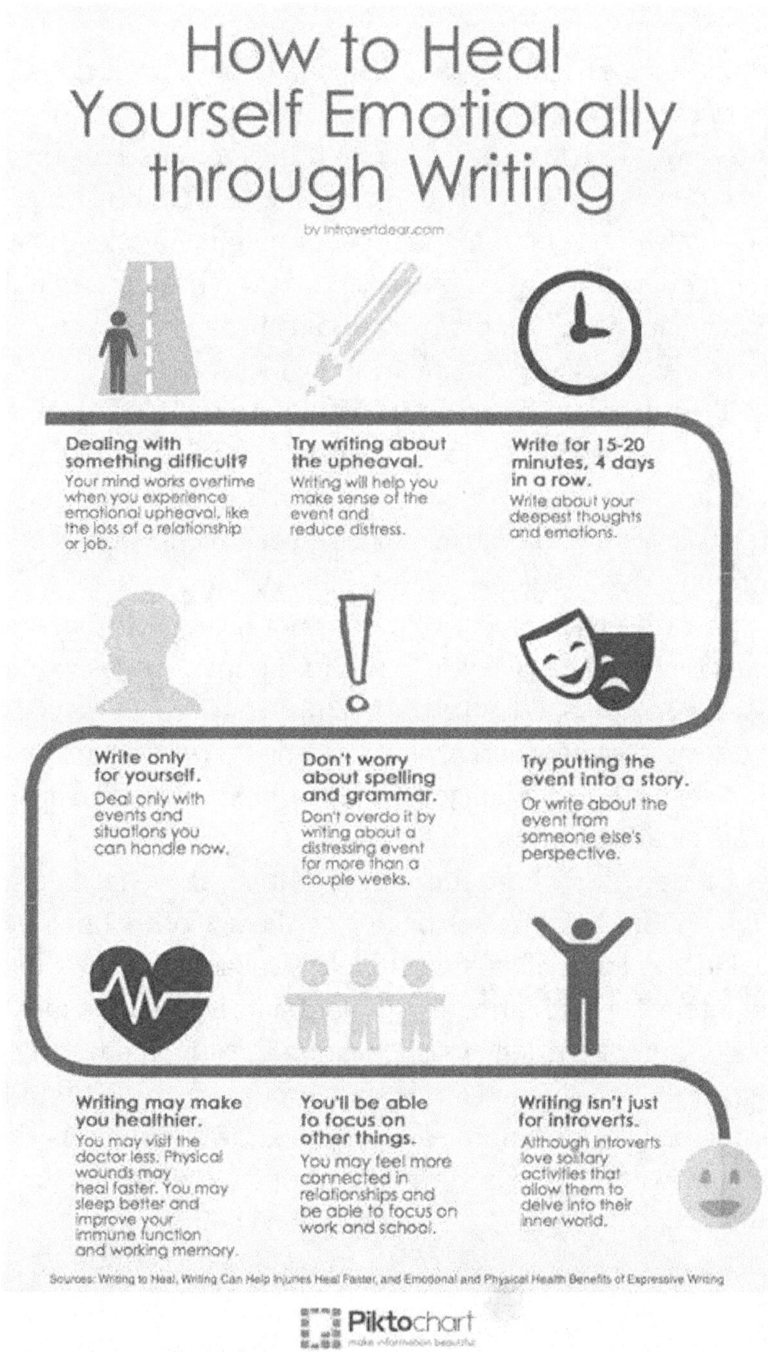
How to Heal Yourself Emotionally through Writing
by introvertdear.com
Dealing with something difficult?
Your mind works overtime when you experience emotional upheaval, like the loss of a relationship or job.
Try writing about the upheaval.
Writing will help you make sense of the event and reduce distress.
Write for 15-20 minutes, 4 days in a row.
Write about your deepest thoughts and emotions.
Write only for yourself.
Deal only with events and situations you can handle now.
Don't worry about spelling and grammar.
Don't overdo it by writing about a distressing event for more than a couple weeks.
Try putting the event into a story.
Or write about the event from someone else's perspective.
Writing may make you healthier.
You may visit the doctor less. Physical wounds may heal faster. You may sleep better and improve your immune function and working memory.
You'll be able to focus on other things.
You may feel more connected in relationships and be able to focus on work and school.
Writing isn't just for introverts.
Although introverts love solitary activities that allow them to delve into their inner world.
Sources: Writing to Heal, Writing Can Help Injuries Heal Faster, and Emotional and Physical Health Benefits of Expressive Writing
Piktochart
make information beautiful

Some may not agree with the medical studies on the importance of writing but I personally have seen the affects on the clarity it gives your mind and spirit. All to often we as people tend to keep things to ourselves over how personal certain parts of our life can be, but I have say just write, get it out and if people comment take those comments with a grain of salt and let the healing begin. I find great comfort in blogging because I can be free to express my views, my troubles and just let it out.

The disappearance of Writing in it's form

The sad fact that I see is that writing is becoming less and less reverent as we have replaced much of writing in short form like text messages, social media and other forms to get a message across in 140 characters or less. From a writer's perspective it does not take much to write each day, no one is saying write for hours or pages, write twenty minutes a day to start. Write your thoughts, your feels, your dreams and aspirations and go from there, you just might be encouraged to write more and even in a more creative capacity like a book.

Lastly writing is so important that these are skills our own children may be losing due to the age of technology as kids no longer focus on the physical act of writing using utensils which I find a terrible shame as even the most basic form of writing is disappearing. Again, I am not trying to be over dramatic in my assessment you may find I am wrong and If I am please let me know. Computers do very important things in the hands of a writer and writing but so does using a good old-fashioned pencil or pen.

Just Write

If there's one message I hope to convey here is to write, get in the habit because you will soon see the benefits yourself, untap that mind of yours and bring out the creativity to yourself and the world. Finally make sure we make a habit of reading, pick up that tablet or paper back and lose yourself in a good book, any book, pick your genre and grow your mind in different ways.

Chapter 45

1st Draft Complete of 2nd book - The Menagerie

July 30, 2023

The completion of my 2nd book 1st draft is complete, currently named the Menagerie. This book I started July 2022. What led to this book being written first and foremost is my love for the circus, add to that mystery and throw in the paranormal.

I don't believe I have come across or read a book like mine, but there may be a similar theme that exists. Prior to writing this book, I wrote a series on life in the circus from yesterday to today which focused on how the circus came to be along with those so-called freaks who made the circus so special. Although the traditional circus with

Lions, Tigers and bears cease to exist as now most circuses include acrobats, and light shows created holographic animals which are not the same.

I get that many feel that circuses of the past were abusive to the animals, that animals are not made to entertain, and I guess to a certain degree I understand as often animals were abused, mistreated, and forced to perform all in the name of money. But I think it can be easy to forget how influential and how the circus' long history is important to yesterday.

I get certain things we should try to learn from and move on and not try recreating, but circus is sadly not coming back in the traditional sense. I am hopeful my book will keep the name of the circus alive although fictional with a twist, I think when others read it eventually will hopefully find it interesting and unique sparking interest in the circus and especially those special performers.

In the meantime, I will begin editing some, I believe I need a break and then I will get right into it and I do not believe it will take a year to edit as this book is much shorter than my first book. Stay tuned.

Chapter 46

My Morbid Curiosity with Victoria Photography

July 30, 2022

Living in the 21st century there are many things that we have today , that those in past centuries would never think we have today like cell-phones, technology and computers. I often think about past centuries that lived basically in the dark ages with no electricity, no running water and the basic necessities we take for granted today did not exist back then.

One those areas I tend to think about is photography. Although photography has been around for quite some time I often found Post mortem photography strange and creepy. I guess my first experience of some reference to this type of photography was in the 2001 film "The Others". For those who remember this film has Nicole Kidman. The film centers around Nicole Kidman and her kids in 1945 living in a remote country house in Jersey. Kidman (Grace) hires three new servants-housekeeper Mrs. Betha Mills, gardener Edmund Tuttle and mute girl named Lydia. Odd things begin to happen in the house and Grace fears there are unknow "others" present. She then finds a 19th century photo album of mourning portrait photographs. When Grace asks Mrs. Mills about her previous experience in the house, Mrs. Mills recounts that many left due to an outbreak of tuberculosis.

Mourning portraits

This is where my interest in so called mourning portraits took place and then I began to search the sad cases of why this was done. As you can imagine a deathbed portrait is a portrait of a person who has recently died, or lying in repose. These were not rare in European homes of well-to-do people as a way of remembering and honoring the dead. People where generally laid out in their best clothes with some sort of headdress, and some sort of token in their hands.

Postmortem Photography

Another form of memorial portraiture was a practice of photographing the recently deceased. Various cultures use and have used this practice. The invention of the daguerreotype in 1839 which was on the first photography processes invented made portraiture much more commonplace, as many of those who were unable to afford the commission of a painted portrait could afford to sit for a photography session. This cheaper and quicker method also provided the middle class with a means for memorializing dead loved ones.

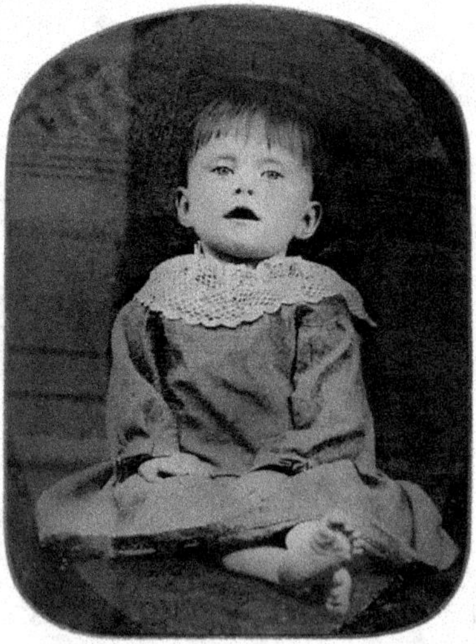

Before this technological advancement, post-mortem portraitures were restricted to the upper class, who continued to commemorate the deceased with this new method.

This form of photography was most common in the nineteenth century when "death occurred in the home and was quite an ordinary part of life. As photography became the new medium, even those of infants and young children were photographed which would be one of the only photographs many would have. The long exposure time made deceased subjects easy to photograph. These photographs served as keepsakes to remember the deceased.

Post-mortem photography as early as 1970's was taken up by artist and continues today. Personal post-mortem photography is considered to a largely private with the exception of the public circulation.

United States

In America, post-mortem photography became an increasingly private practice by the mid to late nineteenth century. Today is not as widely used but I am sure it still exists for private use such as those who attend a funeral wish to take pictures, which I find strange but I can understand the in mourning we want to have lasting images of our loved ones but I doubt anyone would want to look at those pictures in remembrance when one can look at pictures when the person was alive.

I wonder if this type of photography will ever make a come back and maybe there , but who would want this , now that we have cell-phones that can take professional quality pictures that we can keep safety on the cloud.

Yes these photographs were from another time, by looking at many of these many would believe that is how those loved ones captured the souls of those who passed on photos. Many posed as if they never died in the first place.

I would also like to bring your attention to Death, Immortalized: Victorian Post-Mortem Photography - Clara Barton Museum which is a doctoral student by the name of Melissa DeVelvis a student of history in University of South Carolina, specializing in the civil war era. Here is some of she discovered :

"Americans in the 1800s were far more intimately acquainted with death than we are today. Most of this was out of necessity–before embalming procedures became popularized, it was the duty of the family to quickly prepare the body for a viewing and burial. Families would typically hold viewings in their own parlors at home, a tradition that later gave funeral parlors their name. The birth of the funeral industry in the early twentieth century and the growth of large, sanitized hospitals brought about a shift in the way Americans interacted with death."

Thinking about the words of Melissa states why is that society is less comfortable talking about today then in Victorian times, could it be that we just so desensitized to death seeing all the death today in the news, television and film among other medians. Could it be that people tended to appreciate their loved ones more at those times and many times we take for granted our loved ones will be here longer, but we should never take those friends and loved ones for granted.

Much of what they did in Victorian times we certainty would find strange like carrying around a sentimental piece of hair or flesh as a remembrance.

This piece as always is remembering and in no way to creep you out but to educate you as always. Thank you for always going on this wild ride of discovery, you never know with me.

Lately I have been watching the HBO series Carnivale and one of the interesting parts including Death masks. Honestly I have never heard of a death mask before but it was interesting to see how were used a mementos of the dead. I am not sure if these are still done today and who would want one, but I can see that this would allow someone to physically touch and remember ones face after death like a loved one, a child even who dead.

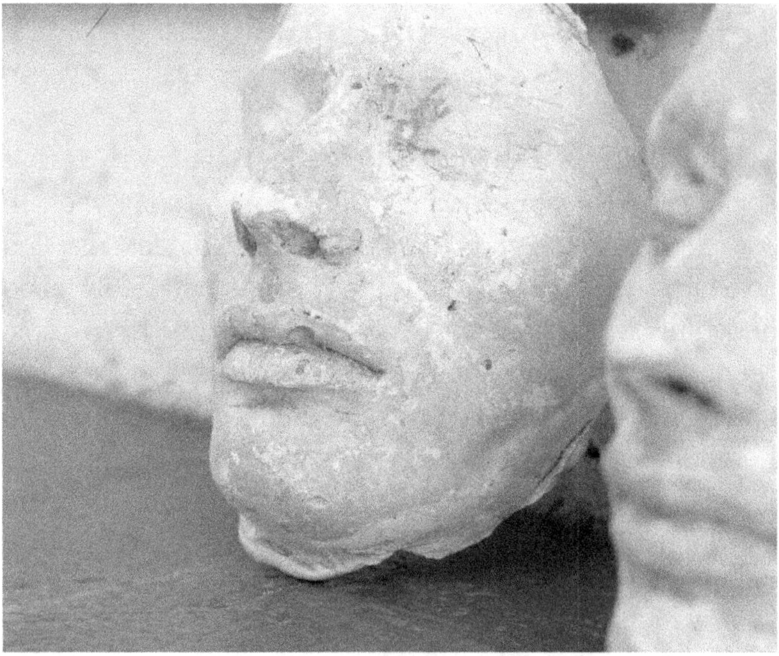

Here's an example of one that I see is very life like and can understand the draw to having these made and probably not every hard to make as they were typically made of plaster or wax.

I have and continued to be interested in the past as many times we try to hold on to the past especially whose who have passed on. I think now today we need to remember the good things in our life and those people in our life we tend to forget about and take for granted.

I am not adovating to bring back death photography or death masks. I am sure people still take pictures of the dead which I have always found strange. I remember when my grandfather passed in 94 my aunts and uncles took pictures of her in her coffin and also my great grandmother as well.

Death is apart of our lives whether we like it or now, Many feel they will never die, but we are not in control of death, we all have an expiration date whether we agree with it or not. I find is especially hard to except when children die becaues they dont fully get a chance to live life and have a real chance to hopefully make some difference, but again their deaths are not up to me. It does anger me when children especially are murdered and killed, but its just as hard when they die of sickness and disease.

Thank you for once again going on these strange journeys that stay deep in my mind, death being one of them as I too have come close to death due to my own hand many many years go. I am thankful to still be here to enjoy my wife, daughter and family as we all should.

Chapter 47

I Did It! My Edited Book Helix 2029 is complete

May 21, 2022

This week I experienced a major milestone in my writing, I have fully and finishing editing my book in which I started back in December 2018 and since have been editing it after finishing the first draft in October of 2019. It has been a journey for me as any writer this is thing of passion.

I have diligently worked on my book on a weekly basis taking occasional breaks and continuing again. The book originally having over 450 pages whittling it down to about 346 as the final version which will be entitled Helix 2029.

As a writer I think about will this book ever be perfect and then I think to myself maybe I should stop trying for perfection and just be content with what I have completed after all the editing has taken place. I would stay the next step would paying to have a professional editor review and provide back to make to make further corrections, but that could be high cost.

Some of the advice out there I've seen is to get an editor, some say you don't need one just try to query for an agent in hopes they will pick it up and then they will edit it.

I do wish to make this book a reality to be published, either to self-publish to have an agent and publisher publish it for me, there are possibilities I think of but will not give up.

Like most writers we feel we have the creative chops to be mainstream, but the reality is not everyone does but I look to authors like JK Rowling who got tons of rejections and others like Stephen King. I am not JK Rowling or Stephen King, I'm me.

I will not be being to see how I can query my book and what that looks like. My book shouldn't be difficult to understand as its partly a mystery, thriller, government conspiracy and even a pandemic scenario all relatable, I just hope it's not too cliché of what has already been written about.

As a blogger and looking at many of your work I can see it's a tough competition out there, there are far more superior writers then me.

I want to thank everyone for always supporting me, I can dream one day to send out a blog that I have been picked up by an agent that would be awesome.

I can imagine seeing my story up on the big screen and or television with multiple follow ups to my initial book. I will not be writing the follow up yet, give this book time to breathe.

For all the writers out there, which is pretty much all of you, don't give up, dreams can happen and I know we get told that ALL the time but we must believe because in each of writing is something special regardless if we think our stories are not be desired, it all came from our creative minds unique to our perspective and mind.

As writers let's not allow ourselves to be beaten down by ourselves being super critical to the point also self-hate, I was there I know what it feels like.

In addition, I have always been incredibly sensitive, and I know being rejected is tough and that is something I will come across when I am being querying my book because of the millions who are trying to get their stories published, but I hope there is light at the end of tunnel.

Chapter 48

Step into a real Asylum - Rancho Los Amigos

August 20, 2022

I have also found the paranormal intriguing especially the spiritual realm which I believe does exist. Having grew up in Los Angeles, there have been and are many hot spots one can visit that you just know something dwells there, most likely evil.

Today there are a ton of shows that dig deep into the paranormal like UFO's, Bigfoot, and Ghost. Maybe you have had some experiences yourself.

One of the cities I grew up in and even worked is Downey, California. Which is a city I haven't lived in and around since 2018.

Some of you have read my previous posts about the house I lived in and actually was my family home until it was sold. This house was a house of evil, though it had a lot of love at times from my grandfathers when they were alive. But this house had something evil that I believe caused he to one day take the drastic measure to try to end it all on February 7, 2007. Strangely on 777, which should be good luck and in a way was because I survived thanks to my sister who just happened to be home as I hung from a noose. In a way that was an eye opening moment as I spent a couple weeks in the hospital, on a 72 hour hold and of course lost my current job at the time, but also was right in the middle of graduate school.

The house in Los Angeles also affected my wife and daughter whom lived there for a few years, as a dark entity. Some of the most frightening times was in the middle of the night around 3AM a loud pounding on our bedroom door. A pound of hate as we opened the door nothing was there, no one was awake. Another time was I was in the shower when I heard a voice from outside the door calling for me that sounds exactly like my wife, but she was a sleep. The was also footsteps at night, things that when bump in the night and a dark force that would stand over my wife as she slept. This force prevented my wife from yelling and a great pressure on her from moving.

Ill admit I would play with these dark forces, no in the sense of doing seances or calling for evil , but the things I would watch, being a horror lover I believe these things would invite those spirits. I would also love watching Ghost Adventures. I guess you could see I always had an interest as I loved as a kid the film "The Craft" and all the classic horror Freddy, Michael, Jason, Pinhead, Chucky.

I guess I never truly realized what doors we open when we watch those types of films, although its hard not as it's a big part of our culture especially in television having just watched Stranger Things.

But what really triggered this post is a place called the Downey Asylum but officially Rancho Los Amigos Rehabilitation center. This place has existed since the 1800's but has been closed down for over 30 years.

Recently there was a major fire which destroyed parts if not all the Asylum. From what I have heard it was going to be torn down to make way for stadium of some sort, so maybe it was planned.

Here is the article:

Massive blaze rips through abandoned Downey asylum once known as the Los Angeles County Poor Farm - ABC7 Los Angeles

The origins

Hollydale was built in the late 1800s for the mentally ill, disabled, and the homeless. With its success came thousands of patients. In the 1950's this town became a part of the city of Downey and thirty years later it was shut down, because it had fallen into disrepair. It's a shame that they couldn't keep it running, because it seems like it truly helped thousands.

The southern campus of the Rancho Los Amigos Hospital is often referred to as the "Hollydale Mental Hospital" or the "Downey Insane Asylum". Built in 1888 as a catch-all institution for the Los Angeles County medical center; a place to care for the handicapped, homeless, insane and elderly. The hospital located in the former town on Hondo, which was absorbed by Downey in the 1950's. Funded by the county bond money, it was simply called the County Poor farm. Here, able-bodied residents could work on a large farm which sustained most the hospital's dietary needs, in lieu of paying for room and board and medical care.

The 600 acres if property also encompassed an aviary, zoo, and rail lines used for freight and passengers. Unclaimed bodies of residents who died at the poor farm were buried at a potter's field nearby, which has since been relocated.

In 1918, the Spanish influenza epidemic hit the area and the facility began to treat all victims rather then just the indigent and the word "poor" was simply stricken from the name of the facility. The hospital expanded greatly in the 1920s to alleviate over crowding conditions and rebuild flood damaged structures after flooding in 1914. In 1932 the name of institution changed to Rancho Los Amigos, which translates to "Ranch of the Friends". Becoming place that offered activities to receive physical therapy and occupational therapy; swimming, woodworking and weaving provided to help restore broken limbs and spirits.

During World War II, the U.S. army turned part of the hospital grounds into Camp Morrow, and at the same time the facility operated as an emergency hospital. It was reorganized once again as a long term care facility after the war, mostly for the victims of polio. Entire wards filled with Iron lungs in the 1950s. The discovery of the Salk polio vaccine in 1955 put most of the machines in storage, a few operated at Rancho for children who were given a bad batch of the vaccines years after.

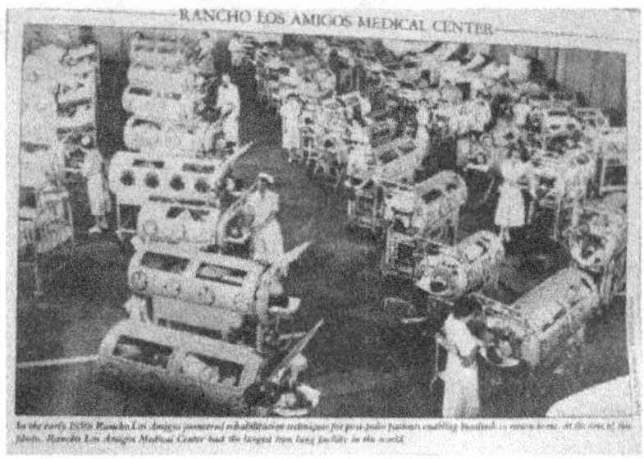

By the late 1950s, the farm, dairy and mental health wards had closed and most of the 600 acre property was divided and sold. Rancho continued to operate as a modern chronic-disease hospital, and later a world renowned rehab center. All of these operations were consolidated and moved to the north campus, a 62 acre hospital that still operates today. The 70 acres became a ghost town with shuttered treatment buildings. The actual date of the closure of the south campus is uncertain, but it is known that the buildings there were used as storage by 1988.

Today the U.S. marine corps occasionally uses the south campus for military drills. At one point during one of the exercises, a freezer in a former pathology building had a full package of mummified body parts. The coroner's office identified 10 legs, feet and brain matter and determined these were amputated medical specimens. Here is an article on the findings : Decades-Old Body

Parts Found in Abandoned Downey Hospital; No Foul Play, Officials Say - Los Angeles Times (latimes.com)

Chapter 49

Learning on a Budget and Still be Successful

April 9, 2022

At a very young age, many of us are encouraged to go to college, get an education so that we will have the earning potential needed to be successful in our life and be self-sufficient. As someone who went to college, I agree that college can help you be successful in your career, but it's more of a tool used to assist you.

Now there are certain fields like Medicine or Law and even engineering that require a degree because of the complexities of what you would be learning and doing.

In those situations, I would say you definitely would need a college education because to enter those fields you need to proper licensures and training, but what if you can't afford college or you have no interest in spending all day going to school.

Choosing a Path That Fit's You

We are all different in that sense, not every individual wants to go to college and realistically that's ok, there are other ways to learn, which is what I would detail to you.

As someone who went to college and received both bachelor's in business administration and a Master's degree in Business, I can say over the course of my life, a degree has helped but feels now there are other resources that also have benefited me now. These outside sources are ways you can self-learn and see be successful in whatever you do.

So you may be saying to yourself, well I have always been told an education is a key to my happiness in my life, and it's true that from a young age we are told that, but there are things we are not told and that could be that those gave us advice just used the same advice their parents gave them.

I have been in my career for over twenty years, which includes my college education because that is part of your career. From a young adult, I have always wanted to learn so college was a natural fit for me because I just happen to like the structure of school and sitting in a classroom, but everyone does.

Until recently within the last few years, I have really opened my eyes to see that many of the most successful people today did not go to college or have a formal education. That's not to say they didn't work hard for where they are today, they just took a different route. Some of those non-traditional routes include the following:

Start a Business

Why Not? , Starting your own business is a great way to learn skills on your own terms, even if you are not the most business savvy, but have an interest in having your own business; this would be a good option. You may be saying to yourself, Well I don't have money to start a business and honestly, you really don't need a lot to start one.

The most effective type of business is what's called a sole proprietorship, but there are other business structures like partnerships which are basically you running the business by yourself or with a partner, which can can be done completely online with a few simple steps.

- Choose what type of business you would be interested in.
- Research places to place your New Website, I personally use Wordpress
- Choose a great Theme, which is a structure to how your business website will look; there are literally thousands of themes and templates out there to choose from without having to build your own.
- Create a marketplace on your new website with what's called Plugin's that all you to take payments on your website.

- If you have the financial resources, you could have someone build you a website from scratch, which can cost anywhere from $1000 to $10,000 dollars, yeah you read that right $10,000.
- The web has plenty of resources to help you do this, which will make it simple to understand and keep you on a budget.

Taking Courses Online

Yup, you can do that, but you probably knew that already. What I am referring to is yes you can go to a college or university and take actual courses online, but there are other sources like:

- Udemy.Com
    - Offers hundreds and maybe even thousands of different topics to learn from Web Design, Business Management, Creative writing, it has a topic for almost most interests.
    - Variety of subjects to learn such as web design if you have an interest in building websites and programming. In addition, there are courses like creative writing, business programs like excel, word, and powerpoint and much more.
    - Courses are very reasonable in price anywhere from $10.00 to 30.00, some a little

higher taught by professionals who either work in certain fields and teach because they have a love for the subject.

  - You can even get a certificate of completion to add to your resume.

- Cousera.Org
  - A different type of learning that is more traditional as this website offers courses from Universities around the world where you can learn specific topics of interest. For example, you may want to learn about computer programming, you will have college professors teach you online.
  - In comparison to Udemy, those are not always college professors but professionals in the field like you and me. I have taken courses here, the difference in these courses is that much of the course is FREE, that's right free, but if you want the certificate of completion you will have to pay, which varies in price ranging from $40.00 and up.
  - These courses are incredibly valuable giving you the ability to take courses with actual students and with the ability to interact all online. Just like Udemy.com, there are literally hundreds of courses of interest.
- Edx.Org

- Similar to Coursera, you have the ability to choose from hundreds and even thousands of courses taught by universities, even allowing you to earn a degree for a price. This service I have also used as a free resource, but I would review it to see if there are programs, courses, and degrees you may be interested in.

Trade School or Technical College

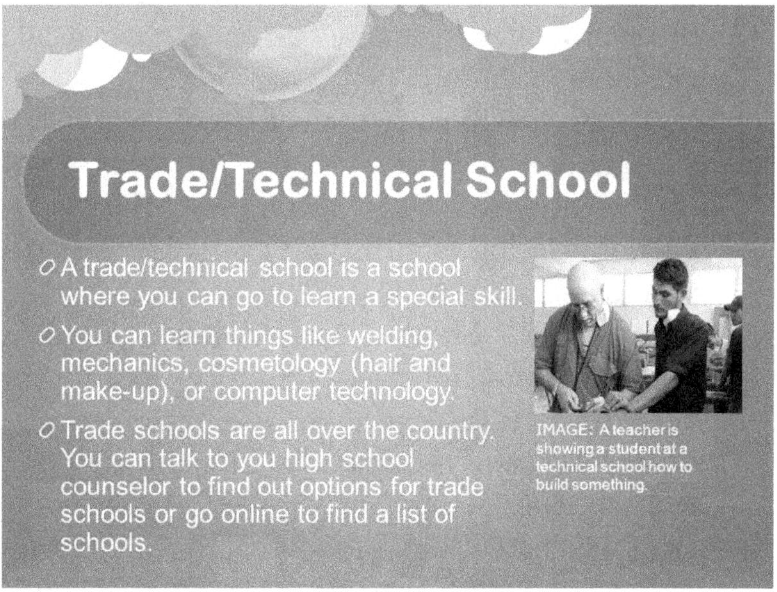

Another great and affordable option that allows you to in a classroom setting but for a shorter period of time allowing to go to school for a year or less and earn a certificate training you for only what you need to get a job. Some of the benefits of a trade school include:

The Benefits of a Trade School

- Time – Courses and Training as long as one year to complete and start your career.
- High Demand – Learning what is in demand only such as learning electrical or plumbing, but a blue-collar and white-collar fields are available
- Money – Programs cost thousands less than traditional colleges, many times Financial aid available to those in need.
- Smaller – Small classrooms more focus on you the student.
- Job Experience – Start gaining job experience sooner, waiting months and not years to begin your career
- No waiting – Shorter times to get started in your program, instead of waiting months or years to get into a certain course or program.
- Career Services – Available to help you find work quickly
- Good Placement Rates – Solid programs and advice to help you choose a career with good placement rates to find jobs quickly in your field of study.

Be a Consultant

This option may be one most don't consider, not really knowing what a consultant is, basically is someone who hires you to provide advice in exchange for money. Consultants can be really anyone and you don't necessarily need years and years of experience to be one.

Many organizations need consultants to advise them on areas such as Social Media, Marketing, Computers, the lists goes on, but to do this there are few beginning steps to review first you would look into companies online that can provide you guidance on where to begin, and don't be afraid to put yourself out there, companies are in great need of those with certain knowledge who have reasonable prices.

Get a Job

This may be the option many end up taking at first, but I am someone who knows the power of being educated whether it's in the traditional sense of self-learning, there are ways for you to succeed and still be passionate about doing something fantastic with your life. Getting a job can allow you to transition into great roles giving you access to learning new skills, meeting new people and networking for better positions.

There is nothing wrong with getting a job to learn some basic experience especially if you are starting out in life, most of us had too, personally I have worked for a student bookstore, I was a delivery driver assistant delivering Televisions, I have worked in Fast food, all of these positions allowed me to learn something that has helped my career.

Where to Go From Here

Where to go from here – All of these are options that will allow you to take a non-traditional route to your career, but all equally viable to your success and would look at ways if you are on a Budget and if traditional college is not an option right now.

In life we all need options, our lives are not cookie cutters and you have a choice, choose what is best for you, on your budget, success is around the corner no matter what route you take, so make a choice.

Chapter 50

Thankful for a Man of God Pastor Jeff Johnson

November 24, 2022

Being thankful is so important today. Often people get so wrapped up in what they do not have in this life like a huge paycheck, a fancy home, expensive clothes. All sounds pretty superficial but is what people tend to put stock into. I was never one of those individuals, growing up although I had a roof over my head, clothes on my back and food in my tummy, I was never wealthy in the material sense of the word.

I had love of my mother, father, grandfathers (When they were alive), sister, dogs , cats, now daughter, wife and others I may have left out no intentionally.

A Man I give Thanks to

But Its important today to thank a man who I do not wish to forget. This man does not know me, we've shook hands years ago, but he was the man that brought to Christ, Pastor Jeff Johnson of Calvary Chapel Downey.

Last nights service I watched online, which I do not always get to do because I am teaching at that exact same time. But this service was special, it was more of a tribute to the senior pastor who started Calvary Chapel Downey in Late seventies. Take a look at who Calvary is : Who We Are — Calvary Chapel Downey (ccdowney.com)

This man changed my life at a time when I was lost but It was also an incredible time as I had just met my future wife Delia and I had made new friends, something I hadn't had for many years. One new friend was also a new co-worker I had met who would be the person who would introduce me to my future wife. This friend who shall be unnamed because we are no longer friends, invited me to her church.

I had been to church before but not this church as I had driven past it all the time, having grew up in Downey as a teen. I did not the protocol for going to church which sounds silly but I stopped off at our local Starbucks so I could bring my new friend and co-worker only to be told when I got to the door that outside food was not allowed so I tossed the drinks in the trash, which now I think of it was foolish and a waste because I simply could have place them back in my car, but I was in a rush not to disappoint my friend who was waiting for me.

Pastor Jeff as we called him was a another gentle with a beard, gray/white hair, a kind face and an easy-to-understand voice spoke to me. I personally do not remember the message I am sorry to say I do not recall. But what I do remember is the feeling that something that was missing within my soul was being filled by the words from the pastor. I felt a sense of relief that I did not have to suffer or worry about where my soul may go when I die one day.

Gods Perfect Timing

Thinking that if I had died on February 2007 at my own hands I would be in hell as I would not have had a relationship with Christ Jesus. At this time in my life I was working of course, living in the house of hell in Downey with the devil incarnate my grandfather Raul and mother. I made a choice right there any then to continue to come back. I did not give my life to Christ on that day, but would come back every Sunday and Wednesday and even come on Thursday for a Men's bible study. I remember those days clearly in a way coming to church on my own and weeping in the pews hearing the words of Jesus speak to me.

Calvary Downey became my home church. It was here that I also met new people, pastors and even a time when myself and Delia temporarily separated that I met other single adults. I continued to attend bible studies and eventually I even joined a home bible study with an old friend Joe and Dora Chivira who were a couple who I met in High school parents of a couple class mates. Yes 2008-to about 2013 I was deep in the word of God, not that I am not today.

Pastor Jeff did not die , but was handing over the reins of senior pastor to Art Reyes who I feel is a good fit for pastor, looking around my age maybe younger. Being that I live over 45 miles away from Downey now, I watch on-line.

Pastor Jeff and his ministry will be missed. Hearing and learning that he came to Christ when he was invited to Calvary Chapel Costa Mėsa attending Chuck Smith's church at the time. This was during the Jesus revival when many hippies came to Christ. Jeff was no different in the sense, he was actually a drug dealer at the time, newly married and a child having a come to Jesus moment and then a movement where GOD would move in his life making incredible things happen.

When in my relationship with my future wife Delia, we would attend Church together and we would also attend her Spanish speaking church called Tabernaculo Baptista of Los Angeles. When we had our daughter Mikaylah we would bring her and attempt to put her in the nursery but at times she refused to go and when we would leave her she would cry and we would have to be called to pick her up, ending up in the overflow room.

Those moments were special nevertheless as we spent time together in GOD's word. Today we are still a Christ following family but often find it difficult to attend physical service as my wife works on Sundays, Mikaylah I am sorry to say does not wish to go, but I MUST, and I do.

Jeff taught us that Christ is the glue that holds us together and I believe that. I remember leaning on the church when I lost my jobs and pastors would pray for me and in time it did get better. It was incredibly difficult in the years of 2014-2018, where I struggled financially , being a new parent and husband was challenging and often I would cry out to the Lord for help and he did come to my aid.

Many of you out there may not be believers but for me and my house we serve the Lord. I know I fail at times teaching my daughter the word of God. I do have bibles for children and books relating to the bible I've read to her at night, but I must do better, I must her soul depends on it. Since giving my life to Christ I have followed many ministries and have gone to different churches in the Calvary family such as Chino Hills with Jack Hibbs and Greg Laurie of Harvest and others. Christ is always in my life, but I know from many years ago I can do better with my relationship, something I think about every day.

My life was changed in 2008 due to Pastor Jeff and I am forever thankful for his teachings , love , kindness and warm soul when I did meet him, embodying a true Christian. I know he is still a man and he fails like any other man and women and I understand he is not perfect, even has even mentioned that in his services have prodigal kids.

This is a man I will forever be grateful for and hope that others including my wife and daughter know this man is special in my eyes and the Lords.

God Bless you Pastor Jeff and your family , Thank you, thank you for I am forever grateful for your love for GOD and your teaching.

I pray that Pastor Art Reyes will be a great lead to Calvary Chapel Downey as Pastor Jeff was called to bring him aboard a few years ago. Here is a recent article of the passing of the baton to Art Reyes : https://www.calvarychapelmagazine.org/downey-pastoral-transition/

For those interested in Jeff Johnson Autobiographical book , as I have read this personally and its excellent called "The Seeker"

https://www.amazon.com/Seeker-Johnsons-Search-Clear-Light/dp/1931667683

Chapter 51

Surviving Being Laid Off in 2023

March 3 , 2023

The pain of being laid off is affecting thousands, but mostly in big tech. It saddens me to say I was just laid off and although I did not work or one of the major big tech companies like Twitter, Alphabet and others we were still apart of financial tech. Here is a recent article on big tech lay off numbers in 2023 : Largest Layoffs of 2023 (investopedia.com)

In a way I was no surprised, but shocked that the company notified us the day of the layoff followed by an e-mail and then a zoom call of those affected.

Waking up early Tuesday for a meeting, checking my e-mailing and finding I was one those being let go, it was painful to say the least.

I have grown over the years to experience this more and more in the last few years of being laid off due to restructuring. It's painful because I do suffer from depression and anxiety along with have a wife and daughter to support, add to the fact that I am over forty years old.

Many who experience see the cavalier way companies make decisions to just cut people as its just business right. We are taught that being loyal to a company is vital and companies command and demand it but where is the loyalty to the worker, frankly there is now.

What's also infuriating is the complete lack of empathy and fake words the CEO's say just to make themselves seem like the victim of the times, often blaming the economy. In the case of the company, I worked for they simply say they are working to "Recalibrate" their workforce and be stronger in the future. Forget the fact that many of us let go, got them to the point of success with how we worked with the clients and made the clients successful.

Having started my career in early two thousands, over twenty years have seen how companies have grown quite heartless in the pursuit of a buck. I get the argument is well a company needs to make profit to survive, they to make sure they survive and cuts need to happen. This I can understand, but what about those companies many millions and even billions in record profits that still cut the workforce. I get it, it's not a charity but still where is the humanity for caring about the workforce, I do not see it.

I am sorry to say that when these situations happen, I immediately got to the worst case scenario of being homeless, penniless or worse yet dead. My depression mode immediately kicks in where I look for a way out such as if my family would be ok, if I ended my life tonight.

My thought process is yes, I would be gone, but they would be able to survive without me and not have the worry of me bringing them down. I would have peace not to worry about them that they would not eat or live on the street. I often toss and turn at night thinking of where I went wrong in this life, how I failed as an employee, as a person, a father and husband.

During these times, there are strategies and can implement to have a better frame of mind and get through this transition.

Relax

This is counterintuitive to how you actually feel. Here is what you should do after you lose your job:

- Sleep in
- Catch up with a friend.
- Go to the gym, take a walk
- Do whatever you want

Self-care needs to be your one number priority because this is a transition that no one wants and likes and must try to do the best we cant in a tough situation.

Avoid application burnout

Without a job we are on survival mode, waking up going directly to our computer and sitting down for 8 hours apply, apply , apply day in day out. You think you are being productive and proactive but you are not by apply for jobs left and right, hit the pause. Its easy to get stuck into apply as many of the sites today like indeed make it effortless and simple to submit our resume, but it can suck us in and drag us down. Remember that applying for jobs online is apart of your job search , just not all of it.

Ask for help

During to your network, being your best bet and much more then applying online. Anyone who can make an introduction for you or provide a personal recommendation is key.

Shift your perspective

Could losing your job be a good thing? I can see the eye roll now. Getting laid off can actually be a great thing for your career. In fact, I owe my present success to every single job that kicked me the curb. Each time making me reevaluate my job choices and what I wanted to do next.

Sometimes you realize you were at the wrong job. That why its so important to take inventory of what you want, where you want to be.

Stay on course

It will probably happen again. No longer do people work for the same company for 40 years and retire with a pension and a nice pen. "The Likihood you are going to get laid off during your career is high, let alone laid off once, but multiple times.

Not exactly what many of us want to hear but take solace in the fact the were all in this career rollercoaster together.

We are going to hand these situations differently, many of us living in regret about the past choices we have made that got us to this point. But a laid off can be a new beginning, a fresh start to reinvent yourself. To correct those mistakes, we may have made previously in a previous position, a real chance to grow again. Yes its difficult, stressful, painful but in the long run this should make us stronger.

Remember to take care of your mind, body and soul during these times because that's is what's going to get you through future lay off's and unpredictable companies who could care less about your well-being as we need to care ultimately about our well-being.

For those who have been laid off especially recently keep your head up and remember this is just temporary. Spend time with those you love and remember to focus on your well-being each day, your worth it.

Chapter 52

Remember The Reason For the Season!

December 18, 2023

What is truly important in this time of year, the season of giving, a season of joy and for myself, the reason for the season JESUS!

All of look at this time of year differently, some absolutely hate this time of year over the sear reason that it's a time of being forced to give and you may say no one forces anyone but truly people feel forced to give out of what they do not have in the form of gifts and when they can not give or will not give they are called scrooge.

I'll admit this time of year is difficult for many who struggle to keep up with giving, often having family members, friends, co-workers and also those we do not know like your postman or women, the homeless, random strangers. I personally find that my words often have meaning when I give anyone anything so if sI give a small token to others I write a personalized card which most appreciate.

I have always celebrated the traditional Christmas as you can say, the tree, presents, Food, cookies sprinkled in with some kindness and love. But as the years go on my feelings for Christmas in general have changed as I no longer see the importance of gifts but know I will never skate by NOT giving especially to my daughter who is only ten and my wife. My father, sister and other family members could care less if they get anything from me.

What I see when I go out today, is pure unadulterated consumerism people spend, spend, and spend on gifts that will go unappreciated, unused and wasted.

I often think of my favorite holiday films, "The Grinch who stole Christmas" with Jim Carrey having fond memories of watching this in the theater with a co-worker and friend at the Irvine Spectrum AMC. Why is that memory in a way so clear is because it's a time when I was at my most free, going to college, with no responsibilities and I was the young age of twenty.

But back to my story, I like the message and how the Grinch tries to teach the WHO's all of the waste they throw in the garbage, and he is the one who gets it. I can understand why, as if you have watched the film, he literally gets all of WHO Villes trash gifts. Cindy Lou, Who is actually the one who, helps open the heart of Grinch and the people of Whoville.

Sadly we here in the United States and parts of the world fail to see the importance of Jesus, Love , Kindness and that Gifts are not what's important, but we are so programmed in our world to equate this time of year as gift giving and who can blame us because the story of Christmas and Saint Nicolas who was an actual person would take his wealth and literally give it to the needy.

I get angry going to shopping centers, malls and just going out in public during these times because people are at their worst, unkind, pushy, manipulative, rude, hateful and the list goes on. Yes I know I can shop online and avoid the stores but that is beside the point because its more about how people act during this time of year truly showing their true character, which is scary.

I'd like to think we are living in kind world, country but truly we do not. People are tired, fed up and living paycheck to paycheck and this time of year pushes people over the edge and not just for financial reasons, but the way people are treated and how we treat our fellow man, women and child. WHY I ask must we treat each other in this way, because gain we have been programmed to be greedy, take advantage of people, get what is ours.

I am truly tired of how we treat people , what is it going to take because we ALL treat everyone with more kindness and respect. Do we need a national disaster, do we need a war, do we need more hardship like a full blown depression before we wake up, I hope not but feel we are ripe for that. Only GOD knows what the future holds, but feel we are ripe for a full blown dictatorship and full authoritative state and then it may be too late. Will we not learn from history on the path we are on about focusing on things that are not important.

This time of year, love more, treat others with kindness, put aside the importance of expensive gifts for 1 time in year. Instead give your time, bake something, embrace people with your words of kindness and what they mean to you.

I am sorry to say during this time of year I too have gotten wrapped up in getting the perfect gift, charging it up on my credit cards, buy, buy, spend, spend only to discover it meant nothing but what I bought would go unused, regift, trashed and for what. Why not spend quality time together this time of year and truly appreciate what you have in this life.

Truly remembering the reason for this season!

Chapter 53

A Stealth Job Search While Employed

February 12, 2022

Looking for a new job can be one the most nerve-racking experience one can experience, but how about adding in the fact that you are already employed. For many out there you will soon realize that your current employer may just be a pit stop to bigger and better opportunities. The challenge is how do you search for that new position while working. A very tough challenge indeed as many work during the day, have limited time off and a demanding life.

To search for a new job while employed is considered the smart thing to do instead of quitting and then searching. As someone who has done both look while working and leave a job and then search there are positives and negatives to each. From a perspective of just quitting your current job maybe due to feeling burnt out, an impossible boss or co-workers that may a good option for you. But if you can just hang on and search while employed you will see that this will allow you to have no gaps in employment and income.

Surely we all have different reasons for wanting to search for another position such money, career growth and even a change in scenery. Some of the primary reasons I choose to search for other employment elsewhere included more money, lack of professional growth and even boredom. Yes you read that right I was bored and uninspired I felt like I was wasting my time.

When searching for that next opportunity there are a few techniques one can take to be successful in your search called a Stealth Job Search. Regardless of how you feel about your current job I say don't disrespect your current employer even if things are really bad, we can all rise to a higher level at these times

Don't search on company time

When we feel its time to go, we may feel the need to just stop caring about current employer, which means we may start surfing the web for new opportunities while you should be working. I would say don't it because of the obvious that the company can track and monitor which sites you are visiting which could give the employer a reason to get rid of you.

The responsibilities of your current job come first, so it's important for you to dedicate time outside of work hours to search for that new position

Keep it to yourself

One of the most important rules to searching while employed as much as you want to tell your co-worker, don't do this. This information will have the tendency to get around which could put your current job in jeopardy. Your job search is a personal decision. Even if you trust your colleagues, you can't control what they share with other's.

Play it safe online

Be careful when visiting job boards or using social media to conduct your search. Many times your current employer could be searching for employees like yourself. Imagine if your current employer found your resume which may cause your employer to be alarmed. Leave your banter and news about job searching off social media as employers in many cases have ways to see your online activity. If you do choose to post on social media adjust your privacy settings so only your followers can see what you post.

Schedule Smartly

Hiring managers understand that when you are searching for work while employed, they will need to make some adjustments to communicate with you outside of business hours, on your lunch or when you have free time. Be considerate of your employer to arrange any interviews, phone calls on your own time.

Know your talents

Know that you have talents to start with and you have value so when you go searching for those new opportunities put those on full display. An employer who you are looking to leave can make us feel worthless at times due to not feeling appreciated for our role in the company but know there are companies out there who will appreciate your talents.

Continue to work hard

Feeling like its time to go can make us feel like just giving up on our current role, don't do it. Continue to focus on your current job, work hard and be patient until that next opportunity comes along and believe me it will come. However, loyalty to your current employer shouldn't prelude you from looking for other opportunities if you are not satisfied with your current role or company.

Where to look for a job

There are tons of websites, job boards and search engines that provide you the tools you need to search for a job. Many of them are easy to use and allow you to refine your search based on specific criteria such as job title, location and salary. I recommend going to LinkedIn and use your network for that next opportunity.

How do you start looking for a job?

When looking for a job its important to have a plan, a strategy of what kind of job you are looking for, the type of salary you would like. In addition, get specific over the location you would like work in and how far you are willing to commute. Lastly keep a list of companies you want to work for and go apply, follow up and never give up until you reach your dream job and its out there. Create a portfolio comprised of your resume, references and anything that can be used to display who you are in physical form ready to provide to employers interested.

Be Patient

I can't stress that enough, it will take time, but sometimes it may be quick where you find that position you are having been searching for.

Finding that next role can be stressful especially when you're already working but be thankful you are still working in your search and still bringing in some income.

There are many out there today who are not working search, desperate for an opportunity. Just continue to stick to the plan, create a strategy and follow the rules to a stealth job search.

Your Journey is Your own, Make it Count!

Realizing you have an issue of self-acceptance is half the battle, but if you look at yourself in the mirror and see that your truly can't accept yourself, then you have work to do. Going back to the film Rocketman Elton John struggled to accept who he was as he felt he always had to hide his sexuality, his fashion sense, his delicateness as people in his life told them those feeling are bad such as his mother and father. Accept yourself, your quirks, differences, strengths and weakness and embrace them right now.

Our lively hood depends on accepting ourselves and because we have a long life to live why live in agony over those feelings, its not fair yourself as you deserve the best. I encourage to look within but if that's hard at first look to those who have fought hard to get where they are today like Sir Elton John accepting himself and never looking back.

Chapter 54

Keep pushing forward and remember never give up!

June 18, 2022

Finding our place in the world is so important to many, including myself, but the world is a big place, even if you're living in a small town, the world can seem even smaller. Going through years of education from kinder to college, a lot can be packed in all those years. Depending on where you live your education will be different, some of which will teach you the life skills to succeed in the job market and some will not.

It would be nice if in your years before going to college that certain skills could be learned as there are two major influence in our life, Parents/Guardians and Education.

Going to Elementary, Middle and then High school or Secondary school, those skills were not strong areas I was taught, and my parents didn't really seem to learn it in their education.

Coming out of secondary school I honestly was in a haze of what I wanted to do with my life, as naturally I was set to go to college, education my education a degree and I guess hope for the best afterward in the field I studied.

Finding my place after high school is probably what I needed at that point, knowing I had choices, but really those in my life did not speak to me about choices. Such as if I didn't go to college, how I would be impacted and If I did how my life would be impacted, sometimes it's just good to know.

What was drilled into my mind throughout life is if you don't go to college, you will not make it, you will not be successful. Truthfully I considered that a lie in the sense that those who don't go to college still can be successful, you just have to take a route to get where you need to go, which may including getting a job to learn certain skills and building up your career right out of high school. Whereas in college, you go to college, get your degree, and then start your professional career in the field of study you choose.

What many will not tell you is what happens after you leave college or High school, how do you find your place in the world. When it comes to finding your place, you may say, what does that mean?

Finding your place is simply finding your purpose in your life and making a difference in the world. Going through life you want to feel like what you're doing has meaning, that you are working towards something.

Everyone is obliviously different but for myself, it took me a long time and I mean years to feel like I was finding my life's purpose. One of the ways this happened for me was when I had a family a wife and daughter. Others look to find meaning in their careers, focusing solely on your career, trying to reach the top before they feel a sense of accomplishment.

I will say that we all have a life's purpose and at times it's not always clear especially going through those formative years of trying to discover what you are good at. There will be times that you will have to try different jobs and careers to have a sense of fulfillment in your professional careers.

It is said that you will change careers every five years, why is that? That is because you are changing, your skills are growing and when they grow, you essentially outgrow where your place of employment.

I can contest to changing jobs every 5 years, because simply I outgrew that role and if there were no place to grow within the organization it was time to move and there is nothing wrong with that.

I will not speak for everyone just myself when I say I worked in Jobs, places to gain skills when there were no prospects of growth after a while, my own timeline to determine this is two years, after which you will see if there are growth opportunities for you and if you will be allowed to grow.

Having a master's degree, I am very capable of doing a lot for an organization, but that's not how many organizations think, they do look at your skillset, but they look at other factors that may not have anything to do with the job, such as If your likable, your age and even your looks. You may think that sounds preposterous but it's true and studies have shown that to be true, it's an area that many struggles with.

Part V -Family

Chapter 55

Happy New Year 2022

January 2, 2022

Hard to believe its 2022, it literally feels as though we just began 2021 and now that year is good and gone and for good reason who wishes to remember this time in history, I certainty don't want to remember the raging pandemic we live in today and how our lives have shifted dramatically in some ways where many continue to work from home, many have experienced COVID and some have even left this world.

I often reflect on what I am thankful for especially having a stable job or Jobs, my wife working, and our daughter being in a school and staying healthy. None of us really know what the year will bring for 2022, some will experience great success, and some will experience great failures which make up our lives.

Each of us hope the year will be great but often times people forget the failures make us stronger, give us patience and perseverance to be better in the long term, a push we all need. That is why many of us probably create new years resolutions.

I like to think we can all have each year banging with success but often times many are just hoping and looking to survive the day, the month and then they year holding on at times.

What is amazing and sad is that years past I don't often remember, its possible those days are not very memorable and there are times I just want to forget especially certain years in my life.

For 2022, it does appear bleak with the Pandemic still year, governments faltering and even the citizens of this great country will continue to make choices that put us in ruination. Each day we have a choice to make to be better, but often times people are doing the opposite, making choices that go against science and even GOD.

One thing is for sure I believe our societies will get worse not better because many appear to have this ideology that once can and should be able to disrupt society, peoples lives as we society continues to believe what is blasted in the media and in social media.

We are living in dangerous times as I believe many do not think for themselves although they like to think they do, but really believe would majority rule says and since millions and billions follow society media with the likes of Twitter, Facebook and Tic Tok, society will continue to believe the lies that many present as truth.

Sorry not try to rant, but just to say that hopefully 2022 will be full of hope for the best in hopes COVID will wind down and we can live somewhat of a normal life but doubt it will happen in the next couple of months.

The problem is that many continue to believe that COVID has no teeth, its just a flu, its harmless and although the vaccine exists that's part of the big lie today, which causes many to go about their day like it doesn't exist, a real sight I witness is last week when I attempted to take my daughter and wife to Knotts Berry farm for family and holiday fun only to leave an hour later leaving the packed crowds many of which did not wear masks and did not social distance, a real disappointment.

For the last weeks I have been on a complete vacation unplugged from work and boy it has felt great to rest, recharge, spend time with my family and enjoy this time, although I didn't go anywhere it was still nice. Surprisingly and I am somewhat disappointed is that is that I didn't feel the urge to edit my book, but know I need to continue to pick it up again in all honestly, I am very tired not of the story but of the tediousness of editing for the last two years, I would like this book to be finished.

For 2022, I wish to continue my weight loss goals, finish editing my book in hopes of find an agent to publish my book god willing. I hope to continue to save money, build on to my current position, not necessarily looking for a promotion but that would be nice, but ultimately would like my wife to change jobs to something that offers better opportunities for her.

I want to continue to be a better father and husband and just a better overall human being. I could not and will not do all these things without my continuous relationship with my GOD Jesus as said in

Matthew 1:23 – **God is with US!**

My wish and hope for all of you to have prosperity in the new year. This year may be tough, it may be confusing, but it may have success too, but fill this time with love and kindness, patience and come end of 2022 you should be a better person.

I am say that from the beginning of 2021 to now, I am healthier, leaner (Having lost 55 pounds) and meaner but not in the rudest sense.

The last few years have been good in the sense that I have not struggled like I did in years pass and I continue to get wiser and older as the years appear to tick away as this last year, I celebrated 42 years old, 43 this December.

I continue to be thankful for all I have especially my family, my work, a place to rest my head each night, clothes on my back and food on my table, something many of us can take for granted as these times continue to get increasing difficult and especially so for myself who lives in California.

What I also say lastly don't let the times of today get you down, its easy to look at the times, our society, what you have and don't have equate that to a life a of value, you and I choose what we consider to be valuable in our lives, society doesn't, and we shouldn't let it.

I know I lived for years looking to society to tell me what they equated to a successful life whether it was how much money I made, where I went to school and even how I lived, you write your own chapters as in the words of Doc Brown from Back to the future III and I quote

I often am reminded of times of the past when I was a child, where those times the best times, maybe there they were for me as a child, but for my parents they could have been the worst. Growing up in the 80's those were not the best decades for prosperity. Even though we didnt have to deal with Pandemics, we did have to deal with the changing of politics in our country, wars and the changing landscape of what what our country looks like today which is not always a good thing. Yes we have great technology, but we are still behind in a ways especially in how we treat one another as kindness and respect have gone out the window but greed, selfishness and contempt. I pray the new year will bring people closer but I doubt that as I see now society is on a melt down and not to get over dramatic we are on the verge of a civil war maybe and hopefully not literally but our society is imploding.

Ok I will stop now as I wanted this post to be about how good 2022 can be, not sure why when I write 2022 , I start writting 2002 maybe subconciously that was a good year for me , which is was when I graduated college.

Anyways, Godspeed and God Bless to all and to all a good Night! Heres to a great 2022.

Chapter 56

Happy New Year 2022, Stuck at Home with COVID

January 9, 2022

As I celebrate the new year stuck with COVID, but doing better as I attempt to relax but its difficult as I am deep into my thoughts about my Job(s) and not working due to my illness, which I know is only temporarily but still giving me a moment to self-reflect.

Now that I have experienced COVID, not that I wanted to , I can truly understand how many are affected by this sickness although I am sure many had much more severe symptoms and even death.

For many who have gotten COVID already you can relate, but what was most difficult is it happening right after I came back from my two-week Holiday vacation and not being able to work for a week to recoup.

I am certainly working to push myself to get better, although COVID is perfectly recoverable for most there have been many who have died since March 2020.

My story of control, a pademic written over three years ago

Since this has happened this has really opened my eyes when it comes to my book which I have been writing for a few years now with a pandemic type theme. My two characters Jack and Penny who live in Oregon are currently suffering through covid like symptoms.

Jack and unsuspecting victim who suddenly gets sick one day and his path crosses with Penny his future partner who is indirectly connected to him but a key part of what he is going through.

COVID which many of you are aware began in China, but not to get into an conspiracy's I believe COVID was intentional in a way to affect the world especially the U.S. There are truly bad actors in the world, and it just so happens in my book the main antagonist Chu which is an American doctor like Chu has been plotting for years with the United States to release a deadly virus to take control of the world. Although the idea was from the United States governm

ent to be used to fight our enemies abroad Chu had other plans. Chu grew slowly to want to dominate and seek control taking the experiments to new levels with Jack, Penny and others. Those others were child experiments who are inject with a type of virus that could be used to control the world when time. Over decades Chu perfected his creation and eventually released it upon the world. Jack and Penny fight for their lives as Jack and Penny look for answers only to find none at first. Chu sits comfortably monitor Jack and Penny as they soon go through physically ailments, their bodies changing growing sicker. Jack and Penny experiencing many of symptoms you and I would experience, Fatigue, loss and smell and taste but also physical changes such as lesions and boils all over their bodies, deformities to start.

I will tell you how it ends but I think about what many are going through today, some fighting for their lives literally. Many are just trying to live their lives, go to work, survive, eat, pay the bills and can not because somewhere in China, someone thought it was a good idea, probably the Chinese government to really fuck up the world and get even. But I will not say US is not part of the problem, since the pandemic began they have done well, very well financially having records profits especially companies like Amazon, McDonald's and others.

Do We Really Need it all?

We are too believe we need these companies, we can not live with them but the truth is we can live without them, we can make do and in reality we have the ability to create our own companies that can thrive allowing us to be financially independent, but companies want us to believe we need to depend on them for support when we are all capable we just need to give it time. Most will not become billionaires; many don't need billions or even millions to thrive but enough for each of us to thrive in this life.

What am I trying to saying here is that this pandemic should open our eyes to the belief we need society to survive , that we need the educational systems like colleges to be valuable to society, but the reality is we can survive and thrive without them. Part of the problem is we will in a consumeristic world, world that wants to keep us poor and dependent on them, a world of control. You may say no one controls you , but really we are being control in this moment in time, I know it sounds like some conspiracy but there are parties each day who only want us hooked , dependent on them, a big part of the world is social connection like social media that is used to feed people information, millions of people each day to believe a lie that we can not survive on our own, you need to login each day , plug in and play, sit at home, watch TV, watch Netflix with the guise of being for entertainment but really there is a sinister purpose behind it, which is it to distract each of us from the truth of living a life of value and purpose, don't get sucked into the lie.

Red Pill Vs. Blue Pill

I often love using movies as references to us and one movie I think about is the Matrix films and the reality we live in. Thinking of Neo taking the red pill or the bull pill, may people choose to take the blue pill each day.

In the original film Matrix, Neo is offered the choice between the blue pill by Morpheus's who says" you take the blue pill, the story ends, you wake up in your bed and believe whatever you want to believe, you take the red pill, you stay in wonderland, and I show you how deep the rabbit hole goes,"

The red pill represents uncertain future, unknown to Neo at the time, he takes the red pill it would free him from the enslaving control of the machine generated dream world and allow him to escape the real world, but living the truth of reality is harsher and more difficult. On the other hand, the blue pill, represents a beautiful prion, it would lead him back to ignorance, living in confined comfort without want or fear within the simulated reality of the matrix.

The blue pill is our fabricated reality, which many choose to live in today. This blog is not meant to debate that but that is where these thoughts take me in the world we live in today. Life truly does imitate art when we read books like 1984 and watch films like Matrix about what the future could hold if we are not careful. What we see in film and books could happen and will happen which is pretty scary because the thought or idea is begin displayed in the pages of a book and or film so those ideas exist.

We do live in a very sick world, a world full of depravity, hate and greed which will not change ever. Many are taught we will are not good enough, will never be good enough, but you are more than an enough you just need to believe, believe in yourself and make your dreams a reality you can do it.

Lets not let these times define our lives but lets be the definers. I wrote this blog under the influence of COVID, being at home, sick, tired and trying to ease my mind during a time when the world is in chaos.

May the new year be a year of awakening for all of us! Here is to 2022.

Chapter 57

Happy 9th Birthday Mikaylah !

January 10, 2022

Happy Birthday to my daughter Mikaylah who on January 5th, 2013, came into this world. Forever changing my life for the better. I never imagined each day I would look at a splitting image of me, although she is her own person, I see so much of myself in her its scary.

Every day is a gift watching her growing up from newborn to toddler, to little girl and beyond. She drives me crazy at times, but I love the person she has become, her laughter and joy. Over the last 9 years have been life altering and although some think having kids is just a part of life, we should remember that those little reflections of us are reminders of us when we were once children their age. I truly do get to live through my daughter's life.

I hope each day to give my daughter a better childhood then I had and I believe I have and I only want her to remember these precious years because they go so fast. In a matter of time my daughter will be teen one day then an adult and although my job is never done, I hope I was a good provider to her.

Happy Birthday and many more to come!

Love you Papa!

Chapter 58

New Year Resolutions Yay or Nay?

January 29, 2022

The new year is upon us! Honestly, I feel your hesitation to see if it's worth getting excited about. I can say for myself I am more of Nay to resolutions, not saying there anything wrong with having them but I personally do make those promises.

Making New Year Resolutions

We hear all too often my favourite is this year I am going to get in shape, lose twenty pounds and eat healthy all admirable goals for the new year. Being someone who has been going to the gym for years I always see a new flock of new year resolutions walking in the gym door come January and not return February. We all have good intentions when we create them but may not have realistic expectations over the results.

There are so many out there like create a budget which is important, stop smoking very commendable, find a new Job perfectly doable. But for me we should not let a date push us to change what we are not ready to change it should come more naturally. I think it's so important to think of our goals throughout the year really plan for those goals instead of making those goals on a whim.

Goals Should be Calculated

New year resolutions should be calculated to what you hope to achieve in the new year, but planning should take place beforehand. Noting wrong with holding off to the new year to make those plans officially take place at least you are going into ready and prepare to succeed and not fail. Most of us have made resolutions with good intentions, attempted for a short time and either quit or failed without proper thought, don't let that happen to you.

In today's day and age, you have the ability, the tools to succeed at what those goals are such as if you want to get educated, go to college, get a degree. Some goals can be costly like going to college to work towards a degree, that can be a costly error if you go into that goal without the already intention of getting a degree, so definitely do your research, make sure you are not being controlled by an arbitrary date which may set you up to fail.

Now if you are someone who just loves resolutions and you are crushing your resolutions year after year, good for you, you may be some of the small minority that has the discipline to succeed which means others can too.

To make the goals happen here are few tips to make that happen for you too:

1. Choose a Specific, Realistic Goal
2. Pick Just one Resolution
3. Don't wait until the last minute
4. Start with small steps
5. Avoid Repeating past failures
6. Remember that change is a process
7. Get support from Family and Friends
8. Renew your motivation
9. Keep working on your goals
10. Don't let small stumbles Bring you down

Stats Don't lie

These tips without a lot of explanation can help keep you on track to succeed in the new year but I will say be kind to yourself because new years can be both exciting as you start a new year, a fresh start so to speak so be patient, take your time no need to create progress goals as certain goals will take time like losing weight, getting a degree or quitting smoking or alcohol, but you can do it.

Know if you do fail just pick yourself up again and start again and again and again until you get it right just try to remember why you want this goal, what the purpose of the goal was and what you hoped to accomplish. For myself, if I was to choose a goal that wished to accomplish to finish my novel and put it on the market by end of next year, it's quite possible, but there are factors that can delay my goal most definitely.

You are meant it Succeed Make it Count

We all have goals, something in our heart we yearn to accomplish, and I am here to tell you it can be done but go out and start planning. Now depending on when this is published you may read this after the new year and that's ok, start planning and still set out your goals for 2022.

Chapter 59

Happy Birthday Delia, My Beautiful Wife!

March 19, 2022

Happy Birthday to my beautiful wife. A woman I can truly say saved my life and continues to love me despite my flaws. I have known Delia since 2008 and married in 2010 and had our daughter in 2013. In 2008 when I met my life, I was beginning to get my life together due to spiraling out of control in 2007, a dark period in my life when my life almost came to an end due to my own hand.

For most my teen and adult years until I met my wife, I searched for the perfect women to fulfil my life. At the time I met my wife I was 28 years old. For most of my young adult life I was rejected by women, even though I was and am respectful towards women, women were not drawn to me probably due to my depression and my weight having struggled with being overweight most of my life.

My future loved my imperfections, and she was and is the first genuine person to see me to see my heart. For many years until her I was filled with anger towards not being given the time of day even by the simplest average women who in my opinion had my right to judge me so harshly but did. Yes we all have a choice in who we choose to love and spend time with but I could not have been that unlovable. Back then I was much sweeter, kinder and innocent.

I didn't really appreciate myself back then and due to the years of searching I felt worthless, which is probably one of the reasons I tried to take my life. I know some of you may say well give a shit of a man or women thinks in my me, but I did. I guess I was looking for a connection to someone who eventually love and experience love with and it never came until one day.

The Beginning

I was working at a new company that I started recently and had a new co-worker name Shayna who I had a immediate friendship with. She introduced me to Delia her best friend. Delia is not like me as she was not even born in the US but El Salvador. At the time she spoke broken English but I understood her and immediately we had a real connection. Eventually we spent more time together, dating and falling in Love.

We were not without our challenges even today, she was from a different world then me, but I still loved and appreciated her. She said she always prayed for someone like in her life, but never really went looking herself, we just fell together, GOD's plan in both of our lives. I have not always been so kind to her and even today I'm not always kind, but I apologize to her for who I am. I will always love her, cherish her and appreciate her.

There was even a time early in our relationship I broke up with her, I was scared but I was also because her best friend Shayna had a great influence over her and I. Because you see at the time I met Delia, I met Shayna who became one of the closest friends I had at the time, but we are no longer friends and cut the friendship in 2015. Shayna truly worked to eventually destroy our relationship so that is the primary reason I had to cut the friendship for both of us, she was toxic.

Our LOVE Has only Grown!

Over the years we have grown as people, have had our major struggles especially financial that probably would have broken a marriage but we stuck together through the good and bad times, richer and poorer. She is truly part of me and I love her for that.

Each day I work to be better, a better husband and father and best friend to her, but I am not without my flaws, and I see them.

Maybe I shouldn't dwell in the past and all those women who rejected me but its hard not to forget, but to each there own.

Today we rejoice in her Birthday, although she doesn't want to remember her new age, but with her age I see her more beautifully.

I prayed GOD will bless her with more future years to celebrate in our life and marriage. I LOVE YOU DELIA! Happy Birthday.

Chapter 60

Happy Resurrection Day!

April 16, 2022

For those who celebrate Easter this is a special time for you. Although we as a world and country still suffer through this pandemic, we must not forget these days and what Christ did for us by dying on the cross.

For many you may just flip past this piece because you don't believe in Jesus or even God, but there was a true physical GOD, who was Father, Son and Holy spirit who died for ALL of us on the cross of calvary.

I have to remember that each day I live this life that if I was to die tomorrow, I would have an eternal place to go because of JESUS, because he died for me a painful, excoriating death on the cross.

I live in the reality that I know people forget that everyday even so called Christians and although I am not here to judge I am here to remind you of what Jesus did and not to just remember on Easter but every day.

In America as I see it we are wrapped up with getting even, revenge and just pure hate which is the work of the devil obliviously. Jesus overcame and defeated the devil already and will continue to beat him until the end.

Today we live in divided America that no longer stands by the principles of the bible. For many will say we were NEVER a Christian nation but that is false and please make sure you tell Chris Columbus and the pilgrims because that is ingrained in our history of America which many choose to not remember. This piece is not to talk about the evils of Chris Columbus because I am sure he was but people did really come here to escape to be able to worship God in how they saw fit and not be told in how to worship GOD. I am thankful for those who came to America and made this a Christian nation. All of that has not disappeared completely, but if you watch television or follow social media many of those Christian leaders and political leaders who say they are Christians and follow Jesus display hate and ignorance which is Not what JESUS taught and goes against everything he stood for.

Jesus was LOVE and is Love which is what he would want us to remember today, because he died out of LOVE for all of us. As a Christian we are to follow Jesus example of love for each other but often times fail to do so because of our selfish beings, but still Jesus died for us.

This easter and resurrection day we want to remember the sacrifice Jesus took on himself for us and despite happening over two thousands years ago, the times are not all that different as we allow our country be ruled by immoral people full of greed and hate.

Let's remember what Jesus said in **Mark 10:18**, "*Why do you call me good? Jesus replied, "No one is good except God alone. You know the commandments: "Do not murder, do not commit adultery , no don't steal, do not bear false witness , do not cheat others, honor your father and mother"*

Can we all stay we have NEVER done any of these things , some may say NO I have never done any of these things, then you would be a liar, because most of us have murdered with our tongue speaking about someone else. Murder does always mean we physically kill someone but can murder someone with our words.

Some of you may say what does this have to do with Easter. Its to remember despite our horridness as humans and what we do to each other every day, JESUS said died for us which is a huge sacrifice. If Jesus hadn't died, we would ALL go to hell which exists and sad to say people still go to Hell every day for not believing in JESUS.

Again, I am not here to condemn you and tell you are going to hell, but Jesus paid the bill so we wouldn't have to go to Hell but many choose to not believe and believe hell doesn't exist, but all find out in the end once they leave this earth.

I encourage every person to watch the Passion of the Christ to give you a picture of what Jesus did and how he died. Although just a representation I think it's a good one. Many of us would probably say we would die for those who love but can we really say that, would he die for the unlovable out there, the murders and rapists, killers and most would say No I would never die for them they deserve death and hell, but JESUS died for those people too especially if you look at those he shared the cross with like the thief on the cross.

I honestly can not say I would die for those unlovable people; I would die for my own family and that is the limitation of mankind ourselves and who we are invested in to die for but again Jesus died for ALL.

This easter and resurrection day lets remember how important and special this day is to many and mankind because of what Jesus did for you and I.

Many blessings this day to you and your family!

Chapter 61

Happy Mother's Day 2022

May 8, 2022

Each year we get to celebrate those women in our life who we call mom, it could be our maternal mother, stepmother, grandmother or other. In the United States we certainly have commercialized Mother's Day with flowers, gifts and going out to enjoy a good meal together.

The Happiness and Sadness of Mother's Day!

It saddens me my own mother passed in 2015, but still celebrate the next important mother in my life, my wife who is the mother of our daughter Mikaylah.

As a mother she devotes her time and love to our daughter every day , our daughter is forever blessed to the mother she is and although our daughter is only 9 she may not fully see how much Delia does for her and the sacrifices she makes but will one day.

My mother whose name was Linda was born August 30, 1959, and passed December 9th, 2015, at the age of 56. My mother who I believe lived a hard life, who struggled and sacrificed to take care of my sister and I. Growing up I didn't realize how hard she had until I became an adult myself when I realized how hard my mother work for so little pay at times. Along with that we lived with my grandfather, the devil in carnet Raul who made our lives a living hell each day, may he rest in hell.

The Impact of My Mother

But throughout my life, my mother always tried to appear happy, but I knew she wasn't as she also struggled with her own health issues which only magnified.

My mother did her best, attempting to provide a normal childhood for my sister and I taking us to the movies, the mall and living like any other normal child. Once into an adulthood and having a family of my own which made my mother very happy because she got to see her only grandchild my daughter before she passed whom she loved very much.

My daughter born January 2013; our only child is a blessing to our family giving us a gift to this day. Delia my wife and mother of Mikaylah has not been easy on the account of my changing careers and challenges with the finances, but we have endured.

Mother's Day to me means remembering those women who raised us, supported us not necessarily starting at any age, some gain mothers later in life or gain a mother figure who is there.

I give homage to my wife Delia who is a great mother and to my own mother whom I miss every day but keep with me everything she taught me to be the man I am today.

For many Mother's Day may be a day you rather forget due to your own mother, maybe she wasn't around or treated you horribly or something else that caused her not to be the mother you hoped and prayed for.

Mother's Day History

Mother's Day is believed to have originated in America in 1907 when Anna Jarvis hosted a worship service in honour of mothers at Andrews Methodist Episcopal Church in Grafton, West Virginia. When her mother Ann Reeves Jarvis died in 1905, she voiced her desire for Mother's Day to be recognized as a national holiday. The inaugural Mother's Day was celebrated two years later. It was made a national holiday by US President Woodrow Wilson in 1914. While Mother's Day is observed on the second Sunday in May in India, it is celebrated on different days in different countries.

I choose not to take these days for granted to remember because often we move on with life and forget about this day year after year never realizing that today may be your last mother's day, or your mother may not live until tomorrow or by next year.

May all the mothers have a blessed day as mother's are a blessing to us!

Chapter 62

Happy Father's Day 2022

June 19 , 2022

Father's Day! A day that many out there surprisingly hate due to the nature of their relationship with their father or lack thereof.

I often think of my own father who is still alive today whose name is Moses. A man I love and he has been present in my life but not really present. He as man has never changed, actually I think he has gotten worse. For most of his life he lived in the same family home which was sold a few years ago. He grew up in Los Angeles with his Mother Isabel, Father Moses Sr., Sisters Elizabeth and Rachel (Deceased).

I grew up in my father's and grandfathers' family home, a piece of me was left there when we moved and the house was sold. I hated that house; it was filled with an evil spirit that almost took my life back in 2007.

Here is that house:

Over the years I have thought about other fatherly figures who have only damaged me like my other grandfather named Raul, who I refer to as the Devil. A man who for most of my life spread hate and anger towards me, my sister and mother. A man who I was raised with since the age of five after my parents divorced and my mother felt the need to go search for her long-lost father who had abandoned her in her life. I never fully understood why women especially go looking for their piece of shit fathers who either abuse and abandon them in life.

I have said since I became a father NEVER to become them, those father figures have failed me. I know this may seem harsh. As a Christian man we are to love and honor our fathers. I do love my father despite his many flaws.

The true representation of a father was my grandfather Moses Sr. Although I am sure he had his demons like any man, but he always showed love towards my sister and I. He was so giving whenever we would spend time together.

Since becoming a father on January 2013, a truly life changing event. Over the years I have grown into fatherhood, but I know when I first became a father it was challenging, new, scary but also beautiful at the same time holding my daughter Mikaylah and seeing the complete love in her eyes for me , even today with the same look of love.

Fatherhood is the biggest gift in my life, next to being a husband. My daughter who is a splitting image of me and a copy of me.

I dream of days I can continue to be a better father, but I know I will fail at times. As my daughter is now nine years old and seeing her grow up each day knowing one day I will wake up and shell be eighteen.

This Father's Day I am not the man was when she was born, I am not even the same man from last Father's Day. Each day I grow into my role and responsibility as a father being an example for her. I look at some many good fathers today and honestly, I know there are better fathers out there who have better jobs, make more money, and provide more for their families.

I try not be so hard on myself as a provider, father and husband but apart of me will never see myself as special.

My daughter Mikylah who professes her Love to me each day is something so special and I know that truly am loved by her and my wife each day, I am blessed.

Wishing all of those fathers out there who take the time to spend time with your children, to be in their lives, then you are a good dad! Wishing all a great fun filled day filled with Love.

Chapter 63

Happy Fourth of July 2022

July 3, 2022

Happy Independence Day! I find this day important in our history
as we celebrate most not realizing the significance of this day. As an American
it gets lost on me the importance but many of us Non historians will focus on
the extra day off, time with family, Bar-B-Ques and some sparklers.

Where I live Fireworks of any kind are illegal, but growing
up in Los Angeles in the Hood, that was perfectly acceptable and encouraged
with firework stands everywhere.

I now live in a foothill area where a spark could literally start a wildfire, but for this those who live in the inner city

that is not
really a concern.

But Independence day when think of it , I cant help but to
think of the film with Will Smith decades ok fighting the alien fight. That is
much more exciting Independence Day then most of us think of. But I wish to
give honor to the mean behind today.

The 4th of July represents the birth of a nation, the United States of America, that got their independence from the British and is therefore a day to celebrate the creation of a country.

The Declaration of Independence didn't have the symbolism it has nowadays during its first years of life. It was not until the
19th century. When the new political parties were born that the
Declaration was promoted by the Democratic-Republicans as an important piece of American history.

It was not until 1870 that congress declared the 4th of July a national holiday to commemorate the birth of this American nation.

Many countries today try to mimic what we offer here in the U.S.
such as our laws and liberty, but each country is to their own on what they
feel is right for them even when we don't agree with it such as countries in

the middle east who literally shot and hang people on site for their crimes,
crimes that seem light like stealing. But some countries are much stricter in
their laws and even punishments something we here do not realize although we
have prisons full of people especially minorities and people of color.

Today we have huge problems I don't think are related to the
declaration of independence but when it comes to interruptions of the constitution
from when it was written. Obliviously the constitution was meant to be a foundation
to build from not always to take literately which we try to do today.

Such as if Slavery still existed it probably would be alive
and well, but we have other forms of slavery here in our country like slavery
to corporate America.

This fourth of July lets try to remember the meaning and
purpose much like Christmas and Easter, our history in this country is still
important although society is trying to rewrite our history and eliminate it from
history books.

Have a great 4th of July, be safe, live prosperous and may the fourth be with you!

Chapter 64

RIP Lily - Doggie Heaven Awaits (2007 - August 202

August 20, 2022

Goodbye old friend. Yesterday August 19th 2022 at 8:00 PM was a sad day as I lost a piece a piece of myself, her name was Lily and she was our family dog. Lily who was in the family since 2007 having personally picked her out for my mother whom is no longer here herself having passed in 2015.

Lily had a good heart, loved our family and was in our family during times when we needed love the most having. During this time in my life, I was going through some incredibly difficult times having attempted suicide that year living back at the house of hell with my grandfather who would visit his niece Margie and his sister Lola who at the time their dog just had puppies. Lilly was a runt, small and strange looking with her long slender legs and she had a funny face. This was also a time our other three dogs Kevin, Winne and Wrinkles were older senior dogs at this point. Lilly full of energy gave some happiness to our already depressing home.

Mom's Best friend Til the End

My mother loved Lilly from the beginning and slept her last days caring for her and in my opinion giving my mother going in life having something to care since my sister and I eventually no longer lived in the Devils home.

After Mom passed away the devil took her from our family and we didn't see her for a while, but my sister made it a point to get her back. When my sister did get her back, she was in horrible shape, very thin, mal-nourished, dirty and mistreated. It took a good year for Lilly to recover and be herself again. At this time in our life it was around 2016, another time in my life that we were really struggling living in my fathers home, the same home I attempted to take my life in.

Every Girl Needs a Dog

Lily spent a great deal of time with my daughter Mikaylah at the time who was around four years old and she loved her. Lily stayed with us at all times, sleeping in our room at time, being our protector from the dark spirits that lurks at night often barking and warning us evil was in our bedroom. Lily at this point was considered a older dog, but still fully of energy.

When we left in 2018, we left Lilly with our father who cared for her at that point becoming a friend to him and Lily grew to love my father and so did my father.

When my father finally sold the family home moving in with my sister, bringing Lily of course giving the home a sense that my mother was still around since my mother loved Lily.

Lily Was always there

I am thankful for Lily as she was a dog who only loved us even though she could be annoying at times over barking at everything but at this moment in life I know I will miss her deeply and remember her along with my other family members like my other dogs from my past. RIP Lilly. If there is a doggie heaven I am sure your there now and if Dogs do end up in Heaven with people I am sure my mother Linda is there with her now saying hello once again!

Chapter 65

Happy New Year ! Here's to a Prosperous 2023

January 1, 2023

2023 is upon us, for some it already has happened. Thinking for 2022, I am reminded of how this year started for me. January 4th, 2022 I contracted COVID after spending time as a family at an amusement park Knotts Berry Farm. Going against my better judgement, tired of living in fear , stuck inside like most but unfortunately paid the price. From a personal perspective I was affected physically , in bed for days having just come back from a two week vacation. COVID changed me for some reason, I a stricken with covid brain, unable to think at times, not feel quite myself but then something changed in me, like a veil was lifted from my mind and eyes, I could see.

For most of life I lived in fear, doubt, nervousness, low self-esteem, questioning myself at every turn, but for some reason I feel different. Suddenly I stopped, but not completely. Self-doubt will always be apart of me, it always has. Always looking to please people in my life, especially my co-workers, my managers and bosses.

A new change also took place in my job, a new manager and boss by the name of Jill. Replacing my manager at the time Jarod. Jerod a kind soul, someone who I really enjoyed working with, so had been my manager since my start in July 2020. Jerod taking an internal position and replaced by Jill, a women I have never worked with before. Change was difficult for me, deep down I was scared not of her but that she would not understand me, that I would lose the type of relationship I had with my old manager and I was right. She is not like my old manager, but in all not bad just different. Jerod would regularly try to uplift me , say kind things to me. Jill has been strict with me, but in all I feel it has been to retrain me, make me better in a way and I believe she has.

I believe and hope I will have a better working relationship with Jill, but deep down I am not concerned. Previously in 2019 I was fired from a position, which I Believe was due to my current manager at the time not really valuing me as a employee. I will never forget that feeling and that day October 13, 2019, a day my livelihood changed. As one gets older, one starts to fear those times, especially when you have a family to support, rent, bills, and so forth. But that is in the past and each year I work to keep those things in the past, a reminder yes but in the past as a learning lesson.

This year has been good as I have been able to feed my family, be healthy. I look forward to next year hopefully be more financially prosperous.

Truthfully we do not know what the year will bring, most of us hope for best to live in peace, have a financial means to support ourselves and family , to be healthy and meet our goals. But sadly some and even many may not experience that. Some will go imaginable hardships, some may not be here next here as death will come knocking and every which way. We must endure, attempt to be positive in adversity.

This hope I pray that I do not let those things in our country change me, as our country continues to be divided by anger and hate, but all honestly I am not that surprised for GOD fore told these days would come. Its painful to watch as people rip each other to shreds, break down ones fellow man and women and even child.

Our country and world I see it is under a illusion of distraction as people focus their attention on those with power, celebrity and money taking their attention off what is important.

Next year my hope is to finally publish my first work, even if it means publishing myself. Career wise I would also like start my own independent consulting company which would allow me to take on separate projects, but of course fully intending on continuing to work and teach in the new year.

As a person , as a father , as husband and man I hope to grow personally by continuing to learn, grow and be a better version of myself then today.

I hope to continue my health journey maintain my weight, become stronger although since last year I have gain weight most of it muscle, but would like to trim down again next year.

I look forward to hopefully getting a better handle on my mental health, as although I am ok , I find myself thinking dark thoughts at times, specially thinking about my future death. I think of my wife and daughter, their successes, making them stronger in the

new year, but encouraging them, loving them and appreciating them more.

Whatever the new year my bring for each of you, know that you are not alone, you are valued and loved even if you feel you are not especially by those people who are supposed like family and friends and even our employer. Don't allow those relationship to define you, in a way live boldly without fear and you shall see your truly potential. Never any person set your value, never allow society to tell you what your worth is.

The new year is fresh beginning, although our problems, issues in life tend to carry over in the new year, but I don't have to let those concerns bring us down, just know that you have a choice for a fresh start to start a new job, save money, begin new relationships and even treat those in our life kinder for a change.

Whatever you make, make it a good one and may you have a prosperous and blessed new year.

God Bless!

Chapter 66

Happy 10th Birthday Mikaylah - Love from Dad!

January 9, 2023

Happy 10th birthday Mikaylah. Ten years ago, you changed my life forever. You were thought of before you were born. I remember many years before being a father, even a husband. I always wanted a daughter and now that I have one, she is almost my copy, but of course she is her own person and I look forward to see her grow up.

Each year since her birth, I have watched and experienced her life from day 1 and it is a blessing in my life. I pray each day for the well being of my daughter, that she grows up to be a kind, loving person but also a person who knows her value and worth.

As her father I have tried to provide and give her what she needs and wants at times , making sure she feels secure, safe and loved.

I do not know what the future will hold for her, I hope that her future will be better then mine. At her age which was in 1989 I was playing with TMNT (Teenage Mutant Ninja Turtles). Today she along with her friends on in iPad, Facetiming, zooming playing Roblox.

Like many parents we tend to live through our children as we watch them grow up , go to school and grow up to adults one day.

I look forward to our days together as I take to school and pick her up, working from home has allowed me to see her grow up right before my eyes.

Happy Birthday and many many more to come! I pray she remembers this day, unlike myself who doesn't remember my childhood birthdays, but do remember mom getting me a TMNT birthday cake.

Chapter 67

Happy Resurrection Day 2023 - He is Risen!

April 9, 2023

Happy Resurrection Day or Happy Easter for those who do not celebrate that Christ has risen. This day is incredibly special to me and should be to many of us, but I understand that many do not believe and can not believe that a man can rise from the dead and save us from our sins but I do believe.

Some who read this may say , well that's you , that's not me. Christians are a bunch of hypocrites who spread hate and division, at least that is what I see in the media.

I will say that all people including those who love Christ can and are hypocrites because we are imperfect and sinners, but its Jesus who saves us in the next life.

I know personally I have never physically seen JESUS, but I know he exists and existed as a real person , who is Father, Son and Holy spirit in one.

Jesus suffered an insufferable death, beaten beyond recognition. We often say that we would die for others, our family members, our kids , even a perfect stranger, but truly would we sacrifice ourselves, If history proves anything many would not. Many would justify it by saying why should I do for another person I don't know, when I have my own family to worry about. Yes there are those who bravely defend others and die as a result. But JESUS knew he was going to die, he was born to die for our sins.

Imagine being born to die , that you knew you would not grew up to be old, possibly not have a family or career, would you still accept your death. I can not compare myself to GOD and JESUS one in the same, because JESUS is GOD and GOD is JESUS. I am just a man , flesh and bone, who will die, but when Jesus died, he died so when I died I had a place for my soul to go, not to hell but to eternity in heaven, THANK GOD!.

For those who do not believe, please do not mock those who believe, actually I encourage you read the bible , understand that we were and are born sinners meant to go to HELL, a true place that exists, a place of torment and pain. Sadly, many people reject God, ignore Jesus although in many cases he is around, there are believers around who work to share the gospel with people, but people often reject Jesus.

Jesus loved every man, women and child, EVERY!. Some would say how can god love me if I am this way, no matter you are gods creation made from LOVE although the world rejects you, you are loved by GOD and you have a place in heaven if you believe in him, which for many is almost impossible because many wish to live in SIN believing in the lies of the world that if you die you will be ok, that heaven and hell do not exist, but that is a lie by devil and yes the devil and his minions , his demons exist to confuse us, but we shall not all them to, because JESUS died and beat the grave and devil.

I am by no means perfect, I sin today and I seek GOD's forgiveness each day and he forgives me. GOD will forgive us and takes us to heaven on our last breath. One of the most painful things to watch is what Jesus may have gone through in crucifixion having watched the Passion of the Christ, unable to imagine the pain he went through, personally we have would have died with the first strike, but Jesus endured on the cross dying and rising again, rising.

I often think about death a lot, my own death unsure when that will be , but taking great comfort to know that I will be in heaven on day. Can you be confident where you are going when you die, scary to think if you are unsure, put your faith in JESUS.

Thinking of the thief on the cross next to Jesus at his crucifixion, the thief having faith on the cross as Jesus took him to paradise, only GOD can do that. The thief didn't earn salvation, but "Today you will be with me with Paradise" was Jesus's words. His love and mercy are available to ALL of us.

This easter let's remember you are loved, even if you believe it or not, JESUS loves you and wants you to get to know him so one day you can be in heaven with him.

I want to wish everyone a blessed Easter regardless of who you do or who you spend time with.

God Bless,

Chapter 68

Happy Mother's Day 2023

May 14, 2023

Happy Mother's Day!

This day holds a special place in my heart even though my own mother passed away in December 2015. But her impact left me forever changed. I do of course wish she was here today, but deep down I know she Is in a better place, HEAVEN. My mother named Linda born in August 1959, was only 56 years old when she passed, too young in my eyes, but getting the chance see her only granddaughter born, my daughter Mikaylah. My mother who sacrificed so much for my sister and I, supporting us the best she could knowing it was incredibly difficult or her especially financially. Raised with grandfather, who my mother sought years into her adulthood often verbally abused my mother and myself making life difficult, but mom again kept a roof over our head, fed us and made sure we had everything we needed.

It was my belief my mother had a difficult life even from a young age until the day she passed. I of course know she was always there for me, listening to my issues in life, my celebrations, and milestones in life.

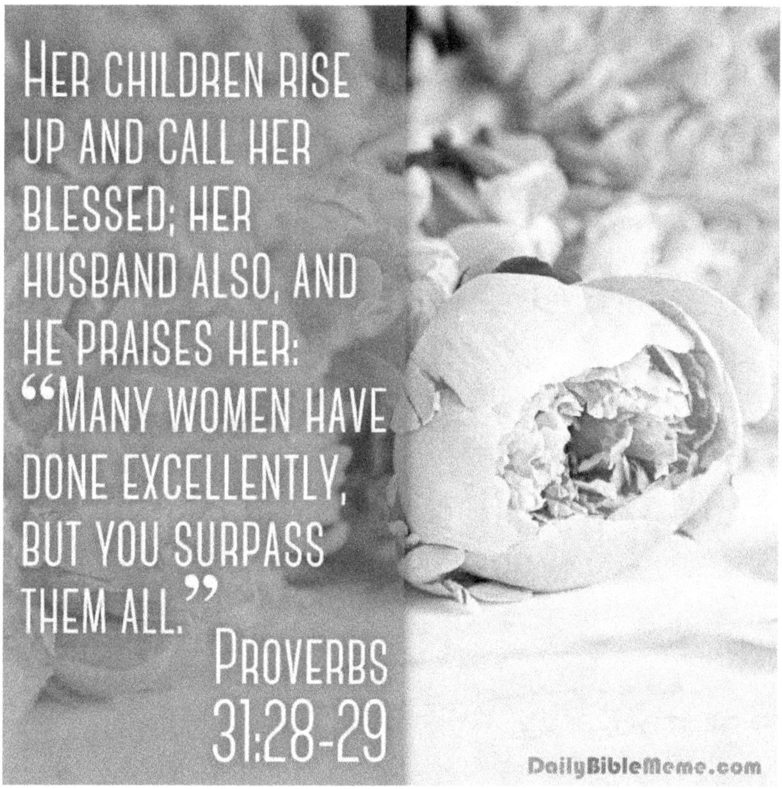

The other women in life are my wife Delia and the mother of our daughter Mikaylah. A woman who each day sacrifices, provides love and kindness to me and our daughter. I honestly don't know where I would be today without my wife's love. I could think of no better mother then my wife who is an incredible mother, providing a true example of a loving mother and wife. I know she worries about being a good mother to our daughter, raising her to be a decent human filled with compassion and love for others and herself. Each year Delia grows to be a better mother, person and wife and I Love her dearly.

What more can we say to but to thank GOD for mothers and fathers too, but father's day is another post.

Chapter 69

A Milestone for Daughter Mikaylah-Growing up.

May 28, 2023

My daughter Mikaylah in a way has passed a great milestone in my eyes but for many its not really a milestone as she completed 4th grade and going on to 5th grade. I have seen our daughter grow up so much in these last years, in a way it's frightening because of how fast time flies.

2022
Last DAY of First Grade AT HOME
2020
Last Day of 4th Grade
2023
2021
End of School
FIRST DAY OF
2nd Grade

I remember so well my fourth-grade teacher Ms. Jean Rothermel of Bell Gardens Elementary School, an incredibly special teacher to me who always showed me kindness to myself, mother and sister.

I remember this time because she would often invite us to her home and take us to lunch. But what makes her so memorable is that she took an interest in me and my interest. At the time It was all rage of Teenage Mutant Ninja Turtles and my love for turtles, and she would collect turtles and gift them to me. She was an older woman at that time, so most likely she has already passed on by now, but she was so special.

I try to remember my daughter's teachers because each of them are very special as well and always try to show my appreciation for each of them.

May we who have children especially appreciate those teachers and the impact they make in their lives because we have or had teachers who had great impacts on us, I remember them even today such as Ms. Marsha Carey who gifted me her iguana, my middle school drama teacher, Mr. David Miller, my high school business teacher and even in college Mrs. Sheila Hosteler my Business law professor, so many I remember.

I am hopeful one day I will see my daughter's high school graduation and even college if she chooses to go.

Here's to another year of growth!

Chapter 70

Happy Fathers Day! 2023

June 18, 2023

Father's Day originated and was celebrated first on June 19, 1910, in the state of Washington. However it was not until 1972 – 58 years after President Woodrow Wilson made Mother's Day official. Fathers day was not always met with the same enthusiasm as Mother's Day, simply because Fathers do not have the same sentimental appeal as mothers.

I agree with this statement as I find that fathers are not considered as important as mother's as I believe it because sadly there are many bad father's who give good fathers a bad name. Often fathers are made to be Oofs , stupid, clumsy, mean, rude, uncaring and in all honestly there are many fathers like that. If you look to the most famous fictional fathers, I look at Homer Simpson. Homer in a way reminds me a lot of my father.

My father Moses was a hard worker and although in my life even after my mom and dad divorced, often they would keep to himself, leaving myself and sister to our own devices whether that was watching too much television, playing too much games and even eat too much and not the healthiest foods.

Dad wasn't the sentimental type, hugging type, lovely dovey type. Dad was the type we saw every other weekend, went to Toys R' Us and then Chuck e cheese or we'd order in and then left to our own during the weekend until we were back with mom again, where we were given where we lived with the worse type of father and grandfather who put us down, cursed at us, spewed hate to my mom, sister and I.

Sorry to say I did not even have a lot of good examples of men in my life, except my other grandfather Moses Senior, who when we would come stay in the weekend, he would go out of his way to stock the fridge with My sister and I's favorite foods, taking a trip to Sam's club.

He was a tough WII vet but had a heart of gold who loved My sister and I, to this day I remember his loss when he died wishing I had spent more time with him.

For myself, becoming a father has been my biggest gift to my daughter Mikaylah who is now 10 years old. Deep down I always wanted to be a father, so I could grow to be the best example of a father breaking the cycle of previous fathers.

I am far from perfect, I do make mistakes and fail, but each day I go to work, feed and support the family as I watch my daughter grow up from infant to child to eventually tween, teen and adult. Watching before my eyes her grow up , growing up so fast as I look at my own life, reflect on my childhood and compare her childhood to mine, but there is no comparison.

These times are much more complicated then those times I grew up as a child, for one we had no social media, add social media bullying and new age problems I did not grow up with. As a father I am truly unsure how to deal with some of the issues today as my daughter gets older, she will experience problems I never imagined would exist.

I find that constantly compare myself to other fathers, better fathers in my view. Fathers who have better jobs, make more money, better providers overall and I look in the mirror at my own failures although I work each day to better myself. I don't know if I daughter sees those differences in other fathers, as she is only 10 but I believe one day she will see those other dads who are more successful, better careers and overall, better in every aspect of the way.

We as dads are ALL different and from what I have seen, what we think and see can be deceiving because those fathers may abuse their families, alcoholics, drug abusers and terrible fathers from the outside they look great, something I need to remember.

To all dads out there, remember that we ALL can be better, kinder, gentler and that it's great to be a great provider but important to be present, involved with a loving touch. Our children who grow up today will not grow up the same we did, but we must continue to self-sacrifice to give them our best because time slips away so fast.

For all the dads out there, have a blessed day!

Chapter 71

44 Years of Life Happened Today! Happy Birthday to

December 1, 2023

Oday is my 44th birthday! Please hold the congratulations, well wishes as I reflect on this day to think about these 44 years of life. More than half of my life has been filled with turmoil, hardships, living in regret and sadly waiting for each day to be my last day on earth. Yet I keep going as I look at my beautiful wife and daughter, think of my sister, father and brother in law and those very few friends I can call friends.

Sadly I wish I had more appreciation for a birthday, but I do not. When many wish me Happy Birthday, I of course thank them because I do appreciate that they did think of me, since many do forget me especially those who say they are my friends and family.

I wish I could be more grateful for my life, I know I should thank GOD and do for allowing me to have breath because you never know when I will take my last breath.

Strangely I think of those individuals I read about who end their lives never to have another birthday, I don't know why I think of Stephen (Twitch) Boss, the dancer from Ellen who ended his life last year. I think of his beautiful life he had, wife, kids, money, fame, everything one could ask for in this life.

Where has myself I have my wife, my daughter and at times struggles to keep my head above water. I feel like I have struggled so many years to get ahead, save money, have a better future only to have set back after set back again starting all over again, I have had too many of those moments to count. Am I healthy, YES. Do I have work, YES, actually two jobs, one full time working in my career field and another teaching. Do I have a place to sleep, a roof, YES I do. Do I live in relativity safe neighborhood, Yes. Do I have food everyday, YES. Do I have money, NO. Do I have a House with a yard, NO. Do I have many friends, NO. Do I have love for myself, NO.

I think the NO's outweighed the yeses, but the yeses are often what we look at when we look at our lives and see that we have NOTHING to complain about. Yes I know maybe I should just be thankful I have what I need to be ok, lack of money of course. Sadly I think to myself when will my last birthday be will it be tomorrow as

I drive on the freeway and someone or something causes my demise. Will it be not waking up for some reason, it will be aneurism or will it one day me deciding when it will be time leaving behind this life.

I know this birthday message is depressing and it should be filled with happiness about life, thankful for everything, every breath and to live another day and year, because frankly people die every day, young and old, natural and unnatural deaths.

What I will do each day is try to create a small legacy that I am here, that is why I blog, that is why I write books, why I VLOG and document my life so my daughter , wife will know who I am.

I do look back at pictures from years past on Birthdays and think , was I happy in this moment in time and at times I think yes I was or no I was struggling at that point in time, but I attempted to be happy. Last year I think about how everything was great, I had work , my weight was manageable and I felt and looked good and now this year its very different as I had a hard year with a layoff in March, But found work with a good company, but along the way struggled , made some choices that affected me and my family financially and I am in regret at times.

I regret that I had a higher paying job in May through July, but was forced to leave and restart my job search. I regret that in May of this year I had two job offers and made a choice taking the wrong role which cost me BIG time career and financial wise setting me back financially hurting our family financially, something I will never forgive myself for, but Must MOVE on. On the bright side,

I am working with a great company which has the potential for lots of growth. But I will say that GOD knows what he is doing as he placed me with incredible people who are kind, respectful, professionals who I enjoy being around and working with instead of the last company that I worked with kind people too, respectful and professional but one very passive aggressive micro managing project manager who forced me to want to leave a good position. Deep down I feel I am good at this new company, I actually feel happy to want to go and be around these incredible people where as the last company although nice, day one I had this strange feeling like something was off as soon as I got there.

But no matter what, I look back on my day of birth and wonder what life would have been like if I was never born, which in my opinion would shape many things such as the birth of my daughter, the meeting of my future wife, but wonder none the less, would life be better...who knows, only GOD knows. I do know that GOD has a plan for me, continues to plan my life even despite that hardships he is there working through me and with me each day.

I know in my heart I need to have more appreciation for my birth, my life, who I am , but at the end of the day I am not special. I look at others and I say Thank GOD they were born, because they seem to have an amazing life, but I know I don't know their life, what they struggle with, if they are happy. All I know is my life, my imprint on those around me.

Here's to a new year of birth, where I look to each day of change, growth, and happiness in the hope that I can appreciate my life further and value it like I should.

Happy Birthday to ME!

Chapter 72

Happy New Year to 2024, Good Riddance to 23'

December 31, 2023

Goodbye 2023 and good riddance! But not completely as I wrap up this year filled with hardship and successes but more hardships than I have needed and even now recovering for this year and wont be made whole again until a year from on and I am talking emotionally and financially. Just like 1 year ago today, everything was gravy, enjoying the end of 2022.

YOUR FIRED!

Unexpectedly February/March would go south and that is LIFE. Without warning, out of a job via an e-mail from the CEO of the company. I guess I should have expected it, we were after all considered a Tech company, not like Twitter, Google, Microsoft and so many others. It was a job I had been after for almost three years, a job I liked especially my customers and some of my co-workers. But it was a job Afterall, no guarantee of employment especially in the good ole U.S. of A.

I along with about seventy employees got the boot, some of them my work friends, although I never physically met them as I was a remote worker which was apart of the perk as I got to spend three full years with my wife and daughter and see their lives in a whole new greater light, which I still miss today.

Staying Optimistic

I was optimistic as I took the first weeks of March off to get some much-needed rest having not taken a real vacation in over a year, the last being in December of 2021. Then in mid-March I had a planned surgical procedure which would allow me to stay mobile with caution for 1 month. I found the successful end of March fairly quickly with interviews, which was a great joy and exciting and got two offers' days apart end of April to start in May and that that point everything was ok until it wasn't.

I stupidity accepted both offers giving my time to really decide as I loved both positions and knew I had to decide, but I really should have immediately let one go and burned a good bridge. This was a time I was not myself as being jobless with so much responsibility on my shoulders was overwhelming, frightening and my mental health flared up as I couldn't sleep, think, full of anxiety about what the future looked like.

New Oppurtuntunties

One position was with one of my old industries in a credit union, the other in Utilities and a company I had wanted to work and, in my heart, knew I wanted the Job in projects working for the utility company, it was well paid and the credit union both paid me 15% higher than I was previously making. There were pros and cons to each position, I guess I should have paid closer attention to what I knew.

One of the reasons I did not take a the Credit Union job was because the job was focused on things I was Just doing at my old company but different, more like a system administrator and for some reason didn't see myself doing that, I wanted to try something new.

My gut told me I should have the credit union job, but I took the job I felt I wanted, which did not pay off. Immediately when I started my new job in Mid-May in Utilities, I was excited, happy and looking forward to my new role. Strangely when I stepped onto the new job, that changed for me, after a few weeks I felt regret about the job I took as it turned out it was not what I thought it was, it was much different then explained in the interview.

I was of course considered a contractor, knowing that going in but I felt different as if I was not truly apart of the team. For many this wouldn't have mattered, I did after all have a job so who cared if I was a contractor. I cared because in time I felt I was not treated the same as a regular employee, I was kind of treated like an outsider.

In a matter of the next few weeks were typical, onboarding, training, getting to know new people and more training. For the first three weeks, I shadowed the current person who was moving to a different division. I am forever appreciative of my trainer as she attempted to warn me about the person I was working under and her name was Blanca, a name I will never forget. I met and interviewed Blanca from day one, felt a good connection and the other two Tabitha and Stephen. I had no issues with Tabitha and Stephen, they were both kinds, professional and respectful during my short time.

Balanca on the other hand turned out to be someone different and when I met her in person being that my interview was virtual, that is when I got that strange feeling, that gut feeling came back and it was looking at me straight in the eye.

What I was told about her came to be true, that she was someone who didn't like mistakes, hard to work with although she would often act like she cared, wanted to see me succeed, work with me was not true at all as by

June, when I officially came on board as her Assistant PM she often went to my manager and complained about my work even thought I was still training and then eventually she would lose patience with me and make comments to me threatening my job, putting me under great stress.

I was a nervous wreak , going home unable to sleep, full of depression and anxiety as IT WAS IMPERATIVE I FEEL SECURE IN MY JOB. Sorry to yell but that to point out how important this is. I often read and read about how to deal with this type of situation, often I would read that its normal to feel this way in a new job, out of place, normal to have people get angry, lose patience, threaten one's position, but I had NEVER experience nothing like this before. The positions I have always held I was given time, patience, kindness to learn my job and this time I was not.

Long story short on July 8th, I was reached out by my contractor contact who had just come back from a month vacation in Singapore that he had spoken with Tabitha, Stephen and Blanca and Blanca was unhappy with my performance wanting to possibly get rid of me, but agreed to put me on a PIP plan (Performance Improvement Plan) for 60 days and after that they would decide what steps to take next.

I stood my ground and said NO and that I didn't feel right, and it was not right being placed on one having only been on the job the only 1 month. I was embarrassed, upset and was given a day to think about if I would agree. The next day I decided and again stood my ground and at that point we parted ways, I was done and gone. After this I was filled with even more anxiety, depression, thinking if I made the right choice, that maybe I could have stuck it out, dealt with Blanca, and went from there, something I wish I would have done, but I saw what was happening.

It was that same week I had gotten an email from the company I am at NOW that they were interested in interviewing me as I had turned down interviewing back in April. In June I had reached out to the recruiter interested in the position I applied for but didn't hear anything until July 11th, yes I remember the day because it was convenient, so perfect in timing, it was GOD and I give him the credit. From there the rest is history interview went great with two of my current managers, one has left the company named Emy and two Director/Managers who are still with the company.

I started September 5th and I can honestly say the experience has been night and day as with my current company onboarding was wonderful, the people wonderful, the experience great as I was treated with kindness, respect, professionalism and has been that way until today. The minor con is I took a 10% pay cut from the company I got laid off from in March and I believe that is because I am working in a new industry, but doing similar work like I did back in March. I now work as a hybrid employee currently 4 days in office , 1 day at home and eventually once I hit my 1 year mark, I can work 2 days at home, 3 in office.

Its not so much of a shock as I used to work in the office five days a week, but I do miss fully remote. I have grappled with anger to this day and I guess what I have been most angry about is those who I thought were my colleagues were anything but never hearing from any of them.

Yes I have my family to support me but its nice when those who say I care, your important don't follow through. Again I should be used to people forgetting about me, ignoring me, mistreating me, but I always hope for the best in people and are always disappointed.

Why do I bring this up in a new year's message, because this is the year that reshaped my perspective, This is the year I felt broken, with no control over the situation.

Although I have been without a Job before, laid off, fired, but this time is different. As I get older it becomes more difficult obtain good employment as ageism is a major hurdle for myself and others. This was the year my mental state was stretched to the point that I was looking for a way out, meaning suicide, death.

Many would say that is not necessary, its just a job, you'll get another job, no need to kill yourself for that. But like I said I am the supporter of my family and when I cannot support my family, I fail them and when I fail them what use do I have for them. Unfortunately, if I was to off myself now my family who is not financially secure so I would need to wait as I don't want to over suffer with my loss and financial insecurities.

I am sure and hopeful next year will be better, I put this year behind me and I will say our family as my wife suffered too greatly with my job loss, her worry, her anxiety and even getting Palsy in May which took about 30 days to get remotely better.

Now I just need to let go of what I gave up this year, the mistakes I made, the loss of more money but I did gain too like a great work environment, great coworkers, stable environment where many of my colleagues are with the company 5,10, 15, 20, 25 and beyond years in the company which is encouraging as long as I don't screw it up or they don't have lay offs and I am cut again, I do not think I can take that again. This year I even made plans to give myself five years of life left, which I still plan of keeping unless something changes over the years.

I want to enjoy 2024, I want to see my family grow, change and be happy, but again things tend to stick with me and this will stick with me for long time, just the thought of it makes me sad and angry again.

For those who have had a year or years that make its mark, I want to believe we get a fresh start in the new year. Each day is a new start, a new job is a fresh start, so I remember that the people I work with today don't know me, I have a chance to build new friendships, relationships. I have some optimism left in hoping for the best as I continue to grow in my career, and I believe only GOD knows my plan and to him I am right on schedule.

I know GOD is in control. GOD Knew I would lose my Job this year, but he had and has a plan for me, I just need to trust him more and I do, but I am still a weak human. I pray the new year brings you and your family's prosperity and if their hardships and there will be at times, don't give up, look forward to each day and know what is truly important and what is not.

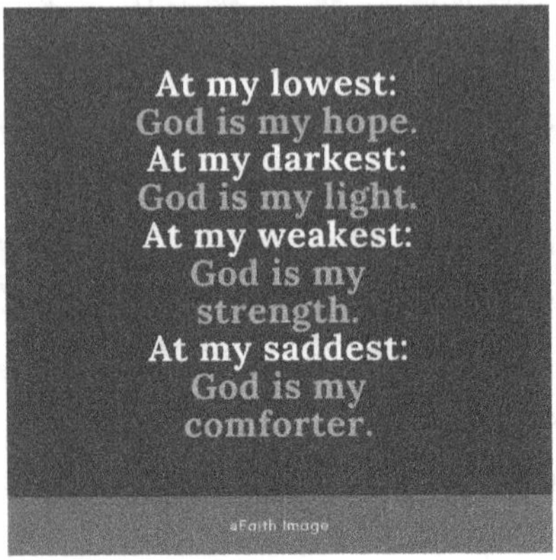

Often, we pay way TOO much attention to the things that don't matter. People will come and go in our life, Companies could care less about you and I we are just numbers on a spreadsheet, but at the end of the day we have control over our reactions, how we think and what we do with our time, which is why I need to STOP worrying, roll with the punches and deal with it and that my mental health, physical health is worth it. I know that is easier said than done as many have far worse problems than I do, but these problems are all I can take right now.

Wishing everyone a great new year, I am sure it will be a real kicker, like a real kick in the teeth but hopefully not.

VI- Career and Life Changes

Chapter 73

My Job Loss, My Job Gain and How I managed

April 29, 2023

Losing one's job is painful, it can be one of the most destructive events happening in ones life. I should know I have been through a few of them. Most recently I was laid off March 2nd, 2023. An unexpected shock as the organization I worked for gave no indication there would be any form of layoffs. It was Tuesday February 28th, six in the morning as I was preparing for a meeting with a client at seven. I naturally check my messages when my team's app did not open which I found unusual. I then went straight to my e-mail when in black and white saw those dread words, "Restructure" , "9% staff cuts" and "Your position has been eliminated".

I was completely numb to the news as it was so early, my daughter and wife were still sleeping, waking my wife up to let her know the news and she was in shock, we embraced and assured each other everything was going to be alright. From there I logged onto my computer as I searched my e-mails to see that the C.E.O sent the whole staff a four in the morning e-mail about the changes. I lost many of my teammates in the cuts, people I worked closely with, people you would not expect to be cut, were gone.

The Rise of Mass Layoff's with No Empathy

I know in today's job market; mass lay offs have been happening progressively since last year from twitter and google to most recently amazon. The organization was a part of was also a tech company and a public company at that. I took me some time to adjust, to not fall into previous traps of self-destruction, self-loathing, blaming myself, thinking what I could have done differently for my employer to keep me on board, it was personal.

I had to realize that although these situations are difficult in most cases, they were temporary setbacks, but one never knows as the job market appeared slow, filled with those who were recently unemployed fighting and competing for the same roles. From day one I knew I needed a break, taking a two week break to recharge, rest and think about my plan of action. Although I have a family to support, I was fortunate enough to receive severance and vacation, last paycheck to help tide me over.

I know I am unfortunate that many do not get this, some literally lose their job and worry about how rent is going to get paid, how they will feed themselves and the kids. What was painful to watch was being on LinkedIn and seeing the incredible amount of pain of those struggling like I was, often worse being out of work for months, some even years.

I will admit that I needed a break, hadn't not take a vacation in over a year and a half as my previous role made it difficult to step away on the account I had clients to support, I often was not utilized fully, even bored at times, but content to be working , working with clients and doing what I feel I do best.

Its ONLY been 8 weeks, but I have gotten some good interviews with companies I wanted to work for, fine tuning my resume, interviewing and presentation skills. Most interviewers were impressed with my background and me as a candidate, but no job offer. I have gotten the typical auto decline e-mails, been ghosted by recruiters, and even coming to the point that a job offer was within reach only to be rejected. Looking for a job is a lot like sales, you get a lot of rejections and no's before you get an astounding YES.

Hope has Come For New Opportunities

Although I have not been working, there has been light at the end, I got TWO great job offers on almost the same day with sizeable increases. The two roles are very different as one is with a financial institution, and another is a utility company.

Although I haven't started, I have been struggling with the thought that one of these roles would be rescinded by the company, even though there is no indication this would happen, it's my brain overthinking.

I am hopeful I will not have to look for work for a while, but you never really know as some organizations tend to follow the trends, which is what I believe is happening in Tech. The job losses are not necessary, but tech companies have decided this is the time to cut the fat of their head count, leaving thousands jobless in an economy that is already in a recession.

What I found really helpful during this time is that my organization enrolled with an Career coach who helped me with my resume, provide resources on branding myself for the job market and finetuning my skills for interviewing and preparation.

Tips for those Searching

For those going through a recent job loss whether a layoff, a firing or restructuring, these tips should help you get back on your feet.

Personally, I have found NOT spending 8 hours a day behind a computer applying for jobs, but be strategic in who I apply with, doing my research the company, the pay creating a targeted job search. Be patient with yourself, network, network and network and have a good support system and in time you will land that role putting you back on your feet. I know I make it sound really easy, but again this is not easy it takes time, diligence, maintaining a positive state of mind.

If you are going through a job loss, I encourage you to not give up, despite the difficulties, keep pushing forward for yourself and your family, which is our greatest motivators. We all love a comeback story, I can't wait to hear about yours!

Chapter 74

My Metamorphosis In New Job and My Change

June 24, 2023

May 16th having starting a new role after a couple of forced months of involuntary unemployment. A role unlike I have ever been in but with some familiarity in my field of project management. It was been stressful, uncomfortable causing me to think of my past choices, especially the position I turned down which was very familiar territory in that it was similar to my last position.

I'd admit I did think and question what I did, did I make the right choice, thinking for a moment that nothing is permanent, that I needed to relax and take the time to remember that many of these feeling are normal, that starting any new position is not always familiar unless you stay in a certain industry and have been in the same industry, but I have not as I have been in different industries from education, finance , software development and now utilities.

The people for the most part have been welcoming, willing to help me and support me, but at the end the day I need to perform at my role in a different way. Most of my tasks are familiar in projects, such as communicating, meetings, project updates but some aspects are very different as I am in a support role, a support to the project and project manager, I am not the shot caller.

I get the opportunity to work with many of legal, regulatory, environmental, engineering and so many others who work on a single project worth over 100 million dollars. The projects are large and complex typically taking anywhere from five to ten years to complete, nothing compare to projects that took four months to complete.

As of late I have been despondent, not fully happy in my new role. Yes I am happy the bills and rent is being paid, but I go to work each day, a new day, new things to learn and doing my best not to make errors, but overall be a good teammate. Working in corporate America is very familiar and I have worked in corporate America for years, where there's a coldness to it, a cut throat environment at times and a hierarchy where I am once again at the bottom.

I came to this company for a purpose, to learn and be apart of industry that can be difficult to infiltrate, but I am here. I am here to learn skillsets you cannot learn elsewhere, but along the way I will discovery if this was all worth it.

Since I was laid off in March, I have been in a constant state of unrest. Even when I got my first job offer, I was still in unrest, I was happy, but I wasn't and then the position that I am at now was offered to me.

Deep down I had my hesitations, a gut feeling but it was a company I had wanted to work for over 10 years, my moment had arrived or had it. I should listen to my gut feeling, the last time I didn't, similar scenario I took the job and eighteen months later I was fired.

The firing did lead to better positions and where I am today, so I can imagine where this experience can lead me years from now.

I have had no real peace in my life for months, even when I should feel better as I stay awake for hours, my brain refuses to turn off, feeling tired in the mornings, but I push through and get the job done.

Sadly it is common for me to take on roles, I am not always passionate about, but do it for the paycheck , gain some experience until I search for something that I will be passionate about.

What I have struggled with and like many struggles with is often I am put in situations where I work with people who are difficult to work with as I personally have a hard time with people who are very direct, finding I tend to take what people tell me personal and internalize that response and carry it with me everywhere.

I am overcome with guilt since turning down the other position, as I held on to both that role and the role I took to the last minute, unable to make up my mind. I regret I continued to give the other company hope that I would start only to renege, burning a bridge. I did follow up with that other company, but they declined to give me another chance, which eats me up.

I have had a few feedback sessions with the project manager, my manager and supervisor providing feedback on areas of improvement which I have taken wholeheartedly and to implement.

I will continue to make improvements, do my best. What has been a relief to me is my co-workers around me who given me positive encouragement, assurances that what I am feeling in the job is normal such as being overwhelmed, learning the system, procedures and being apart of the culture.

Each day it does get a little bit easier, as I adjust my approach to how I do my job, taking the feedback, but always remembering I am not in control of the outcome of my time at this company. I am hopeful I can stay a few years and then move but only GOD knows how long I will be here.

I pray that my mind will come to rest, that I can rest physically and continue on my way to enjoy my life. During this time, my mind and thoughts have been particularly dark.

What I have found comfort in is writing, putting my thoughts out here instead out on LinkedIn as I tried to do that and have concerned coworkers reach out to me. For now, I will push forward each day, give it my best and essentially wait for whatever god has planned.

In this time I need to work to control my emotions, attempt to be content and accept the way things are for now. There are some lessons I have learned during this whole season in my life.

Chapter 75

Lessons Learned in This Time of Joblessness

Septemeber 4, 2023

Job searching is difficult, painful, frustrating, demoralizing, but there are lessons we can learn in these moments. For many I sympathize with reading the struggles many face each day such as Homelessness, depression, anxiety and even suicide.

Here are lessons I learned during this trial in my life in hopes they help others.

Lessons Learned:

- Give yourself time and grace during this time as we can be our own worst enemy which will affect our job search and destroy our confidence in the process.

- Have a strong support system and network, reach out, talk to others about how you feel, how you struggle and if you are the other person listening, just listen, support, show compassion and kindness.
- STOP blaming yourself regardless of if you were #laidoff, #fired or left voluntarily, there were choices others made on our behalf we had no control over and the choices we made were meant to better ourselves such as leaving toxic work environments.
- Continuously learning, I found Udemy to be a great resource to keep learning, self-improvement and getting your mind off the job search.
- Journal your thoughts, struggles, successes, and failures; this will allow you to direct your energy positively. I have found blogging and vlogging and podcasting incredibly therapeutic.
- Save for the future, I know saving is not easy, but make sure you pay yourself first when those future paychecks are, because you're most important.
- Working for any company is a business relationship, that can be cut at any time don't take it personal, move forward and have the mindset that bigger and better things will materialize just give it time.
- Seek therapy if you struggle further and speak to someone immediately. Sadly, when people

lose hope, they can lose their lives seeing no light at the end of the tunnel, there is light but need help getting there.

- Ask for help, there is no shame, we are all human and need a helping hand and should never feel ashamed and others should never shame us for asking.
- Know your value, you are valuable, you matter and have gifts and talents no one else has recognized that and use those gifts in future roles.
- Never give up, even when we feel like it.
- Exercise, get out of the house, run, jump, play. Doing this benefits your mental health, allowing you to think and strategize about the next steps in your job search.
- Don't allow recruiters or companies to tell you what your worth, know it and remember it.

I have so many more I have learned during this time, it has been more difficult than it needed to be as months ago I was working, but unfortunately was not the position I thought was requiring me to job search again. I failed greatly this year, causing self-deprivation , putting myself down, living in regret, blaming myself which affected both my physical and mental health.

I pray for this new chapter in my life, excited for new opportunities, meeting new people and relationships. I will be going back to the office in a hybrid role, having been WFT for over 3 years will be an adjustment, but maybe a much needed one.

Chapter 76

Fighting with Myself Over New Opportunities

May 7, 2023

Over the course of these two months, I have been under a constant state of turmoil due to losing my job due to a tech layoff. This was certainly a company I had wanted to work for for years. Overall, I had a good experience, learned a lot and met fantastic people but in the end, I was a part of the 9% cut leaving in the cold. At first it was a shock, getting an early morning e-mail that I was one of the positions ELIMINATED. It stung as I looked around at 6 AM, overlooking my sleeping wife and daughter unsure what I was going to do now, scared and unsure of myself with the question, what did I do to deserve this.

The depression of Mass Lay offs

I honestly deep down felt this could happen to me being apart of a tech company, where companies like META, Amazon and Shopify thousands of jobs losses in tech : https://www.msn.com/en-us/money/companies/more-than-190-000-tech-sector-employees-have-lost-their-jobs-since-the-start-of-2023/ar-AA1akUXk

Up to this point there has been over 190k tech losses and its heart breaking to see all of the lives affected by greedy corporations who made millions and some billions off talented labor only to cut them. Getting a job is not guaranteed, but what happens to human decency in talking to your employees, understanding they have needs and not being greedy. I understand companies have a responsibility to their shareholders to be profitable, to stay in business.

The fight of Self-Doubt

During this time I have fought myself with self-doubt, self-worth and struggled, but along the way have continued to push forward, interview and even land two great opportunities.

Two great roles offered

Both positions began the interview process back in late March and early April. The first position was with the financial services industry as apart from the credit union. Being in the financial services industry since 2011, I was familiar with applying for a project manager role. I did not get that position but was offered an equally important role on April 18 which I accepted on April 19th. Prior to that I conducted a 2nd interview a few days prior.

Surprise, surprise on April 19th, I was offered the 2nd position, a position I feel I had waited for many years now, but unexpectedly came across Interviewing the first time on April 14th and then the 17th. The second position took me by surprise working for a dream company, but it was disguised because this role was through a consulting firm that works on behalf of Southern California Edison.

Both companies had a great interview in my opinion, I really felt a connection to both. The credit union for instance was a Christian based credit union and SCE is utilities in electric, a company I have been trying to get into for many years now since 2014.

The credit union was the position I was less concerned about from starting to the background, but the other position kind of left me a nervous wreck as I worked through the consultant firm who had the relationship with SCE. This has been a test of my patience, as soon as they offered me the position, it took a couple weeks to get SCE to approval the position with the manager I interviewed with and then background which took place last week, so two weeks to get to this point with a start date of May 16th and May 17th, Hybrid.

The other position which is full on sight for the first 90 days with a start date of May 8th and here is where the story twists.

Making a final decision on Job Choice

As of Wednesday, of last week I informed the credit union of my intentions not to take the role, but they suddenly started to want to work on my schedule. Nothing taking a "NO" for an answer is when my battle began with questions such as "Was I making the right choice?", "Maybe I should have chosen the Credit Union," But This is my dream company SCE, a company that I have strived to get into for years. Can I just walk away now, although the opportunity would be too great.

Seeking advice from those who I trust, all said the same thing, SCE is an opportunity of lifetime, its difficult to get in. I weighed the options, pros and cons, even though the salaries were more than I made at my previous company, the only difference was the benefits and their cost.

One thing I did not want to do is be blinded by my goal of working for a certain company, regretting it later, but I did my research and overall, all I could see it positive comments, good culture, happy employees.

Although I am certain of my choice, its been a challenge trying to decide which path to take. ONLY God knows what will happen with either and I believe GOD gave me options to have a choice, so either path will lead to great things.

During these last two months I have self-reflected A LOT, rechanged my mind and body, gotten much needed rest. I am ready to go back into the workforce, hopefully for a long time until my next long rest.

My mind has tossed and turned in decision, leading me to this point after numerous rejections from companies I thought I wanted to be apart of but deep down these last two companies are the ones I have a choice to make, but really I made the choice in my heart which was SCE, not I must pray further to ask GOD for his wisdom in my decision. Whatever choice I make I know GOD will be with me.

My Journey to Projects and Project Management

I will say that one of industries is very familiar to me like mentioned having worked banking as member services in the call center, worked in the branch, back office, mortgages, branch supervisor, special projects which led me on the road to working for other companies in projects and working directly with clients. The other position with Edison obliviously I have never worked in the Utilities industry and the project management they use I am unaccustomed to, which there will be a learning curve.

I am perfectly ok with a learning curve, although many would stick to what they are comfortable with because the position may be simpler even easier, but I have found that I may not grow as much in the role and that when I choose roles, I am very familiar with I tend to get bored easily.

At my previous company I found the position simple at times, although it had its challenges I think after so many years I was familiar with those type of projects, working with those types of clients. I think with the credit union role It would have been very similar to my last position, which is not necessarily a bad thing, but the position is new, as in newly created and no one else had fulfilled that role before I would be the first person reporting directly to the COO of the credit union.

The other company, I have had a passion to work there for many years, going back to when I worked for my credit union, which serviced those customers. Many of those customers I grew to get to know, respect and they appeared happy and had great incomes. Because of this reason I went so far to go to a school to be an electrical lineman in hopes of working for Edison one day.

The school which I attended 8 years ago today Northwest Lineman College in Oroville, California. The school was incredible with great instructors, but I did not finish, I left after 5 weeks being there. It was incredibly challenging physically and classroom study was tough, but I felt I had a better handle on the academic side of things.

Here is a picture of my time there, where I climbed 50-foot poles and learned some very interesting things.

After leaving school, I went home to rebuild as I made sacrifices to go there like quitting my full-time job, part time teaching job and moving the family from our apartment to my father's home, the same home I grew up with.

From there, I got my job back at the credit union I just left but part time, got my teaching position back and got a new position with another credit union part time in projects. Eventually I left my old credit union AGAIN, started full time at the new Credit union and then years later was laid off, which led me to working on projects, continuously leading me to where I am today.

I know I should not have so much trouble choosing, but part of the reason I struggle is that I don't want to let myself down or the companies that want to hire me. It should be a simple decision to work for the company I have always strived to work for, but deep down I worry that once I get what I want, hopefully its everything I wanted and not the wrong decision.

Up to this point, I feel I have made good career choices, although at times I was left jobless because the last 3 of 4 jobs I have been laid off.

As of now, I should be starting a new position with the credit union Tomorrow, but last week advised them I would not be starting. For the Edison position I have a start of May 16th, which I fully intend on starting.

During this time, I have taken long walks in the park to think, to rationalize my thoughts of choosing he right position, thankful to have these opportunities but afraid of an error. Both positions were in a way unexpected because

I applied for one job, getting a different job and the other job was disguised as something else come to find out it was my dream company. Both options would lead to prosperity, but in different ways, choices, choices.

Wishing me luck on my journey as I prepare for a new career chapter in my life, I am looking forward to it.

Chapter 77

New Job, New Stress and Trying Not to Lose It!

July 2, 2023

This week was one of those weeks where I was about to say F*ck it I am quitting this job. As many of you know I have been in a new role since May. A role that I is completely new and NO remanence of my last role. I now work in Project management as a Junior Project manager supporting the projects and PM in the Utilities' industry.

I have been under STRESS, sometimes extreme stress as I push to learn the job, but what has been even more difficult is the PM I work under. Please note SHE is NOT my boss but she is an important part of my job because I am attached to her and project. Since meeting Blanca, she appeared nice and for the most part she is.

But being that she has been with the company for many years, I am considered a contractor and not a regular employee, but contractors are a perfectly normal part of this industry, similar to the NSA, CIA, where this labor is necessary.

A little dive into what I do. I work in Utilities under Major Projects, which are projects that are over 25 million dollars and a part of the distribution and transmission division, adding another layer I am part of the Licensure and permits division under that. Basically, before anything can be built, our department gets the permission of State, Local and federal agencies to proceed with the project, which requires a lot of time as these projects can take up to 10 years to complete.

There are multiple stages and phases we must get to before any construction can take place, because construction is the shortest phase, sometimes 18-24 months long.

The job is stressful enough just to learn new techniques, new ways, policies, and procedures, correcting past work behaviors. But to top it off, having a manager nitpick, critique , bordering on harassment, because she wants things her way.

I am not saying I will NOT do things her way, I NEED TIME. TIME to learn, TIME to make Mistakes and UNDERSTANDING, not criticism and that is exactly what I have been going through.

This week was almost the straw that broke me, something I have never felt to do in a very long time. What triggered me is a day of errors, errors equated to being new and learning, but not good enough for the PM, she was obliviously frustrated with me and from my observation embarrassed, which from the looks of it doesn't happen often. I have been embarrassed, especially in front of a client, this was in front of fellow colleagues. This PM has already gone into detail with me that she DOES NOT want our department and her to look like fools, like we do not know what we are doing.

I feel honestly, I am in the shadow of the previous person in this role as she has spoken VERY highly of her and now I am her replacement, but I am no replacement, I am my own person, who makes errors, who needs time to adjust. I will also note that I have not gotten a lot of training, as the person filling in before I got there was in this role for 6 months, but she was with me for 3 weeks and then off she went to a different department. The PM is not a Trainer, she has no interest in training me or showing me how to do things that is up to me to learn on my own.

I have had some support from my supervisor and others who do the job that I do which has made my learning manageable.

It was Tuesday that was the day in a way I will never forget, the end of the day when I was specifically told that "I need to get my act together or this was not going to work". At that exact moment, I decided to write an VERY long e-mail to my supervisor. I did hold off, but each let my manager know I was not doing well and was concerned but said we would talk tomorrow.

Tomorrow came and I was stern, ready, focused, That conversation changed me and I was determined to change my approach, my approach to be cold, calculated, unfriendly just a worker robot.

It was all hands on deck that day as Blanca pulled me aside and spoke with me kindly, didn't apologize but explained her expectations of me and we had a good conversation and went on our way to work.

I am still unsure how I feel right now as I really don't wish to give up this opportunity. It really bothers me that she runs to my supervisor and manager, unsure what is being said but having trust that whatever happens, happens and GOD is in control. I just got through a torturous few month with a job.

It has been a very long time I have had these type of personal conflict issues as that is what I equate this too, she has a completely different personality, a women of power, a women who has been doing the same job with the same company for over 20 years, of course she has clout and importance as I am just a nobody there, I know my place but I need to learn and grow and then eventually get the hell out of there as I give myself 3 to 3.5 years in this specific role and then I will move on, so there is an end date to this role before I move on to bigger and better things.

As of late I have been unable to sleep, as the wheels in my mind run all night thinking about how I can be better, be a better employee, stop making mistakes and appease the people around me so they are happy with my work, I am failing in my eyes.

Many will tell me that is normal to feel this stress, it will go away in time and that I need to relax, but in all honestly, I am NOT the problem, the problem is the lack of understanding, the lack of training and lack of time to learn, I am human, not a robot.

Part of me greatly regrets turning down the other role, but this role no consolation prize, it's a tough job with value to offer me and for my career, but just need to stick with it, do my best and let go of certain feelings as like any person worry about the future , tomorrow and where this job will lead instead of focusing on just being better each day and in time, I will stop being hassled and have handle on the role.

I am not completely hopeless, I am doing what is expected of me, attending meetings, corresponding with the teams and doing my job and trying not to miss a beat.

I have to remember each day, time is precious and take this time to learn the job, not to let those negative people, even those we work with discourage us in our pursuit. What's so difficult is why can't we as happy have the ability just to go to work, be happy, enjoy our job, have peace, come home and enjoy life like many do. Instead, I constantly worry, come home stressed, have trouble sleeping, and start the day all over again.

Finally, during my course of anxiousness, stress my mind tends to go dark, so dark that I think about death, thinking would my family be ok. Thinking that my family could have a fresh start, that I could be at peace with the stress I am experiencing, that my mind never rests.

I would like to think that another position or Job I would feel different, that position I turn down for this job, I would be happier, but honestly who knows. At this point I must try to push forward, learn, live, be happy and work towards moving forward.

Chapter 78

Accomplishments, Milestones and Failures

June 12, 2022

In our lifetime we will experience success, failures, and milestones. These are the things that make up a good part of our life and we should recognize each of them as they are all . Throughout my life I honestly did not recognize any of these, but I did focus on my failures mostly although I had successes and milestones like when I earned my Bachelor of Science in Business Administration and my Master of Business Administration. Even though I obtained these twenty years ago and fifteen-year years I really think much of them. They did take hard work to obtain but I never truly appreciated them and to the most part I think of them as tools of trade.

My Goals Realized

Today I continue to work towards my goals, recently earning my Project Management Certification which took months of study and a very challenging test but I passed. I have also had personal success and milestones in the completing and editing of my novel which I hope to publish one day, that would be a major milestone.

Each of us has these to reflect on not just the failures as many of us can count of many of failures in our life which include poor personal choices, career failures like being fired from a job and even choosing the wrong profession for us.

All these are meant to be life lessons we need to take with us to #Nevergiveup as long as we have life running through us we have a new day to beginning and have a restart. I know for some out there its not easy because maybe you have made some really poor personal choices maybe even ending up in prison or have allowed the wrong people in your life, but you can always have a restart and start fresh.

My Gifts Realized

What is sad about my life is that I have all these gifts like my marriage and my daughter who although I love and appreciate spent so much of my time focusing on the hardships and failures and not on the successes of my marriage and being a father because now that I look back I see that I worked hard to be a good provider to have a roof over our head , food on the table and clothes on our backs. I just never saw myself as anything special because to this head I feel I am just an average Joe. Not that there is anything wrong with being average, I just strive to be more now each day like an author, a better father and husband and even a better employee.

To help me realize Success, failures, and milestones I had to come full circle, what is weird is really didn't start seeing myself differently until earlier this year when I experienced a bout of COVID, which for reason woke me up, unclogged the cobwebs from my brain and I see differently now. I wasn't on deaths bed or anything just my perspective changed.

Now as its I see myself differently and I want to do so much more in life and focus on my career more such as working towards being a project manager, even considering starting my own consulting business soon. Things are looking up for 2022 and the future which is great. I don't know if any of you out there have ever felt this way where you finally see yourself in the mirror for how special you truly are, but you should.

Make your Focus on You!

Continue to work towards your goals and look within yourself to see your special gifts and know you are unique. For most my young adult life and adult life, I always saw my self in worst ways, unvaluable, unintelligent and the worst thought one could think. Most if not all of these dark thoughts came on the account of my depression and low self-esteem.

One way that I have found to gain more confidence and self-worth is by my blogging, Podcasts and Vlogs which allow me to provide advise those who also struggle to gain confidence and not know their true. In my opinion we live in a very repressive society doesn't want you to see your value because of what we can potentially ask for especially in your work life. When you come to a point that you realize your thinking is incorrect and correct it you kind of feel like a weight has been lifted off your shoulders, that's how I feel anyways.

Celebrate your accomplishments and milestones, learn from your failures but don't beat yourself too harshly. I have found when you change your mindset you change you and even those failures won't seem so bad but a learning lesson and not a reflection of you.

Keep pushing forward and remember never give up, your goals and dreams are too important!.

Chapter 79

My Road to a Better Me

April 23, 2022

This year has been unlike any other year with COVID, the pandemic and shutdowns resulting in many of us struggling to be healthy. Now if you have maintained an active lifestyle and were not about to let a pandemic stop you then I applaud you. Prior to March 2020 I was regularly hitting the gym five days a week with a consistent training routine of weights and cardio but not eating as healthy as I knew I should have been.

The gym was always something so important to me I would go rain or shine, morning or night it didn't matter, but then that all changed for many of us. Most gyms naturally closed due to COVID, but some did stay open with an attempt to keep everyone safe. Living in California where there is probably a gym in every city that made a huge impact on those of us who said it was not safe to journey to a daily sweat box and risk exposure to COVID.

So like most gyms my local gym was no different, which pretty much has been closed close to a year now. I often think if I miss the gym and to a certain degree I do but realized that I am able to work around the gym by going to my free resource the local park. When the shutdowns started to happen, I was probably like many shocked that society of hording goods, restaurants, malls and many businesses even churches were forced to close which was pretty depressing to watch. Like many my family and I huddled indoors while I have the opportunity to work from home, my eight-year daughter soon took her elementary school online via zoom but my wife who works in hospitality had to still go to a physical place.

Over the course of weeks turning into mouths many of us adjusted how we ate relying on fast food and ultimately trying to relieve the stress of our new reality for many that lead to food and lack of exercise, hey many of us were just try to deal. I was no different with the gyms closed I took the approach of living in fear for a time just ordering out limiting my exposure to people in markets and the outside world which included exercising.

In time I knew what was going to happen to my mental health and my waistline, but I said to myself I will get back on that horse and exercise at my local park and I did but at the same time I was depressed about the situation and the motivation just wasn't there which meant my waistline expanded slowly at first and then over time I was shocked at how much I gained.

When it comes to my mental health, I have seen a direction correlation between a large waistline and my mental health which only made me feel worse. Over the course of my life, I have always struggled with my weight. Bullied for most of my life being the fat kid, embarrassed of my body and my lack of movement when it came to activities like P.E. Part of problem.

I think was that during most of childhood and teens then adult years I lived with a great depression, low esteem and poor self-image which led to me eating more. Mom and Dad who I love where not the best examples for healthy eating and lifestyles, so I learned from them as well. These habits carried with me until today with my love for sweets, fast food and snacks.

For many this is not an usual experience many gained pounds over the course of the year due to the stress of being stuck at home and the stress of no childcare, schools closed for many and having the literal whole family at home driving each other nuts at times, all added to the stress, over eating, lack of exercise and ultimately weight gain. But one of the bigger issues was mental health and the toll it took on many some taking the drastic step of suicide. Although suicide did not cross my mind during this time, I can only imagine what other's have experienced.

This year would be the point of redemption for me as I took a long look at my pudgy self and was frankly disgusted with myself being a role model to my wife and daughter looking, the way I did, It was time for a change.

Losing weight was not uncommon to me, I had done it before as it was going to take time, patience, exercise and eating right. My first problem when I previously tried to lose weight was the amount of effort I was putting into exercise which for me I find running to be the most beneficial to weight loss but I just walk daily I don't tend to see the results I want.

One area I really have to almost eliminate is fast food although I do eat occasionally but unlike a year ago I was eating it almost every day with a lack of what I call real home cooked meals so that definitely contributed to my weight gain.

I also had to drink one think I was not a fan of drinking which was water, now drinking half my weight in ounces for water, eating breakfast, a light lunch and light dinner and eliminating snacks. Now I don't want to make it sounds as if I starve myself because I don't its just that with all the water I brink and certain foods I eat literally make me feel full , foods like oatmeal which take my hunger pangs away.

Since late January I have lost a total of twenty-two pounds, consistent now with losing about two pounds a week which is considered healthy weight loss. My mental health and energy have also improved although we are not out of the pandemic yet, I make it a point to exercise six days a week running for about one hour and that's all it takes for me. My hope is that by July I can lose a total of fifty pounds changing my life and sticking to this lifestyle change.

I believe we all have in us to get healthy if we make the choice and stick with it, be patient with yourself and know there's not quick fix to losing weight. I have literally tried starving myself coming to see that ended severely hurting me physically and in the end did nothing for my weight loss but ultimately led to poorer health by eating more.

As mentioned, this has been a lifelong struggle but I am determined more than ever to get this done right and stick with it for the long haul. For many of you this journey may sound familiar, but I just want to say don't give up. Lastly there is one fictional character I remember everyday in my goals and that is Rocky Balboa ever giving up because anything can happen when you fight for what you want.

Afterword

It is my hope that if you read my volume two blogs, you were not bored, but find my words, my expression, my rawness refreshing. I know much of my writing can be vanilla, simple pleasure one can say as I blogged about celebrating birthdays, anniversaries and other life events. I aptly titled this book unhinged as the first book is named Triggered. Two terms I battle with each day as I am often triggered and how often when people read my work I come across as unhinged and it's a label I have become comfortable with over the years. Although most who know me such as those at work would not see me as unhinged, as that is my dirty little secret that I can maintain my functionality, but at the same time have the craziest thoughts of ideation. My wife Delia truly gets the chance to see me unhinged, full of worry at times, anxiety and my afflictions, yeah sounds fun to be married to me, but all is not bad, that is what makes me, me.

Although I am physically in this world, my mind lives in another world, a conflict mind where I live in the past too much as I live in regret and shame, which is displayed front and center in my writing. As mentioned in my introduction, I wrote this for everyone to read, although my blog is available to anyone to read for free of course, but do I really know how long that blog will exist, when a book can last into infinity. For many of us who hear the word blog, one would think of someone writing about the cooking tips, their travels, their rants and raves, which are all types of blogs I have visited myself which are quite incredible, as you feel a sense of connection with the writer. Unlike a famous author like Stephen King or your favorite author in most cases one could never reach them directly, but with a blog you have access to have a connection and in most cases the writer responds to your questions and comments like I do. This is another way I hope to build a connection with my readers.

Being a no one writer, I appreciate your readership and will never take my readers for granted, these blogs give you an intimate look into me, for those who want to know me, connect with me, this is one of those purest way. I plan to continue to continue these volumes, as you see this volume goes up to December 2023, leaving from that point to current, which I plan for another volume to capture of 2024 and 2025, so keep reading.

Works

Short Stories

- Gutierrez, Joseph., **Short Stories From a Child's Mind – Animal Friends Edition**, Pub. May 12th, 2024, ISBN: 9798869320803, 68 pgs.
- Gutierrez, Joseph. , **Short Stories From a Child's Mind – Swashbuckler & Gunslinger Edition**, Pub. June 18th, 2024, ISBN: 9798869332608, 84 pgs.
- Gutierrez, Joseph. , **Short Stories From a Child's Mind – The Monster's Edition**, Pub. July 8th , 2024, ISBN: 9798869341525, 40 pgs.
- Gutierrez, Joseph., **Short Stories from a Child's Mind – A Collection**, Pub. Aug 30th, 2025, ISBN: 9798348540555, 180 pgs.

Non-Fiction

- Gutierrez, Joseph., **The Forgotten Son-Chapter 2**, Pub. Oct 31st, 2025: 9798348532901, 282 Pgs.

- Gutierrez, Joseph., **The Forgotten Son-Chapter 1**, Pub. June 15th, 2025: 9798348523930, 204 Pgs.
- Gutierrez, Joseph., **The Forgotten Son**, Pub. February 7th, 2025: 9798348211059, 840 Pgs.
- Gutierrez, Joseph., **Runaway, Shame : A Memoir**, Pub. December 1st, 2025: 9798348578039, 256 pgs.

Novels

- Meyer, Joe R., **The Pox**, Pub. June 18, 2023, ISBN: 9781088235973, **First Edition (Out of Print)**
- Meyer, Joe R., **The Pox**, Pub. January 18th, 2025, **Second Edition**, ISBN: 9798330560424, 420 pgs.
- Meyer, Joe R., **The Menagerie Locket**, Pub. March 17th, 2024, ISBN: 9798869186348, 254 pgs.
- Meyer, Joe R., **Pounds of Flesh**, Pub. October 2nd, 2024, ISBN: 9798330371617, 246 pgs.
- Meyer, Joe R., **Doll Parts**, Pub. September 7th, 2025, ISBN:9798348559441, 294 pgs.

www.ingramcontent.com/pod-product-compliance
Lightning Source LLC
LaVergne TN
LVHW052217200926
848481LV00001B/133
* 9 7 9 8 3 4 9 2 1 4 4 9 3 *